The Myth of Progress

Yvonne Burgess

D1035990

First published 1996

Wild Goose Publications
Unit 15, Six Harmony Row, Glasgow G51 3BA

Wild Goose Publications is the publishing division of the Iona Community.
Scottish Charity No. SC003794. Limited Company Reg. No. SCO96243.

ISBN 0 947988 77 7

Cover and chapter opening illustrations © Marianna Lines, 1996.
The cover art is hand printed on fabric, from stone in natural dyes.
The Ouroborus (the snake eating its tail) denotes the cycle of the year
or any other recurring process, as well as signifying circular oneness
or totality.

Cartoon illustration © Jim Whelan, 1996.
Photograph of Yvonne Burgess © Paul Turner, 1996.

Designed and typeset by Iona L Macgregor

Distributed in Australia and New Zealand by Willow Connection
Pty Ltd, Unit 7A, 3-9 Kenneth Road, Manly Vale NSW 2093.

Permission to reproduce any part of this work in Australia or New
Zealand should be sought from Willow Connection.

A catalogue record for this book is available from the British
Library.

Printed by The Cromwell Press Ltd, Melksham, Wilts.

The Myth of Progress

Yvonne Burgess

The daughter of ex-missionaries to West Africa, Yvonne Burgess has worked as a columnist for *New Internationalist* as well as teaching English and working in community development in Zimbabwe. She has worked in the voluntary sector, for Oxfam and Campaign Coffee. The author now lives in Fife, playing in a ceilidh band and giving music workshops.

This book, my 'firstborn', was written at several sittings in Africa and in Scotland. Progress is such a vast topic that I have had to leave out far more than I have put in. Readers are invited to fill in the gaps themselves, and to pursue their own connections - or objections.

Acknowledgements

Without Ed Katso, I would never have written this - the whole argument is, in a sense, one side of a conversation with him. In the book's earliest stages, I was greatly helped by the loving support and perceptive comments of Paul Bain, who gave me a safe, comfortable haven to begin writing in. Such a debt cannot be repaid. Gwen Egginton helped to focus my thinking, and found the time to work through the manuscript and give me valuable feedback. Debbie Chapel and Jaap Boender have cheered me on tirelessly over the years. Simon Taylor read and greatly affected chapter two by sharing with me his deep understanding of early medieval history. His enthusiasm and kindness have been an inspiration. Martin Jeffcott showed me how to use his computer to type the book onto disc, and he, Anne and Sarah made me warmly welcome in their home during those weeks. Marguerite Nesling laboured with me during the early stages of editing. Thanks to Jim Whelan and Paul Turner for their generous contributions of time and skill, and to Marianna Lines for her lovely artwork.

I owe a huge debt to my friends in Africa - especially the Mpisiri and Msasa families, Erika and Michele - who allowed me to share in their lives, and taught me so much.

To David and Sally Greck, this book is dedicated with love.

Contents

Introduction

A Conversation

Threads, knots, layers - Attitudes long, economics short -
Who is a Westerner? - Writing ourselves out of the picture -
Seeing ourselves as others see us

ONE AFTERNOON LATE IN 1988 I found myself sitting on the verandah of a mountaintop hotel in Malawi, one of those exquisite
monuments to settler arrogance that independent countries often
seem to look after with a strange nostalgic pride.

I had been in Africa nearly five years, most of it in newly independent Zimbabwe, a land of strident revolutionary rhetoric and
pragmatic get-rich-quick values. I had been exhausted by the contradictions of my life there and had come to Malawi on my way
home. Gradually I was relaxing in the gentle, gracious atmosphere
of Hastings Banda's sorely oppressed, yet dignified and tolerant
country.

Beside me on the hotel verandah sat a black Zimbabwean with a
Cambridge accent, and I was asking him about the private school
he was teaching at outside Harare. In Rhodesian days it had been
for the country's white elite, and eight years after independence, I
learned, it was still virtually whites only. He told me, however,
that its board members now ranged from white captains of Zimbabwean commercial farming and industry to 'the other extreme'
- and he named a prominent member of Robert Mugabe's government who had spent time in jail during the years of white rule.

Knowing this man's affluent jet-setting lifestyle since independence, I spluttered with cynical laughter at the idea of this man
being cited as 'the other extreme' to the settlers. But my friend
checked me with smiling seriousness, 'Does it surprise you that
people want the same things?' 'No, it doesn't,' I admitted, blush-
ing. 'At least,' he continued, 'the apartheid of the 1970s is no longer
possible in Zimbabwe: We are progressing'.

At that moment, I could find no words to answer him, though
questions and arguments were struggling to find form in my mind:
What do you mean, 'progressing'? By whose measure, in what
direction? Progressing in what sense? It has taken me years to
articulate my response and the relevance of this book to our conversation may not be clear throughout. But 'progress' is a big word.

What follows is an explanation in story and argument of what burst out as laughter in that conversation on the verandah. I want to look at the underlying myth of modern Western culture, namely that history is Progress, that this Progress is measurable - economically, technologically and in other ways; and especially at our idea that we Westerners, inventors of the myth, have progressed more than any other culture on earth.

These are the main threads of the argument - firstly, a critique of the concept or myth of Progress, as Westerners usually apply it to ourselves and our Western history of 'civilization'. This will involve looking in some depth at our habits of thinking, including their historical and even religious origins.

Next comes a critique of 'development' ideology, which we could define as the myth of our own Western Progress graciously applied to other societies and their cultures. The essence of development's message is 'You too can become advanced like us, with a little financial help and lot of hard work'. The arrogance and wilful blindness implicit in this attitude to most of the world completely escapes most Westerners, most of the time, so I will resort to anecdote as well as argument to try and shake this idea loose.

Thirdly, I will look at Western racism, which is firmly based on the myth of our superior Progress. In story and polemic, I will consider the moral knots we tie ourselves in over colonialism, slavery, South Africa, human rights - in fact over almost everything, as a result of our unquestioned and unrepentant conviction that our society is the most advanced on earth.

I will also look at the limits of the apparently irreconcilable conflicts between left and right, for both political philosophies prioritize the material benefits of modern industrial society above all else, and both accept the same basic model of intellectual and technological Progress.

As in a conversation, the argument in this book is conducted on several different levels. I will use memories and stories to tell my own story and to give a taste of life outside the West, as well as to illustrate historical events and cultural attitudes. There are passages which deal with the political and economic realities of the world we live in, following the threads of sense and continuity that run through our complex and troubled common history. There are more philosophical passages which seek to name our Western cultural errors and false turnings, and more psychological ones which ask what these errors do to us, or make us do to each other and ourselves.

I mentioned threads of sense and continuity, and a tapestry or embroidery may be a helpful image. For it is not the threads themselves, but their intertwining to make a pattern that reveals the meaning in our history. Therefore, having named the main themes, or threads, I will work with one or other, or with combinations of them, throughout the book, lifting and laying them as I go. At any point in the book they will all be present, though some will be out of sight at the back of the fabric.

Do not expect to read this book as you would read any other. The writing does not move smoothly, in a linear way, from a to b to c and so to two, but comes in *layers*. Changes of level are indicated by a break in the text and a large capital letter to start the next section.

Besides looking at how our current cultural atmosphere has come into being, I want to consider how our attitudes would need to change for us to gain a more balanced view of ourselves in relation to the other cultures of the world, and to live more fulfilled lives within our own culture.

The attitude of mind I advocate in this book is not something new that I have thought up. It is as old as the crannogs and burial mounds of our European ancestors, as well-established as weddings, and as currently widespread, on a conscious level, in our culture as for example the network of organic food growers. But for the last few centuries, this approach to life has taken a beating in the West, and it needs to be nurtured and given more air. This book belongs to a huge array of efforts - practical, social, spiritual and intellectual - to express, and more importantly, to *live* alternatives to the dominant, destructive culture of so-called Progress.

Ars longa, vita brevis is a true and well-known adage. The motto over this book could be 'Attitudes long, economics short'. Material circumstances may change almost beyond recognition in a single lifetime, or even in a decade. However, it takes generations to prepare an attitude of mind.

I do not claim to have discovered which comes first, the chicken or the egg, the cultural attitudes or the political and material circumstances. Obviously, there is mutual influence between attitude and action, and between economics and both of these. To reflect this interweaving, the main chapter headings follow historical periods and events, while sections within each chapter focus on states of mind, cultural attitudes and habits which inform and arise out of, and in turn lead into more political-historical events.

To put my own cards on the table, then: it must already be clear that this book is being written by a Westerner, for a mainly Western audience. I am a white woman, a middle-class Scot. Therefore I am connected with the Scots settlement of Northern Ireland (my father is from County Down), of North America and Australasia (where I have relatives), and of Southern Africa (where I don't). My background is strongly Presbyterian, and missionary. My mother grew up in a manse, and so did I. The four happy years my parents spent on mission compounds in West Africa up until just before I was born are probably the main reason that I felt impelled to go to Africa myself, thirty years later.

There is much more of course, some of which will emerge in this book. My ancestry, and the atmosphere within my immediate family and wider local and class culture have all shaped my ways of thinking and feeling.

These days, being 'Western' does not mean being born in a 'Western' country. Westerners - first worlders - are born and made now in every country on earth. They watch TV and videos, drive cars, make the odd international flight, invest their money legally and illegally in the West. Culturally, many are quite un-Western - and yet they belong firmly to the Western economic system. Things are getting complicated; or rather, more integrated. The forces of economic development (or underdevelopment) are tightening their grip worldwide. This is the backdrop against which I write and in which we all live.

Nevertheless, in this book I will use the word Western to refer to the European diaspora rather than to this ubiquitous surface-layer Westernization, which usually masks something very different that goes much deeper.

Before I go any deeper, however, let me pay my respects to the way things were left on the hotel verandah; for there was much wisdom in my friend's challenge to my laughter about the ex-freedom fighter on the elite school board. My mute embarrassment and inability to take up the argument at the time acknowledged that wisdom, and I am relieved, looking back, that I didn't launch straight into an analysis of Progress with him.

Certainly, my laughter sprang from awareness of the increasingly blatant hypocrisy among Zimbabwe's 'socialist' leadership - but as my friend so subtly yet frankly reminded me, a white visitor in Africa is on shaky ground when it comes to mocking or criticizing African aspirations to affluence.

It is too easy for white commentators on Africa to forget this. So often Westerners assume the right to observe and criticize other societies, and take issue with injustices and absurdities introduced and still exacerbated by our own dominant presence. Used to our powerful roles as professional experts, and thinking of ourselves as 'objective' observers, we are very good at *writing ourselves out of the picture*, as if our own participation as customers on the hotel verandah were neither here nor there. We sit in lush surroundings, sipping the cream of colonialism, and talking 'development', socialism, grass roots participation, appropriate technology and so on, with no sense that our behaviour itself is inappropriate - not to say downright arrogant.

Though we admit that Africa has been oppressed and exploited by Europe, we count ourselves (you and me) and our organizations out of this unpleasantness. We prefer not to see the continuity between the colonialists and the missionaries and ourselves.

We admire and frequent the gorgeous hotels built by Europeans in spectacular African or Indian settings but we overlook the embarrassing fact that these people were our ancestors. We drink the coffee and tea, and smoke the tobacco that colonialism was all about - yet we deplore the racist settlers who stole the Africans' land. And we regard African customs and beliefs as rather weird, if not downright scary, and as clearly inappropriate to 'modern life'. Yet we complacently criticize the missionaries and administrators who tried to bring Western civilization to the 'benighted heathens' as they called them, and to persuade them that their ways were backward and even evil.

When we Westerners, pretending to be 'objective', write, talk or think ourselves out of the picture like this, I believe we let our own need to maintain a positive self-image determine what we see and what we fail to see. It is too uncomfortable to contemplate the all-round effects of our expatriate presence in Africa - and besides, one thing leads to another.

If we start to consider these implications, it is a short step to questioning the appropriateness of a 'normal' Western lifestyle anywhere on earth. And soon nothing might be left standing. Better to keep looking the other way, with benign exasperation, on the trials and disasters of life in the 'developing' world. Better to keep feeling separate and superior.

I am not suggesting that Westerners have no right to observe, analyse or criticize what is happening around us: after all, that's what I am about to try to do. But I believe we should restrict ourselves to places and situations we have experienced first hand, and resist the temptation to rely on others' assessments.

And we should always frankly acknowledge our role as part of the problems we are looking at. Real objectivity must start with honesty about ourselves.

It is not easy to cast fresh eyes on one's own culture. But through living in Southern Africa, I have realized that in fact many practices which we in the West accept as belonging to life in 'advanced' society are regarded as immoral, degrading and subhuman by people in more traditional cultures. We need to learn to *see ourselves to some extent as others see us*, in order to realize how twisted we have become.

Throughout this book I will refer to people I have known and things I have learned through living and working in Africa. However, this is not a book about Africa, any more than it is a book about Scotland. It is a book about the strange, lopsided condition of the world we live in, and of ourselves in this world, where a single economic system rooted in our own Western culture increasingly dominates the fortunes and livelihoods of every people in every continent.

The stories and examples from Africa are nonetheless important: for while such extreme scenes may only be experienced by the few Westerners who go to 'poor' countries and spend time there, the shocking contrasts and contradictions in those places reveal things which are harder to see, but no less true at home - and they reveal the hidden heart of our own wealth. Many Westerners find that they return home from their stint in Africa, India or South America acutely sensitized to the decisive forces at work in their own society. Connections are made visible by travel: or they can be, if we have eyes to see.

Likewise, the stories and examples from my own upbringing and primary-school history lessons remind me of my roots in the cultural assumptions with which I now take issue. In common with my schoolfriends and teachers, these assumptions shaped my early thinking and idea of myself, and who can say to what extent they still do so.

When we start looking at ourselves like this, it is important to keep a sense of perspective, for it is easy to become self-absorbed and discouraged. The rational mind is a very sharp cutting tool, which can hurt us deeply when it is carelessly used. Rational thought is both the triumph and the scourge of our Western culture, for it enables us to collate and analyse information about the world, including ourselves - but it does not help us to make emotional sense of our prodigious knowledge, to make emotional sense of it. We have much information, but little truth.

We need to remain interested in and open to other people and other peoples, in order to learn things that will enable us to grow; and we need to *accept ourselves as we are* in order to grow through what we learn. But this involves first *admitting how we are*. Love and a sense of humour are indispensable.

When I read a book that challenges me and calls me to think more deeply about unfamiliar or uncomfortable themes, I often find myself putting the book down and staring into space, or getting up to put on the kettle, or going for a walk. For me, such 'looking away' belongs to the reading process - just as all the various displacement activities of washing dishes, washing clothes, tidying the room and so on before sitting down to work all properly belong to the writing process! Breaks from reading for reflection, disagreement, or just to get away from the text for a while can be very helpful.

So: what has become of Western society? What has our collective obsession with Progress made of us? And how did we 'develop' to this point?

Genesis *Ambivalence Lost*

A chosen people - Being right - Them and us - True or false -
Adam and Eve - Ambivalence v the patriarchal takeover -
The Christian view of history

OUR WESTERN MYTH OF PROGRESS goes back to the Hebrew Bible, which tells the story of a people moving forward through history. For Westerners, the Israelites were the original religious settler-pioneers. Christianized Europe took over the Jews' idea of themselves as God's Chosen People. This idea fired the Crusades, and much later, Europe's colonization and Christianization of the Americas and of Africa.

First the story was about a wandering tribe of released slaves, then about warriors and knights protected and inspired by God, then colonial pioneers, all of whom were guided by God through hostile territory to the Promised Land. In our century, the myth has been secularized and rendered scientific so that God can be left out: now we tend to think that we guide and propel *ourselves* through history, by the light of our 'advanced' Western intellects.

Though we may feel the Old Testament version of the myth of Progress is rather naive and dogmatic, not to say bloodthirsty, it does contain much wisdom and subtlety, as I would like to demonstrate by looking closely at the myth of the Fall in chapters two and three of Genesis.

In the Hebrew Bible (what Christians call the Old Testament) the people of Israel are shown repeatedly falling away from God, choosing to rely on their own strength, disregarding warnings, and having to return, repent and be renewed in relationship with God in order for history to move forward again. Even while the stories of conquest and murder would seem to promote a boastful and militaristic attitude towards other, neighbouring cultures, the ups and downs of the Hebrew heroes and their followers warn against human arrogance and hybris. Jahweh always keeps the upper hand. History, in terms of the Hebrew Scriptures, is the developing relationship between Jehovah and His Chosen People.

Paul and the early Christian Church fathers proclaimed the end of history in this sense of spiritual-psychological progress. Jesus, as the risen Christ, was proclaimed as the guarantor of God's reacceptance of sinful humanity once and for all. As long as the Christian message, and Christ's divinity, were acknowledged by the individual believer, nothing else was required: you could be sure of redemption. Membership of the Chosen People depended, in this framework, on religious affiliation to the Church of Christ rather than on race.

Nowadays, in the largely secularized modern West, most of the Chosen People no longer have a God to relate to; and so, for most Westerners, there is no longer anything to bow down before, no-one to whom we can, should or must confess our failures or crimes. This strikes many people in our culture as a blessed and timely liberation from oppressive and discredited religious dogmas - another step in humanity's progressive emancipation from 'superstition' and passivity. But seen from another angle, our very godlessness traps us in the role of God.

Since there is no higher instance for us, we ourselves must bear full responsibility for guiding history's progress - that is, for being right, all the time. This is not a healthy state of mind in which to live, either for an individual or for a society. Many people, especially Western feminists - have commented on the obsessive need to 'be right' which characterizes our culture, and distinguishes it sharply from more tolerant, traditional societies which value consensus and harmony. A Malawian friend once told me, 'Even if I know I am right, I cannot beat my own drum'.

Yet the compulsion to be right was not born with modern atheism or agnosticism. Dogmatic intolerance has informed centuries of Christian persecution of heretics and heathens, including the Inquisition, the witchburnings of the early modern era, the Thirty-Years War that ravaged post-Reformation Northern Europe, the expulsion of the Puritans who fled to the New World, and much sectarian oppression and violence in Scotland, England and Ireland.

As religious belief has faded from our culture however, dogmatism and intolerance have continued to flourish. Often, new (materialist) dogmas have been used to debunk old (metaphysical) ones. For cultural habits run deeper than changing world views, and much deeper than economic history. Our dogmatism seems to be both a root and a fruit of our culture.

Indeed, I am not suggesting that the Hebrews were free of such dogmatic intolerance. On the contrary, the Hebrew Bible is a chronicle of atrocities and desecrations which were conducted in the conviction that Jahweh was superior to the gods of surrounding peoples, and that therefore Hebrew customs and beliefs were superior to those of their neighbours.

However, the chronicle retains quite a realistic sense of proportion - the Hebrew heroes often have faults, and the enemies sometimes have redeeming qualities; even Jahweh is depicted at times as all too human.

By contrast, many early Christian writings, such as the Gospel of St John, the Book of Revelation and the letters of Paul the Apostle, are formulated in abstract terms and make categorical claims about the nature of human life and death and the universe.

These writings encourage an uncompromisingly black and white, 'us and them' view of the world. You are either in or you're out. And it's no longer enough to be born into the faith: you have to make your choice.

The first three Gospels, while being full of teachings, have a sense of humour and light and shade, as well as a sense of real events involving real people. But on the whole, I find the stories of the Hebrew Bible more realistically differentiated, psychologically richer and therefore more convincing than the disembodied spiritual exhortations of much of the New Testament.

Besides giving imaginative satisfaction, the complexity of the older stories honours the mess and confusion of human life, which cannot be neatly defined or confined in simple categories of good and evil.

Christian theology has been uncomfortable with mixed motives and real-life characters, preferring unambiguous distinctions between good and bad, with victorious heroes and happy endings.

Symbolic, multi-level thinking has become difficult for modern Westerners. We tend to divide literature and life into 'fact' and 'fiction' and so we don't see how the most important things can only be expressed *between* these categories. Therefore we are ill-equipped to deal with myths, as demonstrated by the spectacular claims of the Genesis-based 'creationist theory' in the USA, which states that the world was created in six twenty-four hour days, a certain number of years ago, 'as written in the Bible'. In the 1980s, while the campaign to get this 'theory' onto the school science curriculum was under way, a bumper sticker proclaimed 'God said it - I believe it - that settles it'. This theory is now on the school science curriculum in many states. This theory now stands alongside all the archaeological and other evidence for evolution, as a 'theory of equal validity' - to be taught by bemused biology teachers trained in highly scientific, secular surroundings

The hidden logic behind this cultural absurdity is that such a literalistic reading of a creation myth could only be raised as an issue of religious faith in a culture which had flattened out its spiritual experience into a series of true or false statements, and then got completely caught up in measuring and counting everything in the world.

The story of Adam and Eve's expulsion from the Garden of Eden is another myth which modern Westerners find hard to read intelligently and attentively, with our whole imagination. In itself, it is a complex and adequate myth, told by the Hebrews about their own cultural roots. But in Christian hands it has been turned into a blanket indictment of corrupt human nature - and particularly, female nature.

The Book of Genesis in fact begins with two stories of the Creation, followed by the story of humanity's fall from an original condition of harmony and ease. In the first account of Creation, God creates all living things, 'male and female created He them'. There is no hierarchy, and there is no Fall.

The second - later - Creation myth is the self-explaining story of a community in which men have seized and then assumed power - the beginning, perhaps, of patriarchy in that region of the world. Since power struggles change things drastically, they create a sense of movement, of history. When the winners tell the story, the history usually becomes a self-justifying narrative of Progress - as Western history mainly is - but in Genesis, the pain of the conflict and the loss of harmony and unity are still clearly remembered and acknowledged. This complex awareness of something lost as well as something gained is what makes the story so rich.

Genesis chapters two and three are the basic myth of a people - or more precisely of its male rulers - who feel themselves to be historical and 'progressive', in contrast to the more traditional peoples around them. They feel they have expelled themselves from a relatively unselfconscious, simple and cyclical existence (the first human condition) into an endless quest, a journey, by deciding to eat the forbidden fruit of the Tree of Knowledge.

The Garden is wistfully remembered as Paradise, but *the wisdom of the myth is in its ambivalence.* For the Fall is depicted both as a disaster and as a responsible decision. (The question of who is held responsible for the decision is very telling indeed about the gender relations in patriarchy.) On the one hand, the eating of the apple is a breach of sacred trust, which spoils the original intimate relationship between God and humanity, and a severely punishable crime; and on the other, it is a reasonable, even courageous response to the serpent's cogent argument and challenge.

The serpent, let us remember, is not the Devil, and is only condemned later, by God, along with Adam and Eve, for their conspiracy together against His absolute power. The serpent is described in the King James Version, as 'more subtle' (not evil, or lying) than any other creature. In fact, the serpent catches God in a half-truth. For when Eve says that they have been told not to eat of the tree in the middle of the Garden lest they die, the serpent replies with another half-truth: 'You will certainly not die. God knows that the day you eat of it, your eyes will be opened, and you will be like gods, knowing good and evil' (Genesis 3, vs 4-5).[1]

If we read the myth carefully and open-mindedly and avoid the Christian temptation to take sides, God's commandment not to eat of the tree in the middle of the Garden appears, at least from one point of view, arbitrary, and his anger in vs 14-19 vindictive. It is also clear from the phrasing of the serpent's advice and the way it comes true (they do learn the difference between good and evil, or at least they learn shame) that the people who told this myth of themselves, though they may have longed for paradisal reunion with their God, would never have wished the fruit of the Tree of Knowledge uneaten: for then the whole subsequent relationship between Jahweh and His people, documented and celebrated in the Hebrew Bible, would have remained unwritten. In this myth, as in many of the Hebrews' stories and songs, Israel's pride and Israel's shame are shown to have a common root.

The same could - and should, I believe - be acknowledged of Western Progress: why do we resist a paradox that stares us in the face from every daily newspaper?

Having said all this, the myth of the Fall contained in Genesis is already a very sophisticated piece of patriarchal ideology. Like every new social order, patriarchy had to rewrite the myths of the previous culture to bring them into line with the new balance of power.

The treatment of Eve in the myth of the Fall is so blatantly ideological and full of contortions that it takes a society equally bent on justifying or excusing male dominance (as ours still largely is) to overlook them. The story of Adam and Eve in the Garden of Eden thoroughly reconstructs not only the relations between the genders, but humanity's relations with its Creator and with the rest of Creation. It does this in the self-consciously masculine voice of Progress.

By relegating Eve to a second, dependent level of Creation, in contrast with the earlier Creation myth which knew no hierarchy, this story puts a gap between womankind and God which reverses the early human apprehension of God found in all cultures, namely of the life-giving, cyclical Mother-Creator who waxes and wanes with the moon, tides and seasons. Man, of course, jumps into the gap, masculinizing God and making himself the original human being, who was merely given a female companion, to serve and entertain him, and belong to him alone.

The story goes on to link woman with the forces that separate 'Man' from his God; and turns God into a man's man and a severe judge of women ('In sorrow shalt thou bring thy children forth'). Gone with the Mother-Creator is the pre-patriarchal awe of motherhood, the holiest of holies. The victorious, armed men and their God are stern, authoritarian, prepared to resort to violence (more in sorrow than in anger) to uphold their own view of order and justice.

Even the words we use to express this in English tell the same story. In direct contrast to the natural order of things, where the mother precedes the child, of whatever gender, the root forms in our language for human beings and for divinity (man, male, God) are masculine, and the derivative forms (woman, female, Goddess) feminine. How the world has changed! Or rather, how Progress has changed the way the world is described!

It is interesting to consider how Adam and Eve behave in this story, and how God responds to each of them. Although Adam is supposed to be the first human being, Eve is the one who acts like a grownup, while Adam acts like a dependent child. Eve has the starring role: she gets the lowdown on the Tree of Knowledge from the serpent; she decides to risk death for the sake of awareness, and she persuades Adam to follow her example. Adam's performance, on the other hand, shows threefold weakness, in his initial laziness and passivity, in his willingness to be led against his sense of what he ought to do; and in his cowardly betrayal of Eve when confronted by God - blaming both her and, by implication, God himself, for his own disobedience. ('The woman you gave me for my companion made me do it.')

Does the myth preserved here perhaps hint that, in this early period in Hebrew culture, women were still acknowledged to be the main initiators and workers, the fearless ones? Were they, rather

than men, seen as the responsible actors who took their own decisions and got on with things while the men lay about moraliz-
ing, or napping, when they weren't having intimate conversations
with God, or wars on His behalf? The story certainly suggests
that male assertiveness and subjugation of women still had a long
way to go before they reached recognizable European standards.

Changing cultural attitudes is a very long process, and it is
probably impossible to stamp them out altogether. This means
that although we have to dig deep to uncover the roots of modern
patriarchal consciousness, it is not a hopeless quest. For non-patriarchal attitudes and practices persist alongside the dominant
patriarchal ones, even in the West, where the denigration of women
and their values has been taken to such systematic extremes, and
yoked to the consolidation of male monopolies in church, business, science, medicine and finance.

The older values persist in family dynamics, in stories and say-
ings, in beliefs and skills and social practices. These values tend to
be stronger among those who have less stake in the dominant world
view. They also occur throughout the Bible, and Jesus' own words
and actions often express the non-patriarchal view very clearly,
though they have been routinely used to bolster and legitimize
the hierarchies of Western power.

In the myth of the Fall, the non-patriarchal consciousness is
expressed, I believe, in the sense of two-sidedness, the implied
human protest against The Divine (authoritarian male) verdict of
guilty. This protest is not to be confused with Adam's feeble attempt to protect himself from blame: it is a protest which emerges
from an open-eyed reading of the story itself.

Firstly, Eve's action does not seem altogether reprehensible. The
intelligence and power of discernment she uses can be maligned
as 'female curiosity' or else praised as the courageous spirit of
discovery. Whichever way, these are recognisably human qualities, and in the myths of many different cultures they are depicted
as motivating human rebellions against Heaven, and getting us
into trouble.

Again, God's response to Eve's misdemeanour seems
disproportionate in its massive violence. The God of the Hebrews
appears, here as elsewhere in the Hebrew Bible, in a less than flat-
tering light. His wrath seems to stem from injured pride, and His
original withholding of knowledge from our progenitors in fact
seems to deny their distinctive humanity.

It is as if the tellers of this myth accepted that life is beset by
irresolvable conflicts. On the one hand, Eve's action was under-

standable - not simply and unmitigatedly evil; and on the other hand, given God's character and commandment (that is, given the nature of things) it was only to be expected that trouble would follow her all-too-human exploration of the unknown. The myth presents us with the timeless law of something gained, something lost. Knowledge of good and evil (no mean feat) is paid for by the loss of eternal, work-free life, and pain-free childbirth. In other words, *there is no such thing as unmitigated Progress.*

When we try to deny or escape this inherent two-sidedness of life, I believe we put our individual and our collective sanity at risk. Yet this is exactly what Christian theology has sought to do since the beginning of our era - to separate God and good from Devil and evil. As believers aspire to be godlike and to exclude all evil from their thoughts and actions, they often become both arrogantly self-righteous and tormented by guilt. For life refuses to be cut in half, to have its integrated ambivalence wrenched apart into two dissociated worlds.

Guilt is not, as some have suggested, a mean-minded invention of Christianity designed to keep the flock in subjection: it is simply a by-product of the 'cowboys and Indians' approach to spiritual life - the notion that there are 'goodies and baddies', and that people can live either side of the dividing line. We, of course, like to think we are the 'goodies', while *they* are the 'baddies'. But every time we point the finger of blame at 'them' (the sinners, the Protestants, the Catholics, the Communists, the capitalists, the blacks, the whites) three fingers of our hand point back at us. Guilt is the spirit's revenge for our denial of part of ourselves.

Christian tradition has misread the ambivalent spiritual truth embodied in the myth of the Fall and therefore the nature and meaning of human progress - the journey after the expulsion - has likewise been misinterpreted. Perhaps the distortion happened because Christianity was born at a time when the Jewish tradition was exposed to Greek and other Middle Eastern influences. Sophisticated minds tutored in the idealistic philosophy of the time formulated and organized the new faith. They laid out the new doctrines and reinterpreted the Hebrew Bible in the light of what they understood Jesus' death and resurrection, rather than his life and teaching, to have meant in terms of world history.

God, it was now asserted, allowed 'Man' to fall, so that He could later reconcile humankind to Himself through the redemption of those who accept His only-begotten Son as their Lord and Saviour. This grim, manipulative reading of world history and of God's relationship with humanity apparently barred from heaven everyone who had ever lived without hearing the Word. It also promised misery and damnation for those who knew the Christian message but either rejected it or failed to accept it fully enough. Even the saved were not spared psychological torments, since they were always targets for the Devil's wiles.

The Christian view of history encouraged a desperate evangelical urgency which has trampled upon other people's beliefs and traditions in the name of God and has elevated us, the bearers of 'Western Christian civilization', to the role of world saviours. The Christian version of world history has paved the way for the modern ideologies of development and Progress which regard Western social, economic and intellectual norms as the highest realization of human potential hitherto achieved in history.

In a disturbing and dangerous cultural development, Christian doctrine places the individual Christian above the events of history. Scripture no longer draws us inside an ongoing process of developing relationship between God and His people as it does in the Books of Samuel, Ruth and Kings. The New Testament does not call us to participate in irresolvable tensions between knowledge and innocence, pride and submission, sensual pleasure and spiritual fulfilment, as do the beautiful, moving stories and myths of the Hebrew Bible.

As a child in Sunday School I responded spontaneously to the stories of Joseph and Moses, of Samuel and David and Ruth: I learned the unstateable truths they teach about life by getting involved in the ambivalent, inconclusive emotions which the stories stirred in me. 'Grownup' Christian doctrine, however, leaves no room for ambivalence or inconclusiveness - and it is not surprising that only the stories of the first three Gospels tend to feature in Sunday School lessons.

Paul the Apostle pioneered the Christian habit of referring to the Hebrew Bible in a rather patronizing tone. Our very term 'Old Testament' declares it obsolete. For Christians, history is already a foregone conclusion: *we have arrived*. All that ultimately matters has already been achieved for us through Christ's sacrifice and resurrection.

The same self-satisfied story of Creation, Fall and Redemption has been applied to the history of our Western dealings with the rest of the world. Africa, we reason, *had* to go through a stage of being carved up and colonized so that its people could later liberate themselves into self-government as modern nation-states;

Africans had to be convinced of their ignorance and unfitness to govern their societies so that they could, through formal education (laid on by us), emerge from 'ignorance' and 'unfitness' into knowledge and professional expertise. Whole peoples have been humiliated so that individuals, by struggling up Western-erected ladders, can eventually earn respect and status (and money), none of which are granted by 'developed' Western society as a birthright to all its members.

Put as bluntly as this, such a justification of colonialism appears crude and cynical, and even those who subscribe to it would probably try to qualify it somehow. But although it is seldom stated so explicitly, I believe this is the subtext of almost all 'development' activity and socio-economic striving in Africa. It is the view of colonialism which has been generally held by missionaries and colonial administrators since they arrived in Africa, and it has now been taken up, with some modification, by their black (and white) successors.

What makes this approach to history so frightening is that *its holders are raised above good and evil in the cause of Western-style Progress* - the only remaining absolute. Even while we acknowledge the crimes of colonialism, we tie our minds in knots to justify them as part of an overall Progress package. We pretend that the end (a life like ours) justifies the means (exploitation and degradation), in order to avoid the idea that the means might irremediably discredit the end.

Although the language is now economic, I believe that the cultural attitude which allows - and indeed necessitates - this self-justification, is theological in origin. The religious doctrine has faded, but the mental paradigm remains intact.

In psychological terms, I believe that our Christian and post-Christian view of history makes it harder for us Westerners to learn from our mistakes. While justifying our actions saves us the pain of shame and the humiliation of admitting ourselves to be firmly in the wrong, it also denies us the chance to seek and receive forgiveness, including self-forgiveness. Instead of taking the risk of such a change of heart we Westerners, the cultural relatives of colonialists and missionaries, carry the white man's burden into our socialist cells and development education campaigns.

For Westerners, the psychological repercussions of our deep-rooted and long-standing Progress myth are tremendous. We cannot believe one thing for the world out there and another for ourselves. What we do and have done on the world stage, we do and have done also in our own families. And often, the way we treat our children is not a pretty sight. We tend to regard them as we have regarded people of other cultures and continents - as unruly wild creatures, who 'need' to have their wills broken, be reduced to dependency and then taken in hand, disciplined, trained and educated to be well-behaved participants in civilized life.

We have not respected our children, or accepted them as good, loving and beautiful creatures, so convinced have we been of their (and our own) sinfulness and need to be improved on.

The things we inflict on our children we inflict unknowingly, meaning no harm, 'for their own good'.[2] We may do it because this is how we ourselves were brought up, and we cannot help how we were brought up. Likewise, we cannot help having been born into an affluent culture, with all its history, its norms, prejudices and assumptions. However, though it is hard to swim against the tide of one's own past experience, or of our peers' opinions, once we understand what is going on, we can decide what we think and how we want to act within our culture. We do not have to repeat our parents' mistakes on our own children - not if we acknowledge what those mistakes were, and how they hurt us. Adults, at least in our Judaeo-Christian cultural context, are responsible for their own values.

Just as there are parents who, remembering how they suffered as children, break the pattern of oppression by consciously treating their own children differently, so there have been missionaries and colonial administrators who were open-minded enough to fully respect the people they lived among. Of course, it is possible to be a Christian and to honour others' beliefs and ways of life - their full humanity and otherness. This has not, however, been our traditional attitude to other cultures, and theology has conspired with an unequal balance of power to reinforce the West's cultural superiority syndrome.

But it is lonely at the top. Our culture is in an unhappy state of mind, as we are seeing more and more clearly every year. We have to change from within, for history is changing anyway and will not wait for us. The danger is that if we do not turn our minds to welcome the changes before us, we will become even more paranoid about losing our privileges, and end up fighting desperate wars to preserve our unfair advantages.

We need to recover a more ambivalent awareness of our religious traditions and our modern culture. I believe we Westerners are now finally beginning to acknowledge, as the Genesis myth does, how much has been lost as well as gained in the course of our Western Progress.

2

Class-based Culture

The Roman umbrella - Dark Age confusion - Feudal consolidation - The pyramid as Progress - Awe and contempt - The myth of the happy ending - Reassessing our past - Land, survival and dignity - Externalizing oppression - Feudalism, East and West - The ladder up the pyramid

CULTURE IS OBVIOUSLY A CONTINUUM, so any 'beginning' must be arbitrarily selected. In chapter one, I chose to examine the story of Adam and Eve's expulsion from the Garden of Eden. The Hebrew Bible belongs to a Middle Eastern culture, yet it has informed our own.

This chapter deals with Europe proper, in the time between the decline of the Roman Empire and the end of the medieval period. During these centuries, Europeans were learning habits which are still with us twentieth-century Westerners.

We human beings retain an imprint of our whole cultural history in the way we think, use language, relate to one another and see the world. We learn all this from our parents and elders, who learned it from theirs. This means that in a crucial and everyday sense, *history matters.*

In one sense, the Western idea of human Progress would seem to have ground to a halt during the long period between the Roman Empire and the Renaissance. During the Middle Ages, an unchanging world order was explicitly cherished and the hierarchical status quo was claimed to reflect God's eternal plan for mankind. A longing for stability after centuries of Germanic migrations and conquests was the impulse which allowed the establishment of a feudal system in Europe. (Though even the Middle

Ages probably felt anything but stable to those who were swept up in its incessant wars, local and foreign, or to those involved in the power-mongering in Church and court.)

However, Medieval *ideology* was about hierarchy and stability rather than about change and Progress, and the question that interests me here is how the basic, simple idea of a Chosen People's walk with God was adapted to encompass, and to justify, an overtly elitist social order that ranged from fantastic extremes of wealth to abject, never-ending poverty and degradation.

The Hebrews of biblical times, though they kept slaves captured in war, were a fairly egalitarian people among themselves. Their prophets were always urging them to take care of their widows and orphans - in other words, their poor. Women were presumably expected to live under the protection of a more godlike man and not to fend for themselves economically.

Hebrew culture was small and integrated, with everyone referring to the same sources of authority and the same history and customs. So their cultural innovations could be quickly assimilated and everybody drawn 'ahead' at the same pace. The Roman Empire, on the other hand, included hundreds of different peoples living in completely diverse ways, spread across thousands of miles. All these people and territories were joined by Roman military might and organization, and a thin layer of Roman 'civilization'.

The various peoples ruled by Rome were affected by Roman culture mainly through paying their taxes, and through their young men being posted as soldiers to far-flung parts of the Empire. So the different European cultures under the Romans retained their distinctiveness and their ancestral usages, values and beliefs, while sharing the Roman umbrella of security and administration.

Given that European patriarchy represents a historical innovation and cultural shift from an earlier cosmology, sociology and value system, we may suppose that most of the cultures embraced by Roman arms were a lot less rigorously patriarchal than the Hebrews or the Romans, so that women would have continued to play their traditional roles in childbirth, healing and religious practices, and to enjoy their traditional social position.[1]

On top of the local cultures, however, sat Roman society - or as much of it as was represented in the colonies. This society was very strictly patriarchal, and stratified into classes with different rights and obligations, all the way down to the slaves, who had nothing but duties. So, throughout this vast area of Western and Southern Europe, for several centuries there was the experience of two cultures co-existing - a traditional, local culture and a foreign culture which ran things and considered itself vastly more sophisticated and superior. This was a very complex social situation, which was not simplified by the loss of centralized Roman power and the rise of the various Germanic kingdoms.

There is, it seems to me, a delightful irony in the fact that Northern Europe's recorded history begins with two Southern European imperial civilizations, classical Greece and Rome. In particular, it is ironic that my people, today's middle-class Westerners, who have been running the world with such confidence in the name of human Progress and technology, are the racial and cultural descendants of the so-called 'barbarians' who smashed up the Western half of Rome's affluent and 'civilized' empire.

Our ancestors, these warriorlike Germanic tribes and their indigenous victims, dominated Europe from roughly the fourth to the ninth centuries (different dates are given for different parts of Europe). These centuries have come to be rather dismissively referred to as the Dark Ages, and are thought to have been a time of terrible upheaval and bloodshed in regions which had enjoyed relative peace and security throughout the Roman era. After conquering a region the Goths or the Franks would set up their own parallel society alongside the local 'Romanised' population. For example, they maintained their own and the Roman legal system.

The warrior ethos of these peoples had a profound effect on the medieval European imagination, and hence on our modern European consciousness and temperament; but at the same time the Germanic nations were also deeply affected by the cultures they encountered within the ex-Roman empire - including Christianity and Roman civilization itself. (Several Germanic kings issued codified amendments to Roman law which were used throughout the Middle Ages.)

So 'European culture', whatever that might be, is a very complex tapestry indeed, created by many peoples through many periods, with strands (among others) of Celtic, Roman, Germanic and Judaeo-Christian values, usages and attitudes woven into it. The ideology - religious and/or secular - that seeks to embrace and express such a bundle of cultures, will have roots in many different local histories and power struggles.

Compared with the clarity and unity of Hebrew faith, ethics and socio-religious practices, Europe's are inevitably going to look like a huge muddle, or a random patchwork, until some cultural event or process occurs that is recognisably and originally European, to give coherence to the muddle, and let a pattern emerge.

It is hard for a single idea to make headway in such a diverse cultural atmosphere. And if credit is to be apportioned for nurturing European single-mindedness, or cultural coherence, it should go to the Christian Church based at Rome, which for centuries schemed and negotiated, and fought and persecuted, to bring order and unity and establish its centralized authority over the whole of Western Christendom.

As Roman imperial structures and authority declined, the Church remained the strongest institution linking the parts of the old Western empire, and linking 'Dark Age' Europe with its Roman past.

In my Scottish school history books, the term 'Dark Ages' gave the impression of a long historical lull, when nothing of note happened, or a curtain of secrecy or ignorance had been drawn over whatever did happen. The books stated laconically that during this time 'Europe descended into barbarism'. As a child, this phrase suggested to me scary images of naked, hairy apemen on their haunches chewing at human bones - a brutal and subhuman condition, where life was worth nothing.

It was only when I went to live in Zimbabwe and began to notice the grace, courtesy and psychological sophistication that co-existed there with bare feet and floors and walls smeared with cowdung that I began to consciously question categories like 'civilized' and 'primitive' which I'd grown up with, and the value system that underlies them.

I now believe that life beyond the library walls, and behind the history of wars and sovereigns, is well worth living; and that people in oral cultures live full, balanced and stimulating lives using extremely sophisticated systems of knowledge - social, medical, spiritual and psychological - that have been built up over many generations of observation, reflection and practice.

It seems to me likely that, when they were not being hammered by Goths or Franks, the peoples of Europe who had been ruled by Rome may well have had a good deal of fun camping in the ruins of villas and fortresses and living their own lives again, unsupervised and untaxed. I imagine they were quite relieved they no longer had to build roads for Roman armies and walls to keep invaders out. There would doubtless have been less wealth, and less opportunity for young men to travel long distances (with the army), and there was certainly a lot more insecurity, with the warrior tribes on the move. No doubt 'standards fell', (as Westerners are fond of complaining when local populations succeed to power). The state of the roads must surely have deteriorated, and the baths would no longer have been properly maintained. But life, and fully human social culture, would have gone on much as normal, with storytelling grandparents, cooking and childcare, ceremonies and festivals, herbal and magical practices for health and good fortune, and work in the fields and building houses and bringing in firewood.

Christianity was around (but not yet obligatory), with travelling monks and monastic settlements, various communities and sects, and all sorts of local saints, myths and legends, festivals and practices that mixed the older beliefs with newer doctrines. The Christian Church based at Rome had not yet managed to establish its religious monopoly across Europe, so there was more room for local variation and different interpretations of the Gospel.

Variety extending into eccentricity is a hallmark of nature and of communal village life and oral cultures. But it is the enemy of authority, discipline and military effectiveness: and ultimately, *variety is the enemy of Progress, with a capital P.*

In the Middle Ages (circa 850 - 1450), European culture began to be forged into one monolithic structure. Several factors combined to bring the European free-for-all to a close. Historians tell us that the feudal system was set up as a form of self-organization, self-militarization, to replace the order and protection imposed earlier by the Romans. It cannot have been easy living in a settled society ruled by a nomadic warrior tribe who were used to raiding and feuding; and it seems as if the peoples of Europe were prepared to settle for some order - any order - to relieve them of the incessant upheavals.

Inevitably, the order established was merely a consolidation of the status quo - and while the kings and chieftains and their followers jostled for position in the feudal pyramid, the Rome-based Church was busy securing its authority, with the aim of eventually imposing a single theological currency on the whole of Europe.

The interests of Church and Christianized kings coalesced and the new political structure was somewhat incongruously christened the 'Holy Roman Empire'. Its first acknowledged ruler, Charlemagne the Frank, probably hoped to gain both papal approval and enhanced credibility by association with that earlier era of European stability and glory, based on military conquest.

Charlemagne's papal investiture at Trier marked the crucial relationship between Church and State that was to characterize the European Middle Ages, a relationship sometimes cosy, sometimes murderous. Those who benefitted materially and socially from the establishment of feudal structures throughout most of Europe were the Roman Church and its hierarchy, and those who ended up with land, power and titles in the new order.

The majority of Europeans, meanwhile, were reduced to serfdom and used as a hard-pressed foundation for a structure that reached, ideologically and architecturally, up to heaven. It was a high price to pay for a quiet life.

Consolidation of power relations may make for stability and peace of a kind, but it also means that the weight of the powerful is borne squarely by those below them. Also, the more massive the structure that supports them, the more those at the top come to appear like gods, to others and to themselves. This observation leads us to one of the meeting points of Church and State: the divine right of monarchs to rule. Where exactly did this brilliant idea come from?

When we read the book of Samuel in the Bible, we learn that the Hebrews were deeply sceptical about the wisdom of having kings at all. Saul, their first king, was appointed by popular acclaim the book says, but against Jehovah's express advice (a polite way of recording posterity's better judgment?).

This suspicion of kings seems to have been shared by the Romans, who expelled and murdered a good few in their time. However, the Roman Church had no such doubts: its Pastor was - indeed still is - believed by the faithful to be appointed by God, in direct succession from Jesus' friend Peter, its founder.

So the Hebrews, together with the Roman Church, passed on to later European kings and emperors the idea of divine right: that kings were chosen, in the last resort, by God - and that therefore royal power was in itself proof of divine favour. Incredibly, this myth has been clung to, at least in Britain, throughout all the skulduggery of the last 1,500 years, providing a corruptive precedent of hypocrisy and double standards at the 'highest' levels in our society.

The idea of divine right has no New Testament basis beyond the instruction to 'render unto Caesar what is Caesar's, and to God what is God's', and Paul's advice to the Romans to obey earthly masters while regarding everyone as equal 'in Christ'. However, New Testament indifference and Hebrew Bible caveats about kings were both swept under the red carpet in the Middle Ages, which could only conceive of the Kingdom of God in feudal terms as a spiritual power pyramid like Europe's earthly and ecclesiastical power pyramids, with ranks of archangels, angels and saints, priests and sinners.

Europe had already experienced several centuries of class-based society: the various ranks of Romans and their slaves; the Germanic conquerors and the indigenous peoples they oppressed. But feudal logic viewed these effects of conquest and politics as a divinely-decreed system of social relations, like the Indian caste system.

What has happened - what *can* happen now - to the idea of Progress?

In fact, European feudalism has itself been generally regarded by Western historians as an *achievement* of cultural Progress! Order, efficiency and consolidation of power are values we applaud and understand, even while we deplore the conservatism, elitism and religious credulity of the Middle Ages.

To give the label of Progress to such a baleful social process as the construction of the European class pyramid calls for a high degree of repression, or 'for your own good' thinking. Indeed although we Westerners think of ourselves as liberated and democratic now, *we still sanction oppression (our own and others') as a stage in that 'liberation'*.

While the Dark Ages have been generally passed over as backward and forgettable, the Middle Ages have been fawned over as fascinating, with their heroism, romance, intrigues, alliances, wars, persecutions, their magnificent cathedrals and courtly literature. The microscope has been turned on the lifestyle and 'culture' of the rich, and the rest have been regarded by posterity with the same weary contempt and occasional pity which they received from their oppressors at the time.

It is worth stressing that this winners' eye-view of Progress accepts ever-increasing disparities of wealth and power as evidence of advances in human 'civilization'. We *expect* yawning inequality and subordination of the majority to form the foundation of empires, and of what we regard as the greatest achievements of human culture, be these pyramids, palaces, astrological systems or whatever. We refuse to call the imposition of such privilege and injustice by their true names: socially and ethically regressive - even barbaric.

Karl Marx himself regarded the feudal era as a 'progressive' stage in Western history. This may be surprising, given the efforts he and his followers have made to right the wrongs of feudalism, and turn the spotlight from the lives of the rich onto the lives of the common people. The trouble with much of this social history is that, until very recently, it has tended to be bland, boring and materialist.[2] Statistics and general descriptions of living conditions replace the familiar faces and characters of traditional history, and do not make for riveting reading; schematic, reconstructed daily routines replace court intrigues and decisive battles.

But the history of 'ordinary' people does not have to be boringly written. Lack of more detailed, personal records to work with is surely part of the reason for its frequent blandness, but it may be true that even social historians have been culturally prejudiced against the lives of 'ordinary' people.

Contempt for the masses (the Germans have a word for it, *Massenverachtung*) still characterizes our culture, and is one of the most persistent attitudes we have inherited from the Middle Ages. The very word 'masses', to describe the majority of people in our culture, is contemptuous. Instead of suggesting great numbers of people with all their rich variety, complexity, interrelationships, skills - and their inherent sacredness as human souls, the word 'masses' suggests huge heaps or too much of something - of any old inanimate substance, that is. In revolutionary politics, the word 'masses' carries overtones of an irresistible, potentially violent force of numbers - but still it lacks any tone of respect for the people referred to.

Any social hierarchy is bound to engender contempt for its 'lower' orders - it needs to. The 'upper' orders retain their privileges and status by virtue of this contempt and its corollary, ordinary people's awe of their assumed superiority. Besides feeling awe and contempt for each other, those at the 'higher' and 'lower' levels of the power pyramid internalize this socially-prescribed awe and contempt as pride and shame - the feelings 'appropriate' to their social rank. To resist this emotional disfigurement is to put yourself outside the prevailing social structure, to make yourself an outcast, eccentric, a rebel or worse - unless you have a separate social group to identify with (a church, for example, or a group of pub regulars), where proper dignity and mutual respect are observed, and the prevailing social rules are irrelevant.

It was in Zimbabwe that I began to recognize these things about the social hierarchy I grew up in. That recognition depended on the leverage of contrast. The atmosphere of mutual respect I experienced in rural Africa was so pervasive and strong, and so unlike anything I had previously known, that it spurred me to consider how my own culture had developed so differently. This atmosphere also revealed to me for the first time the extent of the psychological bruising I myself had received in a fairly average - though more than average 'churchy', middle-class upbringing.

I am convinced that the cultural memory of feudal power relations underlies our persistent debilitating sense of rank and station in the West. Whatever we are doing, we compare ourselves - are we better than her, than them? Where do we stand on the ladder of wealth, status, skill or merit? Medieval awareness of hierarchy has been modernized into the competitive streak in Western culture so nurtured in the USA, and now more and more also in Europe.

All of this seems so opposed to egalitarian values that it is hard to see how a socialist like Marx could have 'approved' feudalism at all. But Marx's approach to history had two angles: the first angle used economic analysis as a weapon for change. Marx radically criticized injustice and exploitation, pointing out the brutality underlying supposedly respectable society, and the self-serving motivation behind the high-sounding ideologies of the powerful. This critical, protesting impulse in Marx's work has since inspired people all over the world to cast off the mental and political chains of their oppression by their own ruling classes or by foreign colonial powers.

The other angle of Marx's theory said a great 'yes' to history, *including* all the degradation and alienation suffered by the dispossessed majority, by declaring the whole of history to be 'progressive'. History, Marx claimed, would inevitably culminate in the socialist revolution, which would lead to the end of all exploitation and injustice. This complacent and fatalistic aspect of Marxism has been used to sanction all sorts of new oppression in this century.

There may be wisdom in apparent contradictions, so we should not automatically assume that this one is nonsensical. However it is confusing. The revolution is held at one and the same time to be an inevitable event *and* something to be actively struggled for. This produces an irresolvable dilemma: if we consider ourselves to be 'progressive', are we therefore the instruments of historical forces which are inherently progressive anyway - or *does history depend on us* to carry it 'forward'?

Questions like these bring us close to the endless wrangles over free will versus predetermination that have dogged Christian theology since it began. Even though Marxism purports to dispense with Christian categories of thought, it is still dogged by the same old either/or dualism.

In the dualist Western tradition, first you divide something whole (like life) into two mutually exclusive concepts, like good and evil, or physical and spiritual reality. Then you veer about perplexedly between the two mutually exclusive categories you have created, or spend a great deal of energy trying to explain away the gulf you have opened up. So both Christians and Marxists struggle endlessly with the irresolvable tension between predestination, or historical inevitably, on the one hand, and free will, or activism, on the other.

Marx's confident (yet unscientific and unverifiable) declaration of faith in socialism's 'inevitability' recalls the Hebrews' belief in the eventual, promised coming of Messiah as well as the Christian belief in the Second Coming. Note that the cultural continuity is expressed in the *idea*, 'We've been promised a Happy Ending', rather than in the *content* of what is believed.

Pattern is stronger than colour, form more durable than content. The Jews chose to reject Jesus, so they could go on waiting for Messiah; the Christians who accepted him than had to replace *that* longed-for event with another promised culmination - which Jesus reportedly encouraged them to look for - in order to fulfil the deeply-imprinted pattern of confident expectation.

But besides the general cultural context in which Marx lived and wrote, there is also a more specific influence on his work which helps to explain the contradiction in his approach to history.

I believe the reason for Marx's ambivalence about the nature of history lies in the clash between his own essential motivation and the world view of his main intellectual predecessor, the German idealist philosopher Hegel, whose system Marx took over and modified for his own purposes. Marx's gut-level starting point was outrage at the miseries and degradation inflicted on working people in the early years of the Industrial Revolution in Europe. Hegel, on the other hand, can be seen as a self-satisfied apologist of the emerging late eighteenth-century Prussian political identity - a loyal servant of Frederick the Great.

In her own eyes and to the rest of Northern Europe, Prussia represented a go-ahead, disciplined and efficient fighting force, a young society on the march, sweeping away outdated superstitions, customs and beliefs which stood in the way of Progress and rationality. In the ears of Poles and non-Prussian Germans, the word 'Prussian' still has a chilling, militaristic ring to it.

Hegel 'absolutized' Progress. He placed philosophy in the service of history, and conceived of historical Progress as humanity's ultimate spiritual and objective self-fulfilment. Such ideas obviously have a strong attraction for committed and idealistic minds, such as Marx's and many others. But if the twentieth century has taught us Westerners anything at all, we must surely realize by now that systematic ideas are both invigorating and deadly dangerous. They are most dangerous when they jump to universal conclusions about human nature from their own limited social and historical frame of reference - particularly when, as is usual, the leap is unconscious. (Writing like this is rarely immune from such Western habits, and readers should beware.)

Besides the well-known horrors initiated under Hitler, Stalin and Pol Pot, the twentieth-century habit of applying systematic ideas to human society has caused a great deal of less publicized suffering from disastrous resettlement and 'villagization' schemes in Tanzania and elsewhere, to US support for military governments in Latin America.

Hegel developed an elegant system to explain what he saw as historical Progress. Any given state of affairs, the status quo (or *thesis)* would gradually produce a force opposed to it (*antithesis)*. When these forces met and joined battle, whether by reform, revolution or whatever, the resulting new order (*synthesis*) was set to become the next *thesis*, and so on.

Applying Hegel's system to the social processes of European history, Marx found that feudalism represented the 'progressive' synthesis of an earlier thesis - the disintegrating Roman Empire - and an antithesis - the warring Germanic peoples who moved in from the North-East.

Later, feudalism in turn became a 'thesis' to a new antithesis when the rising European bourgeoisie demanded political freedoms to match their economic power. Feudalism and industrialization - the bourgeois economic order - were thus approved as necessary stages in Western society's Progress towards 'socialism' - which, according to Marx, was/is the best possible modern form of social organization.

This version of events recalls the Christian view of history described in chapter one - the planned Fall from grace, the sending of the Redeemer and the reconciliation between God and Christian humanity. The model is still one of history heading for heaven, and it still involves an acceptance of injustice and misery as stages in an overall plan which is 'for our own good' in the long run, according to an authoritarian God figure (Jahweh - Marx/Hegel - the early capitalists). As fathers have said raising their hands to their children, 'You'll thank me one day'.

Religious or secular, both biblical and Marxist plans amount to massively deferred gratification. Deferred gratification is a kind of cultural Christmas club or incentive scheme which sacrifices its children's innocence and ease of mind for the sake of more self-discipline, which is supposed to lead to greater effort and achievement. And so, at an unnameable price, the great Western cultural superiority syndrome (CSS) is born.

Seen in this light, our CSS, our habit of deferred gratification, and our idea of a grand plan of history with a happy ending and ourselves in the starring role all seem like attempts to mitigate psychic and social suffering. We have rewritten our history, our mythology and our ideology in order to render the pain of what has happened to us, and of what we have done, bearable - that is, necessary, and for our own ultimate Progress.

The first question to be raised against the predominant Western view of history is whether the way we Westerners treat our own past is fair, either on that past or on ourselves. What exactly do we mean - and what abuses do we approve - when we refer to feudalism, and to industrialization, as 'progressive' stages in our history? Why this applause for the winners - who, as we know from experience, are often the most ruthless and least humane among us? Do our own deep-rooted and sound values, wisdom and humanity not deserve more respect than this? What about the values of the losers, the peacemakers, those who suffer rather than wield power? Do we really believe in the virtue of the winners?

Self-respect and respect for others go hand in hand: we can't have one without the other. If our self-respect depends on being 'better' than someone else, then we have no true dignity at all. This, I believe, sums up the cultural tragedy of class-based society.

I have learned these things from within, by growing up in a class-based society myself, and then having some experience of life in a non-feudal and non-industrial society.

Besides the four years I spent in rural Zimbabwe, I have also noticed distinct contrasts between the social atmospheres on Orkney and in mainland Scotland which I take to be linked to differences between the two places in land ownership as well as industrial history. Many of the insights in Edwin Muir's autobiography confirm and expand on these observations with reference to Orkney and Glasgow.[3]

From what I have seen and felt in Africa and Orkney, it seems to me that societies which have had less direct and intense experience of feudal land ownership and virtually none of industrialization, have retained a higher level of general dignity, self-possession and courtesy, and a more confident public wisdom, than feudal or industrialized societies enjoy. This means that the majority of people in these societies command respect and authority by virtue of being born into the society, which the majority of people in class-based society do not command.

There are concrete socio-economic reasons for this loss of general public respect and authority. The system of land ownership is fundamental to a society's frame of mind, since land represents the original and traditional means to survival. Yet 'survival' is a materialist reduction and trivialization of what is at stake here. For land really represents the means to live with dignity. People who have lost their land have lost their birthright. Henceforth, they and their children must 'earn' their dignity or do without it.

Jobs and careers are industrial society's land substitute. And once jobs and careers are gone, nothing is left. It is no wonder that education became so important to Scots in the nineteenth century, or that poor people the world over now spend money they don't have to secure formal Western-style education for their children: for education is the main route back to dignity for the dispossessed.

Yet there *are* other routes, in a feudal or colonial society. Some of us will have experienced the curious humiliation of meeting servants at the 'big house' in the North of Scotland or in Africa, who identify with the fates of the 'big family'. Their whole working pride and satisfaction is lodged with the honour and happiness of their employers. This is a glimpse of the famous social contract of feudalism, the one whose loss is still lamented by Southern whites in the USA, and by the Rhodesians, and a few older black Zimbabweans, at least when they are talking to whites, who recall the 'secure and happy' days of harmonious master-slave, or houseboy/farmboy - *baas* relations.

We Westerners mostly reject this kind of 'happiness' with a shudder of distaste - *so why should we regard feudalism itself - or the Roman Empire, for that matter - as an advance over 'primitive' peasant agriculture and society?*

Well - because the social arrangements of feudalism facilitated the flourishing of 'high culture' in the manner of great houses, great lords and ladies, magnificently endowed universities, monasteries, cathedrals, crusades, military glory and all. Indeed, the luxury lifestyle of the medieval aristocracy sparked off the industrial revolution - inasmuch as such massive accumulations of private wealth stimulated trade, which led to the establishment of the merchant class, which of course aspired to a similar lifestyle for itself, and political rights, and here we are back in the present again.

The triumph of our economic Progress in the West is truly inseparable from feudalism, just as our present institutions of higher learning and our whole intellectual culture have the monasteries, libraries and foundations of previous privilege to thank for their existence now.

Marx himself was the first to draw many of these historical connections, and he would not have denied the ambivalent, 'dialectical' nature of our Progress. He, after all, developed the concept of alienation, which has become one of the necessary ideas for understanding the way we live now in the West. This is the idea that something fundamental to our life and originally our own - for example, our work or our land - was taken over by someone else, alienated from us and that in turn, we have become alienated from our work and from the land.

When casting doubt on the positive overtones usually accorded to Progress in our society, it is essential to keep sight of our *dual* heritage. *The connections between the better and the worse sides of our history are what constitute its meaning*: they are our story. Ultimately, there is no separating out 'good' from 'bad' Progress, and no siding with the angels, as I think Marx later tended to try to do, and as many of his followers have most definitely tried to do.

However, that does not mean we have to sit on the fence, equivocating. On the contrary, I would suggest that the triumph of class-based culture in Europe represented a catastrophic arrogation of power, wealth and authority by a tiny minority from the general commonwealth of ordinary people who were living in Europe - and who still live in Europe, and elsewhere.

Given all these co-existent strands in any culture, and the mythological nature of the Progress idea, it may be more correct to speak of *tendencies* than *stages* when discussing the cultural consciousness arising out of feudal power relations. In the West, women, urban subcultures, schoolchildren and country people maintain other values besides the dominant ones, values which may oppose, complement, or just co-exist with them.

In Africa, I noticed the cooking-pot-and-soft-drink culture, the interface between Western and rural African norms, but there must have been other interfaces which I couldn't spot, just as there are in any family or community anywhere, which has to contend with class, gender, national, regional, denominational and character differences.

I am suggesting, then, that the class-based *tendency* in European society has been catastrophic, and that Marx's main error lay in accepting the consolidation of the class system in medieval European society as a 'progressive' stage in our history.

Whether or not this tendency is irreversible remains to be seen: but so far, for all the West's democratic self-image, the class-based tendency in our society remains largely unreversed.

I believe that true progress for Western society would mean recovering a sense of personal and communal dignity, identity and interdependence - the kind of easy and utter dismissal of economic pride and prestige, and the self-validating confidence of the kind that Robert Burns expresses in the poem, *A Man's a Man for A' That*. (Though it's a pity there isn't a simple, comfortable, but respectful word in English for a human being, a person, that doesn't rely for its resonance on patriarchal power relations.)

Such true progress would need to be based on completely different ways of living and working, ways which dispensed with inherited patterns of authority and oppression; whereas up till now, throughout our apparent Progress, we have perpetuated the structures inherited from feudalism. Often we have broadened their social base through political reform or revolution. But we have not done away with our underlying models of authority or land ownership or gender relations or exclusivity, as principles of social organization - for to do any of that would mean 'turning the clock back'.

Yet it seems to me that some kind of radical 'turning the clock back' is the only true way *forward* for our society: forward out of feudalism and feudalism's modern forms - the oppressive, exploitative relations both within our society, and between ourselves and other societies, as well as our relations with trees and plants, and with the earth itself. We need to move *forward into survival*, not through more control, management, information and so on, but through *letting go of our need to control*. We need to learn to accept the variety and unpredictability of life as it is in itself, and to respect people as they are in themselves, in their variety and unpredictability. I believe that if we carry on refusing to take these lessons on board, history will teach them to us sooner or later.

We usually think of the last three hundred years or so of growing Western affluence and political enfranchisement in the West as the dawn of democracy, our society's gradual self-liberation from the bonds of feudalism. But I believe that besides introducing fairer forms of social organization, we middle-class Westerners have also been busy transferring the burden of serfdom as far as possible outside our own (middle) class and even our own (Western) society, in order both to maximize our material security and our new global aristocrat status, and to minimize social political dissent and upheaval at home in the West. First slavery, then colonialism and now global economic domination are a continuation in other guises of the oppressive power relations of a class-based society.

Now that I have outlined the beginnings of the European class system, let me clarify who 'we' are. It would be unfair to spread the blame or responsibility for what has been done in the name of Western Progress equally over all members of European society - about as unfair as the Poll Tax. The traditional kings-queens-and-battles approach to history is fairer, in this sense, than the Poll Tax or the undiscriminating 'we' - for usually the ruling class does take decisions and initiate wars, purportedly on behalf of society - but really on their own behalf.

We-the-powerful are the ones who have saved ourselves political, social and psychological upheaval by inflicting upheaval and exploitation on others, at home and abroad - a political form of projection. We-the-powerful are the ones who have carefully maximized our material security at the expense of others' health and livelihoods.

The times when people mutiny, rebel, strike, protest, and manage to affect or change the status quo are the exceptions which prove the rule that the powerful usually decide what happens. These unusual occasions we call revolutions, and interestingly, English historians seem to pride themselves on the fact that England has managed to avoid them for over 300 years.

At times of revolution, the balance of power shifts, temporarily or permanently, until a new normality is established, and a new ruling group or a restored old one, or a blend of both, establishes a new status quo and assumes the continuing privileges of power.

I myself am a member of the privileged strata of European society, privileged by social background (a small-town manse) and by education. Whatever way I choose to live, I cannot renounce my middle-class roots. However tangled and diseased they are, they feed me, and intertwined with the roots of others, they connect me with my main audience - others who have learned the inside of our social history like me, through their middle-class roots.

Owning up to our inherited Western middle-class privilege and power doesn't mean we should sink into swamps of guilt or de-

spair. I am not personally, invdividually responsible for the actions of my class throughout history. As far as I know, I did not
choose to be born middle class; and even if I did, just as my class
has hurt and damaged others, I myself have been hurt and damaged by those actions and their effects. Yet I have also received
benefits and advantages for which it would be churlish not to feel
grateful.

While there is no point in trying to dissociate ourselves from
our class background, people from other classes and cultures can
teach us a great deal. But they cannot do our changing for us.
Only deep within ourselves can new insights germinate, grow and
bear fruit.

At the start of this chapter, I wondered what had happened
during the Middle Ages to the Hebrews' spiritual model of an
onward and upward walk with God. It is hard to see at first how
the feudal era could have accommodated any sort of Progress
model into its world view. Both the ancient Hebrew idea of a
people on the move with God as their guide, and the modern
notion of social change leading to improvements in the human
condition would seem incompatible with the feudal glorification
of an unchanging, hierarchically ordered cosmos.

The feudal outlook in China, for example, as glimpsed in the
philosophy of Confucius or the wisdom of the Chinese Book of
Changes, the *I-Ching*, assumed permanence and cosmic significance in the prevailing social order. The existing hierarchy was
not up for criticism, and not to be tampered with. The highest
wisdom was seen to lie in fulfiling one's proper function within
the hierarchy, observing the limitations of one's situation and per-
forming one's duties with grace and perseverance.

No doubt the feudal outlook in Europe was similar, and for
similar reasons. Feudalism demands rigorous and cosmic self-justification, for in any society, the subjugation and control of the
huge majority of their fellows by an active and powerful minority is a massive social enterprise as well as a deadly crime against
the human spirit.

The setting up and enforcement of feudal power structures means
the wholesale creation of *true poverty* throughout non-aristocratic
society. True poverty has nothing to do with wearing or not wearing silk, or even shoes, or with sitting on the floor to eat, or lying
on the floor to sleep. There is no shame or hardship involved in
any of these conditions, if this is how everyone around you lives.

As long as people have the means to assuring their dignity and survival - in that order, I believe - there is no question of poverty.

True poverty has to be deliberately introduced into society, along with insecurity, which is not so much a material as a psycho-spiritual condition. It must take a great deal of energy, ingenuity, organization and discipline to impose significant inequality on a society previously accustomed to equality, and to persuade people to accept displays of vast wealth accumulated at their expense as the expressions of divine will. To do all this, traditional social morality must be thoroughly undermined and upended, for traditional morality still suspects the opportunist, the bully and the go-ahead individualist alike - 'Who does she think she is?', 'Kent his faither.'

To be truly poor, you must *feel* poor, knowing yourself to be denied the means to full self-respect, in the terms of your own society. *Labelling people 'poor' is one step towards the creation of poverty. Depriving people of land is another.* Both of these policies are being vigorously carried out all over the so-called Third World (in reality the two-thirds world) at present. They were carried out a long time ago in Europe, not so long ago in the Americas and in Australasia.

Wherever we find magnificent and impressive artefacts built by great civilizations, we may surmise that extreme inequalities were present. This is true of Egypt, Greece and Rome as well as of the Aztecs and Incas, and the 'glories' of medieval Europe and Islam. Denying full dignity and equality of worth to most of the members of a community is surely a very high price to pay for such achievements.

Nor does a ruling class escape the consequences of oppression: for its members forfeit their inherent human dignity by resorting to force and fear in place of mutual respect freely given. They also lose their material and psychological self-reliance by coming to rely on their subordinates for all the necessities of life, from breast feeding to food production and domestic maintenance work.

Civilization's crimes against the commonwealth call for massive cultural excuses, and given the religious basis of morality in all cultures, the justifications for privilege have not surprisingly taken religious as well as political forms.

There may indeed be a relationship between the degree of social injustice accepted as 'normal' within a culture, and how complex and inflexible its religious and philosophical systems appear. For every society which has passed into the hands of a powerful minority must already have experienced many, many generations of more egalitarian communal life, and must have evolved a precise sense of the right way of doing things which corresponds with that earlier experience. This ancestral morality would have to be based on respect and tolerance for differences, while maintaining the security of the whole community.

As we have seen (*attitudes long, economics short*) culturally-inherited thought patterns are not easily shifted, though they may be repressed, adapted and overlaid with other ideas and constructs. So it may be that the wider the gulf between the longer-term ancestral morality and the more recent historical practice of a community, the more rigid and monolithic the ideological superstructure has to be, to keep that 'new' practice in place.

If this is so, then feudalism in Europe looks doomed from the start. For in addition to the usual, 'prehistoric' sense of natural justice common to all peoples, Europe had more recently inherited the very consciously articulated 'progressive' ethics of the Hebrews, transmuted into a new, utopian religion starring saints, clerics, angels and all sorts of miracles of healing, justice and revenge. The travelling morality plays may have looked to the ruling classes like harmless, even edifying entertainment for the masses; but the very presence in the culture of such egalitarian ideas as were contained in the Hebrew Bible and the New Testament were bound to lead to trouble in the long run. We are told that Europe's medieval Christians were taught to expect the reward for their virtue in heaven, not here on earth; but I doubt if resignation ever became very deep rooted in the European psyche. And what of the medieval clerics? Did they, as Marx and the Church Reformers later claimed, go along with the oppression of their countrypeople, knowing which side their bread was buttered? Or was everyone, like today, confused by the contradictions between Christian preaching and human practice?

I do not believe that contradictions between our innate sense of natural justice and everyday social practice are intrinsic to the human condition; but they may well be unavoidable in 'civilized' life.

Like Europe, both China and India had long feudal eras, and it is interesting to consider how differently Chinese and Indian religion and society have developed from the West. We in the West inherited, from our Greek, Roman and Hebrew predecessors, an impulse to examine the world and ourselves critically and to seek redress for our wrongs in the world around us. This impulse has propelled us, with great force, out of feudalism and into the nuclear-digital age.

Without recourse to such an extraverted cultural impulse, both Indian and Chinese societies have put their energies into psychologically and spiritually *accommodating* the contradictions between feudalism and natural justice, by developing techniques whereby material suffering can be disregarded and transcended on the road to enlightenment.

To point out this cultural contrast is not to imply a criticism of Eastern 'passivity', though that is the common Western response. Nor do I want to assert that inner mastery is more important than sorting things out in the world, though I believe it is likely to bring more personal peace than our Western attempts at outer mastery do. But we Westerners need to live in ways that feel culturally comfortable to us. We cannot simply ignore the social, political world we have done so much to shape.

I have suggested that our Western efforts to reform the world and ourselves have not succeeded in undoing the damage originally wreaked in our society by feudal and pre-feudal powergrabs. Rather, we have externalized onto other peoples the indignities inflicted within our own culture, and we have also internalized these indignities ourselves, over many generations, by passing on our own mental suffering to our children.

Yet the *impulse* to 'progress' has remained a touchstone of our Western culture, with the acclaimed 'stability' of the medieval world view a mere halt in our historical march into tomorrow.

For the Hebrews of biblical times, Progress has been a linear, historical model of cultural conquest and consolidation, and a deepening, ever more differentiated relationship with their God. In the Roman Empire and in the Middle Ages, this linear Progress was upended and turned into a vertical, ladder-like construct. Henceforth, in Western culture, Progress would be at least as much 'upward' as 'onward' - upward socially, economically, and in terms of authority and power. Social climbing was well on its way.

In different eras our ambitions express themselves differently - in the Middle Ages it may have been more acceptable to harbour religious ambitions than economic ones. For several centuries, the European Jews were left alone with the profit motive, which was deemed unChristian. But this did not stop Christian Europeans vying for power in Church and State, or becoming rich from trade. And the Church itself managed to get very rich indeed without apparently resorting to business.

Many European fairy tales bear out both the age and the nature of our social ambition: *Cinderella, Dick Whittington, Puss in Boots*, but also *Rumplestiltskin* and *Jack and the Beanstalk*, with their fantasy structure of rags to riches, express a tenacious preoccupation with obtaining wealth and ease, and the respect and relief that these are hoped to bring with them from a life of hardship and indignity.

Religious meditations in the Middle Ages were of course also focused upwards. The seven circles of St Theresa of Avila's Castle represent a different kind of ambition and hierarchy, but a Progress nonetheless, from outer to inner, lower to higher levels of mystical awareness and godliness.

And we Westerners still carry a heavy medieval legacy around with us - the ladder of power and influence which, unless we climb it, or knock it over, will forever tower above us, reminding us of our inadequacy and failure. Even the relatively classless North Americans and Australians have their own versions of the European pyramid, based on wealth and career. The mental structure of class has found new content in the European diaspora, it has not disappeared. By the end of the Middle Ages, armed with out class-based model of vertical Progress as well as the linear and ethical Hebrew idea, we Europeans were well-equipped to take on a world less driven by its past.

3

The Age of Discovery

*Meglobmania - Pyramids and tantrums - Shakespeare in
Zimbabwe - God on our side - The Burnings -
Eradicating awe - Insecurity and backlash*

FROM ABOUT 1475 - 1750, Europeans began to go to areas of the world
we had never been to before, and to meet there peoples we had
not known about. Unfortunately for ourselves and for everyone
else, these 'discoveries' of ours soon led to the European conquest of these areas, particularly the Americas and Australasia,
and thence to our innovative involvement in slavery - the sugar
and banana, tea and coffee plantations, the transatlantic trade in
Africans - and even to our takeover of India. This era marked the
start of European imperialism, and the transformation of a great
proportion of the world into 'our colonies'.

The modern West's original sin was first committed in this era. I
refer to the sin of globalism - or meglobmania - in which, despite
decolonization, we are now more deeply involved than ever.

The material and technological circumstances that allowed Europeans to encircle the globe are well known. Navigation skills
were acquired from the Arabs and from ancient Middle Eastern
astronomy, and the forests of Europe were chopped down to build
navies. The Portuguese, the Spanish and later the British vied for
control of the new territories and their untold riches. Our successes must have bred a certain pride in achievement, possibly
even arrogance towards those we were conquering. Could we have
guessed then that we were heading for five hundred years of increasing global power and accumulation of wealth? Now it seems
so natural to us that we in the West were born with silver spoons
in our mouths, born to rule, to teach, to dispense aid and military

assistance. But what were we like as one culture among others, back in those days before all this came to pass?

The values of this era included exploration, discovery and adventure. These values clearly clashed with the values of stability and permanence propounded in medieval Europe, and in many ways the new age did threaten the foundations of feudal culture. It was an era of destabilization and transition.

Besides the excitement of navigation and of discovering distant shores and riches, there was the excitement of the Renaissance and the Reformation, two huge cultural events or processes which were closely interrelated. The Renaissance was kicked off as Europeans rediscovered the artistic and philosophical achievements of Rome and Greece, as well as of Islam, and began to practise using their own intellects independently of what the Church taught. The Reformation was part of the same process of individual self-assertion in the face of the status quo.

Some Europeans started judging their institutions against the principles these institutions espoused, and feeling they had a right to change them or leave them behind if they proved corrupt or inadequate. Others stopped being content to accept the Church's word for other things: for example, the way heaven and earth were constructed. They began to regard their own minds as more reliable instruments of knowledge than the doctrinal declarations of clerics.

The exhilaration of this new-found self-confidence must have injected tremendous energy into late fifteenth- and sixteenth-century European culture. It must have felt like the world - heaven and earth - were opening up before us. Indeed we still cherish many unrepeatable works of genius from this era - by Michelangelo, Leonardo da Vinci, Dante, Shakespeare. The context that produced such creativity as theirs and hundreds of their contemporaries remembered and forgotten was, I believe, the interface between Europe's relatively intact traditional cultures, with all their amassed mythology, cosmology, customs and rites; and a new culture of enquiry, discovery and individual initiative.

There is an innocence about this stage in any meeting of cultures, or time of transition. The real, fresh experience of dawning freedom from ancient thought patterns spurs individuals to express freely things that before remained implicit in the culture, well-known by its members but not requiring verbal expression. Dante and Shakespeare do not explicitly celebrate the new freedoms of the age in their great writings, for as yet these have no content to celebrate. The 'winds of change' are simply felt as scissors snipping away at familiar bonds, leaving the limbs freer to act.

What *is* expressed, so beautifully and profoundly that we are still spellbound by these works, is *the old human condition experienced by the newly self-conscious individual*: that is, the old world view which was being left behind as they wrote.

Something similar is happening at present throughout the world Europe colonized, but this time its main medium of expression seems to be in music, as people from different traditional backgrounds meet the new technology of the West - its sounds, its instruments, its recording equipment, its international travel facilities. The vibrant musical fusions of this era we live in have the same fresh authenticity and cultural depth as what Dante and Shakespeare offered to the world in their more leisured, measured age. And again, African, Indian and South American musicians do not offer us simply their version of the new era - what we and they value in their music is what has come to them *from their past* - the rhythms and polyphony of village life and cultural festivals that are fast becoming extinct, or finding new urban forms.

Renaissance literature and contemporary musical fusions, then, both illustrate a paradox of our Western myth of Progress, namely that *the impulse to liberate ourselves from inherited values can be expressed in celebration of these very values*. Change co-exists with no change.

In passing from the feudal era into the age of discovery, European culture slipped the leash of old authority in science and religion, yet *we carried the structure of that authority within us into the new era*. Attitudes long, economics short. 'Economics', in this phrase, can stand for other rapidly changing, apparently crucial factors in our communal life: however radical the surface changes, inner continuity is maintained.

If we imagine the feudal structure in European Church and State as a kind of social and psychological prison, we first built ourselves a prison, then we broke out of it - except that we found ourselves running away carrying the prison on our backs, or in our hearts. Another image is of a beautiful elegant three-masted sailing ship, on its way to the New World - but among its masts and rigging is clearly marked out the delicate shape of a *pyramid* - symbol of Old World oppression and the dead weight of the past. For better *and* for worse, we carry our history with us, and take it wherever we go - both as individuals and as a culture.

On the personal plane: when I left home at seventeen for my first summer abroad, I thought I was walking unencumbered into the future, leaving behind me all my small-town longings, my frustrations and my unhappiness, my childhood and adolescent inadequacies. Over twenty years later, I realize that my history's been travelling with me all this way.

For good and for ill, *we are who we have become, and who we are still becoming*. There is no leaving history behind. Perhaps the best we can do in the present, as individuals and as a culture, is *to acknowledge and honour who we have become* as fully as possible.

The Middle Ages had a baleful effect on our European cultural expectations. We had become inured to hierarchy and class differences, also to obeying the authorities, whose word should not be questioned. Although both of these feudal tendencies have long been opposed by cultural values we have acquired since the feudal era, the earlier authoritarian expectations still live on. Modern Marxists, for example, have set up rigid hierarchies of command and behaved as self-righteously and dogmatically as any medieval priesthood; while anarchists on the other hand, who take issue with the idea and practice of hierarchical authority, are equated, in our medievally-tinged Western awareness, with terrorist bombers!

Since the UK - and England in particular - has remained more enslaved to class distinctions than most of the rest of Europe, it should be quite easy for British readers to look within ourselves and find our medieval layer of cultural conditioning. We learn authoritarian habits at home first, usually from our parents, and then at school. Then, of course, at work.

So how do we learn the new values that were in formation during the age of discovery, the early modern era in Europe? An example that springs to mind instantly is the eternal question 'Why?' asked by many Western children till their parents feel like screaming. This question is never heard from Zimbabwean children - which just goes to show (say Westerners) that African children are understimulated and not taught to have enquiring minds. Such a question, from an African child, would be regarded as inane, irrelevant, or rebellious.

Yet, sometimes I think it is not so much factual explanations that our children are really demanding of us when they go on and on repeating the question, as more attention and reassurance from us than they are getting. This is why palming them off with absent-minded replies, while we try to keep thinking our own thoughts, is counterproductive. Because adult Western culture is so verbal and information-orientated, our children become pre-cociously verbal and information-orientated to engage us in the only kind of contact we grownups seem comfortable with.

I believe tantrums are another effect of early modern values on our children, and again, these are very rarely seen in Africa. Every Western parent of a two-year-old knows that the tantrum has to do with self-assertion, the discovery of the possibility of saying 'no'. Western parents constantly say 'no' to their children, either in words or by not responding to their signals, while African parents very rarely say an outright 'no' to an infant. They respond swiftly to his/her needs, give way or divert the child's attention.

As long as a child is secure and happy, its expectations are the best indicator of its real needs.[1] This basic understanding is shared by most traditional cultures, yet it has been lost sight of in ours, and perhaps it is bound to lose ground in all hierarchical societies, where the needs of the weak are not met.

We in European culture threw off a great weight of accumulated hierarchical baggage, by learning to say a great big 'NO' in the fifteenth and sixteenth centuries. First we stamped our feet at the religious authorities, then later at the political authorities. Ever since then we have been testing our wills against the universe's, against previously sacred truths and received opinions - against whatever resists us.

No wonder we say 'no' to our children so much, and no wonder they say 'no' to us. As offspring of an insistently questioning, authoritarian yet self-asserting culture, our children accurately reflect our attitudes to the world in their behaviour. All they want to do is to belong and be like us.

The questioning approach was not invented by Renaissance Europeans, for the Greeks had taken it quite far much earlier. But those first stirrings of independent intellectual enquiry in Europe were stifled by a combination of things. The Roman Empire, after keeping the philosophical tradition alive for several centuries, gradually declined and lost power to non-literary cultures for whom Greek philosophy would have held little interest, had they ever chanced to hear of it. Literary culture, during these centuries was maintained by the monasteries, which had an understandable bias towards Christian scriptures and commentaries, lives of saints and other theologically illuminating texts.

(I do not agree with most Western commentators that intellectual innovation is a touchstone of 'civilization' or human culture worthy of the name, for I believe mental originality is a very mixed blessing.)

Europe's reawakening to the joys of independent thought owed a great deal to the Arabs, who had been academically busy (and in Spain) for several centuries. They had preserved and further developed many important disciplines, like maths, astronomy and medicine, with which 'barbarian' Europe had lost touch. When the Spaniards drove them out of Europe, together with the Jews, in the late fifteenth century, Europe grabbed the torch of knowledge from them rather ungraciously, eyes fixed on the finishing line.

Astronomy, shipbuilding and gunpowder from China proved an irresistible combination, and soon we were able to take our enquiring minds - and our religious dogmas - to the 'ends' of the (Zounds! It's round!) earth.

It may seem a strange thing to say, but the spectacular scale of European intellectual endeavour in the last five hundred years probably owes a lot to the Middle Ages. Early modern thinkers in Europe had a much larger object on which to vent their scepticism than the Greeks ever had. Socrates poked fun at cults and mystery rites which, though well established in tradition, were diverse and locally based. The early modern European thinkers, on the other hand, had a massive, monolithic structure to oppose: namely, the Holy Roman Catholic Church, which had already defeated many a greater enemy than they. The Church, with its colossal power and wealth, its claims to absolute authority and universal truth, its patently corrupt practices, and its worldly wealth and political machinations, was the perfect target for the apprentice archers of modern Reason.

The more repressive the upbringing, the more violent the rebellion, if and when it comes. What holds for individuals holds also for groups of people. By the same token, the excesses of disrespect which the West has committed against nature, including our own and other people's humanity, probably owe a great deal to the persistence, right up into the present day, of dogmatic, repressive authority in our culture.

The kind of changes of consciousness ushered in during the age of discovery were spearheaded, often unconsciously, by a very few exceptional people, and the radical implications of what they did - in science, or art, or philosophy - were only very gradually accepted as cultural attitudes by a wider group of informed people.

Cultural change happens very slowly and gradually. Different, even contradictory aspects can and do co-exist, from different eras, like layers in a lasagne. This is a kind of cultural 'trickle down' process, as the sauce poured over a lasagne eventually, but slowly, soaks through the whole dish in the oven.

One of the best ways of stepping inside a past era of our own culture is, I think, to study the literature of the time. As it happens, in my Zimbabwean English lessons, Shakespeare was on the curriculum.

Many might feel that teaching Shakespeare to rural Zimbabweans takes the prize for neo-colonial arrogance, irrelevance and futility. Many of the European volunteer teachers I knew certainly thought so. Others would say that Shakespeare is a timeless and 'universal' writer, and having seen the effect of his plays on young Zimbabweans, I would testify that his work crosses cultural barriers with ease.

I was indeed startled and touched to see how deeply the Zimbabwean students were prepared to delve into Shakespeare's text, unravelling and appreciating the different levels of meaning, relishing both the political thrust of the action and the poetic long-windedness that bored me at school.

I shouldn't have been surprised. Shakespeare's pace of story-telling, his characters' symbolic mode of thinking and dignified way of expressing themselves were far closer to the habits of these young Africans who had spent their childhood evenings round the fire listening to their grandparents' tales, than they were to us TV-watching teenyboppers.

But Shakespeare is also a product of *his* time and place. It is easier to spot the cultural blinkers in a second-rate writer than it is in a great writer who keeps saying things that are true for all kinds of people in very different times and places. But great writers have them too.

The first time I became aware of Shakespeare's (and my own) cultural limitations in the Zimbabwean classroom was in Act I of *Richard II*. In scene three there is a duel whose outcome is supposed to show whether one of the combatants had been guilty of a suspected political murder. As British teenagers, my friends and I would have giggled at the naiveté of the Shakespearean age, but we would have recognized the familiar assumption that the just man wins - or at least *should* win. After all, it is the underlying theme of most Western hero myths and fairy tales, of cowboy films and detective stories, and of our society's approach to war and politics.

The Zimbabwean students were neither amused nor incredulous, they were just baffled. Whereas they were usually enthusiastic and gripped by the action, even if they found the language difficult, and only too pleased to debate and speculate, this scene obviously left them confused and frustrated. It took me a while to realize why the lesson was not going well. They couldn't see how the duel was relevant to the story: what possible connection could there be between the outcome of this combat and the resolution of the question: Who was the murderer?

When I finally saw what was wrong, I explained that the Elizabethans believed that God would support the innocent party in an armed combat: and they laughed aloud. Their laughter was not mocking - it was laughter of shock and disbelief. (In Africa, laughter often expresses strong negative as well as positive emotions, even including anger.)

For these young Zimbabweans, the idea of enlisting God on one side only in a human confrontation was a presumption they were unwilling to believe of any culture, let alone their English teacher's. They were embarrassed, I could see, to have to spell out something so basic and obvious to me, their educational role model. But under the pressure of my evident incomprehension, they did spell it out. This is what they told me, more or less: 'God is not involved in human battles. *People* fight wars against each other for their own reasons. *God is not on one side or another.*'

As I write, I am still exploring what I felt, and what they may have felt, in that oddly charged, mutually shaming moment of recognition. I asked them about their own beliefs - to whom *would* they pray for help, if not to God? Of course, they explained, they would pray to their ancestors, who could be relied on to provide support and protection if the proper ceremonies had first been performed. And fighters might try using spells to make themselves bullet-proof. There were mixed opinions about the effectiveness of such measures. But to imagine God taking sides in a human conflict: that could not be done.

(I am not sure if this still needs to be spelt out to a modern Western audience, but God was not brought to Africa for the first time by Christian missionaries from Europe!)

My students effortless understanding of divine impartiality was a humbling discovery for me. This was only a few years after Zimbabwe's hard-won liberation from Ian Smith's Rhodesia, a war against my own people. Quite possibly, I was only able to live in their country as happily and safely as I did thanks to this gracious, enlightened cultural attitude which I had not even noticed properly.

I had learned and sung many Zimbabwean liberation songs with my local friends, and with the students at school. Moving and often mournful, I noticed now that they never cited God to justify Zimbabwean actions in war, though the ancestors, understandably partisan, featured strongly.

Black South Africans have also refrained from enlisting God on their side in their long struggle against white domination whereas the Afrikaners have been citing the Bible - the word of God - to justify their attitudes and behaviour ever since they arrived in Africa. And as Southern African history has proceeded, an interesting contrast has emerged. For it seems that Christianity alone is not enough to give people expectations of divine sanction for their cause, however just it may be. Most black South Africans are now at least as fervently Christian as Afrikaners have ever been, yet they do not entertain this peculiarly Western superstition.

African culture's different view of God from our own helps to explain why most Zimbabweans and South Africans do not glory in war as we have done through the centuries. Perhaps our belief in 'divine right', combined with our warriorlike 'barbarian' ancestry helps to explain how monotheistic cultures like Christianity and Islam have learned to glory in something so ungodly and evil as war.

Armed with our delusion of divine right, we in the West seem to feel little or no shame for our record of violence towards other societies. On the contrary, we place ourselves without hesitation at the 'forefront of human development', quite unembarrassed by our history of global exploitation and genocide, from North America to Australia and Africa.

It doesn't occur to most of us to feel morally inferior, as a society, to societies who have not enslaved, colonized and misused other peoples, societies which have not excelled and gloried in war as we have done. Rather, we are more likely to feel patronizing towards them; we may even reproach them for not making 'full use of their resources'.

Our idea of ourselves as being on God's side in any quarrel goes back well beyond Shakespeare. It was probably inherited from the Jews' special relationship with Jahweh, who was like a partisan ancestor to them, ensuring their victory as long as they were obedient and properly respectful. The belief in a God who takes sides must have been confirmed by the Christians' early sectarian zeal, and also by the Germanic tribes' traditional worship of Odin, their god of war.

Even before this, the Romans' habit of deifying their emperors would have blurred the lines between religious and political authority, preparing the ground for the colossal medieval European community - the Holy Roman Empire.

Since the early Christian era in Europe, military triumph has been taken as a sign of the divine right to rule. The Roman emperor Constantine converted to Christianity in the belief that the God of the Christians had promised him victory in his next battle. He won, and Christianity became the established religion of the Empire.

All in all, this belief that God supports the winners has been so basic to our history for so long that we Westerners scarcely notice it. We therefore fail to recognize the same superstition in our attitude to the modern forms of our Western power - economic and military dominance. Yet to people in other cultures, our belief that might is right can appear strange and even blasphemous.

European globalism began in the age of discovery, for that is when we started trying to embrace the world with our arms. It may fairly be suspected that only certain cultural personalities would go to such lengths to seek power over other peoples as we have. But no doubt any culture which gains such colossal power as ours has will develop a personality to fit the role.

In the early modern period, Europe was 'emerging' from about five hundred years of semi-stable feudalism: stable, because, like the present system of 'international' capitalism, it seemed monolithic and unmoveable while it lasted; but only 'semi' because, like the present system, feudalism meant deprivation, insecurity and intermittent warfare and upheaval for its ordinary people.

Then in the early modern age of discovery, Europeans began to find areas of the world outwith our own society where we, from the lower layers in the European feudal pyramid, could give vent to our pent-up contempt, envy and ambition with relative impunity. Thus, I believe, was born our destructive relationship with the rest of the world's cultures - indeed with the rest of the natural world: animal, vegetable and mineral.

Cruelty and suffering, once inflicted, do not simply go away. In individuals' lives, they need to be consciously acknowledged and absorbed in order to be forgiven and somehow transcended. But very often, brutality and injustice done to us breed rage and insecurity, and we pass on our hurt to others, usually without even being aware of our compensatory urge to inflict damage, as we ourselves have been damaged.

I have explained this cycle of violence in psychological terms developed by modern Western thinkers and suitable to modern Westerners' behaviour and motivation. But medieval and early modern Europeans did not need subconscious cellars to hide their violence in. They could justify any brutality towards other peoples either as part of the feuding ethic of the warrior tribes or later, with reference to their Christian mission to convert the heathen, drive out devils and bring the light of 'civilization' to their benighted continents.

This theological leap complicates things. Tribal custom is one thing: for good or ill, it is simply the way things are. But totalitarian monotheism is another, particularly when the message preached is of peace, forgiveness and brotherly love. Hypocrisy and double standards are waiting in the wings.

Our increasing European power to travel and conquer was taken, by the Church at least and by the states involved, as proof of our ever extending missionary obligations (divine right again). The missions provided a convenient shield and spear to governments and trading companies. But there was surely less cynicism, and more outright arrogance and downright cruelty than we would like to admit in the first couple of hundred years of this two-pronged attack on other peoples.

When the time came for emigration and *settling* in other people's home areas, Europe's pious, its poor and rejected took readily to the role of brave, hard-working pioneers. Like the Israelites, they had the consolation of being the Chosen in a hostile and godless country - be it North America or Southern Africa. But this was later, after the values and consciousness of the age of discovery had begun to deeply affect our European self-image.

The Puritans and the Afrikaners were post-Reformation Christians. They felt superior to the Americans and Africans in new, more subtle ways than the conquistadors had done. In their eyes, it was not only gross phenomena like European clothing, housing, eating utensils and so on which marked us out as more civilized than the native populations of these places, but our *inner lives*, we thought, were clearly more sophisticated and developed: we had an intimate, personal relationship with God, an active prayer life, a finely-tuned conscience, and other highly-prized 'spiritual' qualities which were features of post-Reformation European culture. Without learning their languages or knowing much about their cultures, we Europeans assumed the peoples of America, Australasia and Africa lacked these inner refinements, and branded them 'savages'.

I am not suggesting that such individual spiritual experiences as our ancestors prided themselves on are in any way faked, 'imaginary' or superficial in those who have them. But neither do I believe that these things are proof of cultural superiority, or even

that they are particularly spiritual. They are simply habits of seeing, thinking and feeling which we learn through our culture.

If someone objects that surely the move from communal ritual
to private prayer life represents an absolute advance in human
culture - a refinement of individual consciousness or some such
familiar phrase - I would reply: judge the tree by its fruit. How
we behave reflects how well-adjusted and adequate to life our
culture is. Where there is massive, systematic cruelty, I cannot see
how we can judge our culture as being in any absolute sense 'more
advanced' than other cultures, particularly when we encounter
cultures which do not rely on such levels of physical and psychological violence. (Economic violence, our main Western standby/
tool is both physical and psychological.)

Our cultural conviction that God supports the righteous and
that *success* is therefore *justification* has stood us Europeans in
very good stead as world conquerors.

But besides our belief in divine right, Shakespeare's plays demonstrate other facets of early modern European culture. For example, the racism in *Othello* is Europe's racism, and the anti-
Semitism in *The Merchant of Venice* is Europe's anti-Semitism.
Both were to get much worse over the next 300 years, during the
massive extension of British and European power that Shakespeare
could not foresee.

Part of the reason that Shakespeare's treatment of Shylock strikes
us so uncomfortably now (unlike his sexism and his racism) is
because of our embarrassment about Hitler and fascism and the
hatred, persecution and wholesale murder of Jewish people which
is still so recent in our European history.

Othello is a more rounded and credible character than Shylock,
who is seen only in relation to his insistence on justice and his
ghetto mentality. It seems to me that Shakespeare's own creative
imagination in relation to Jewish people had been stunted by his
culture's mishandling of them. Segregation, suspicion and prejudice were the norms, and persecution was periodic throughout
medieval Europe. Because of this, when Shakespeare looked at
Shylock he could not see a whole human being. For all his genius,
he stumbled over the 'appropriate' labels and epithets handed him
by his culture in explanation of its inhuman behaviour towards
Shylock's people.

With Othello on the other hand, Shakespeare suffered no such
constraints. Europe had so far had very few dealings with Africans, and had not yet embarked on the systematic exploitation
that was to come. So Shakespeare felt free to depict a strong, well-

developed character who is crucially and tragically affected by racism, but who is in no way a caricature, or product of bigotry.

In order to abuse a group of people systematically, *we have to deny them humanity in our minds* - to render them somehow subhuman, cartoon characters, 'problems'. We cannot address them as people like ourselves *and* use them as means to an end, or as objects of hatred. Judging by Shakespeare's treatment of Othello, sixteenth-century Europeans did not yet see Africans as subhuman.

There were, however, already grave and well-documented doubts about whether *women* were fully human - not surprisingly, since the oppression and exploitation of women by men had been established by various patriarchal European cultures *for at least a thousand years*.

Shakespeare's female figures tend to fall into 'goodies' and 'baddies' in a way the vast majority of his male characters do not. Many of them display his deep distrust of women: they speak, like Shylock, as projections of an uneasy and guilty imagination.

One of the prices we Westerners pay for wielding absolute power over other people is the constricting of our imaginations about them and their lives.

Perhaps the nastiest aspect of early modern Europe - Shakespeare's era - was the Burnings. From the late Middle Ages until the eighteenth century, people were persecuted for living alone, for practising traditional medicine and midwifery, for practising the old pre-Christian religion, for having, claiming to have, or being accused of having spiritual or magical powers not sanctioned by the Church, or for being a threat to the authorities. It seems that the vast majority of these people were women, and that *between six and nine million women* were killed over these five centuries of continuous terror. The Burnings went on for almost two-thirds of the last 700 years of our history.

One of the most disturbing things about the Burnings, for me, is that so little is said or written about them still.

I believe this silence indicates that what happened during the Burnings is still too close for comfort. For some reason, we seem to feel more able to talk about the attempted extermination of Europe's Jewish population a mere fifty years ago. These two obscene and desperate cultural acts have traumatized sections of European society and scarred the perpetrators and their successors to power. And just as anti-Semitism is far from being a thing of the past, so it seems that underneath our confident, materialist cultural exterior there still lurks the same old fear and hatred of female power and secrets.

Shakespeare's attitudes to women are depressingly close to present Western male attitudes. Women still tend to be depicted by men as he depicted them, in one or other of a handful or roles - as seen by men: pure, lovely, marriageable maidens, sexy kittens or sirens, scheming or nagging wives, coarse-mouthed, bawdy wits (less frequent, these, since the Victorian era of prudery and re-spectability) or revolting and malicious hags.

Using women to embody the evil forces that drive good men to commit murder is a technique familiar to the Western cinema-going and thriller-reading public. It never happens the other way round, at least, not in fiction it doesn't.

Once again, Zimbabwe provides a thought-provoking con-trast to the European approach. In Zimbabwe, there are people everywhere who have herbal, psychological, spiritual knowledge that can heal or harm. These individuals are respected and feared, and some are hated for their power. During the liberation strug-gle (1976-1980) the freedom fighters waged a campaign against those accused of casting harmful spells on their neighbours, or ruling by fear.

Many were literally burned to death in the villages, just as women in Europe and North America burned in public, up until the end of the early modern era. No doubt many of the motives for this mass outbreak of vengeance were parallel to Europe's and New England's: it was a time of great cultural upheaval, fear of change, and there was a new order, in this case the freedom fighters, im-posing their authority on a stubbornly traditional and independ-ent-minded population.

But there was a crucial difference between the Zimbabwean and the European witchburnings: in Zimbabwe, *both men and women burned*, for the skills of healing, spirit mediumship and witch-craft are held by both sexes. Only midwifery is a female profes-sion - nearly all the older women in the community are skilled in birth techniques - and there was never an attack on them. It would have been unthinkable.

What reason could there possibly have been to attack Eu-rope's midwives and herbalists, to commit a kind of cultural sui-cide? What proportion of Europe's women were in danger of be-ing branded as witches, and how many of them actually died? What terror they and the survivors must have lived under, and passed on to their daughters and students, together with their life-saving skills. In a supposedly more enlightened age, such fear may go into depression, eating disorders, women's magazines, gynae-cological problems, lesbian separatism and broken marriages.

There are those who argue that the reason for this horrendous persecution in Europe and North America was primarily eco-nomic: that single and independent women were targeted because they threatened the absolute sway of a modern patriarchy con-solidating itself in preparation for a great and ruthless expansion of its wealth and power.[2] Others see it as a cultural and ideologi-cal onslaught on the remaining areas of traditional female power in the name of a male-ruled religion and medical profession.

Since I was a teenager I have known the implicit threat of rape, violence or verbal abuse for not behaving appeasingly or 'femi-ninely' enough towards men, for being in the wrong place (a bar, a beach, a park) or just for being a woman. I date my awareness of this, rightly or wrongly, to the day when a young man passing me in the street hissed through clenched teeth: 'I could fuck you soon enough, hen'. The words were spat out, the violence was palpa-ble. I was supposed to feel - and I felt - scared, ashamed, guilty.

I can't have been much more than twelve or thirteen when this happened. I feel compelled to add that this was in the afternoon, in broad daylight, on my way home from school - but why should I? Would such a verbal assault be more acceptable if made after dark, or late in the evening? Would I be judged as possibly having 'asked for it', having provoked male aggression by walking alone after dark, flaunting my independence? The script of the Burning times is not far under the surface of Western consciousness.

I have never told anyone about this incident, though I have never forgotten it. It may seem a trivial event but it did not feel trivial to me. It seemed to implicate me somehow, I felt ashamed that I had been the receiver of this message, as if I had somehow caused the thing to happen. This was such a tiny event compared to what has happened to so many girls and women, yet its ripples still spread outwards. What storms still rage in other women's hearts and guts, and what fear is still being hissed into children through clenched teeth?

It is still quite common to hear men denigrate women as 'hoors' or 'dykes'. Every insult is a warning to others to keep in line. The more muted warnings of less crassly abusive, more respectable men, come across just as clearly in looks, gestures, jokes and si-lences. The power balance between the sexes is still largely un-changed and I believe that Western women still suffer serious psy-chological problems as a result.

Whatever the true motives for the Burnings, they and their corollaries, the pre-emptive strike and blaming the victim, have become characteristic tactics of Western culture when we feel under threat. They particularly characterize men's behaviour towards women, and the behaviour of the powerful towards the oppressed.

Followers of the psychologist C G Jung talk of our fear of the Other, and of the need to acknowledge our own shadow side in order to stop projecting all our negativity onto an outside object. They may be referring to a split in the European psyche that began during the early modern era with the systematic demonizing and eradication of Europe's wise women. It was a kind of cultural self-mutilation - an attack by the dominant strain in our culture on more ancient centres of power which did not derive their authority from the rulers of the new order.

But in cultural history, as in the physical world, nothing is lost. We can ban certain thoughts, but that doesn't stop them coming. We can even bar them from consciousness, but that merely keeps them shut in the cellar, blind and angry and desperate to get out. Our fear of the Other is our fear of our own banned, repressed needs and impulses.

The Burnings were a sustained attempt to hack European culture away from its ancients, pre-patriarchal and pre-Christian roots so that the new, modern forces of Church, State, science and business could assert themselves unrivalled and freed from traditional constraints of respect, fear and awe. The old disciplines and feeling guidelines were labelled 'superstitions' and 'Devil worship', and dumped on the dungheap of history, where they would later be joined, ironically enough, by most Western theology, philosophy and successively discarded scientific theories.

A Caribbean-English Rastafarian once told me that my people, the whites, seemed to have lost our instinctive capacity for fear. He said this was what had enabled us to take over the world, for we just barged in, as no other people would, disregarding the local spirits; but it also, he said, makes us stupid, and insensitive to real, present dangers.

Perhaps our repression of our healthy instinctive fear and awe also makes us prey to inner monsters - the voices in our heads - and to a kind of aggressive paranoia about anyone who is different from us - fear of the Other.

Africans have not gone in for the kind of violent and wholesale breaks with their past which have characterized our European history. They prefer to assimilate the new into the old, without repudiating anything. For all the miracles of modern medicine, for example, Zimbabwean women still practise herbalism, healing, midwifery and spiritual leadership, and are held in great esteem. No wonder they look hopelessly traditional and 'backward' to us, and no wonder they carry themselves so tall.

This same London Rastafarian had come to Zimbabwe to look for his African roots and buy a plot of land to build on. But he was shocked by the power of women in Zimbabwean households. The round kitchen house is the centre of the home, and is the woman's domain. 'I'd soon change that', he said. This man's Jamaican mother had brought him up, unaided - yet he, an involuntary Westerner, believed women should be kept in their place.

My own parents, on their mission compound in Nigeria, believed that they and their Scottish contemporaries there were liberating Africans from their ancestral fears. And indeed, many Africans received the Gospel in that spirit. However, there is a price to pay for forfeiting your own cultural values, and Africans have had to find their own routes between their traditional belief system and the Judaeo-Graeco-Roman-Christian-Victorian belief system brought to Africa by Europeans.

Our Western siege mentality towards anything and anyone we don't understand seems to me both characteristically Western and linked to the persecution of the 'witches'. Though they seem to belong to a fundamentally different and 'superstitious' age, *the Burnings were in fact the necessary prelude to our modern industrial Progress.* In the age of discovery, Europe needed to rid itself of its traditional awe of nature - whose guardians were the 'witches', the women - in order to set about dissecting, labelling and manipulating the natural world for our own material ends. Five hundred, four hundred, three hundred years ago, we were sowing the wind, and now we are beginning to reap the whirlwind.

The Burnings were also a traumatic experience in themselves for the whole of Western culture. In their excesses of violence, fear and hatred they express a kind of panic which must have been linked with the huge cultural shifts taking place over this long period of dawning 'modernity' in Europe and North America.

For every radical innovation in a culture, there must be a backlash, a reaction of fear and aggression, because human beings, like all creatures, need continuity in order to survive. Discontinuity engenders insecurity, and insecurity stunts development. Therefore, every break with the past will be resisted, as well as embraced.

We Westerners are beginning to realize the tremendous price we have paid for our so-called Progress, and to appreciate the profound confusion of our cultural situation, with its warring impulses, wars played out within our own psyches. On the one hand, our culture has elevated the values of exploration, discovery, innovation, originality and change. We have become more and more infatuated with novelty, less and less capable of resting in the present and being content with what we have. We have made a religion of discontinuity.

At the same time, nature has ensured that we graft as much continuity as possible onto this life-threatening tumour of unchecked Progress. The combination of relentless change and fear-filled backlash has produced all kinds of strange cultural and political phenomena down the centuries of Western 'modernity', from nostalgia and sentimentality to political reason and our obsession with respectability.

Though it is hard given our history, we Westerners should be careful not to confuse increasing sophistication and claims of Progress with real progress.

I am not arguing that there is no such thing as real progress - or learning - in Western history. Slowly, history moulds us a lot more truthfully than we mould history. But unfortunately, we usually have to be forced to learn our lessons. So, for example, most Westerners would now agree that the USA was not fighting such a just war in Vietnam as its government believed, and had most of us believing, at the time. I for one only realized this when I heard about the fall of Saigon.

Nuclear power, which was welcomed in the 1950s as a source of cheap, clean energy, has forced us, expensively and dangerously, to rethink its implications and besides those now actively campaigning against it, many more are deeply sceptical about its use.

Gradually, fears for the ozone layer and climatic stability, for our own health and that of the world we live in, are mobilizing more and more people and increasing support for Green-influenced policies, if not Green parties as such, all over the West.

Not everyone would agree with me that these are examples of real progress. The West is a society of warring ideologies, without much to bind us together any more except our shared lifestyle within capitalism, our shared dependence on the earth, and for most of us the vague but deep-seated sense that we in the 'modern' West are 'ahead' of other societies in significant, even decisive ways.

This conviction was born, I believe, in the age of discovery, which saw the beginning of the modern Western invasion of the international arena. It is easy to trace the cultural continuity between ourselves and the explorers and conquistadors of the fifteenth and sixteenth centuries. Our attitudes towards the rest of the world have not changed so much in all that time.

New, ground-breaking values of exploration, innovation and independent thought became a highly prized part of the European cultural repertoire, while we still retained our social habits of strict hierarchies from the Roman Empire and the feudal system. As frustrated ambition and intelligence met arrogant ancestral privilege, the injection of the new values into the mighty social pyramid exacerbated attitudes of top-down contempt and bottom-up resentment.

The trauma of change unleashed a major backlash of persecution, mainly on women who were branded as witches; and this persecution in turn helped to consolidate the power base of the new forces as well as to break the attachment to older, pre-Christian spiritual and medical practices throughout Northern Europe.

Or perhaps it was the other way round: the persecution was instigated by the authority-seeking forces in the Church and in the new professions; and abetted by the people's craving for certainties in an era of radical change. Most likely, it was a bit of both.

The Burnings, and their predecessors in brutality on a religious pretext, the Crusades and the Inquisition, established in the Western psyche the dualistic split between Self and Other, good and evil, black and white. Though a dualistic world view (and theology) had been around for a long time already - at least since the Greeks - it was not internalized into our European psyches until we became actively implicated in dualism by persecuting those we judged to be evil, heathen or Other.

Shakespeare, writing in the thick of the changes, displays a forthrightness about his culture's attitudes which we can no longer match - for we have since repressed and censored so much of what we think and feel for the sake of halfhearted political correctness. Shakespeare also displays a symbolic grasp of life which we have almost lost - partly, perhaps, because of repression.

In Shakespeare's era, European culture embarked on a voyage of world discovery - words which still resonate with the pride and excitement of that initiatory period of our history. But naturally enough, we took with us on our voyage the prison of our past, and we ended up committing the sin of globalism.

4

Slavery and White Lies

*A history lesson - British pride and denial - The infantile elite -
Breeding slaves - Evil's veils - Porn or pleasure - Breaking the
Beatitudes - Scruples we can afford*

SLAVERY, MORE THAN ANY OTHER SINGLE ABUSE, shows up the cruelty of the West's rise to power; but also of our Western hypocrisy and unwillingness to face up to the truth of behaviour, past and present.

Slavery is now acknowledged by Western culture to be an inadmissible breach of human rights. Yet our present Western wealth and world power are firmly founded on slavery, and our continued economic security rests equally firmly on slavery's modern equivalents: economic (and when necessary, military) conquest and subjugation, racial and economic discrimination, and the systematic impoverishment of other nations, to enforce our continued 'master' status.

Equating the present world military and economic order with the conditions of plantation slavery in the era of European colonialism may seem like wild exaggeration. But if it does, I would suggest that this is merely because we have learned to shrink in horror from the *word* 'slavery', while its *content* - what slavery means for the enslaved - escapes us.

When you are enslaved, your life is lived for someone else's benefit. That someone else has the power to make you work, to make you poor. You have lost the dignity and freedom of self-reliant livelihood, of life on your own terms, and on your culture's terms. There is a master race, or social group, which calls the tunes - without paying the piper properly.

If this, the *content* of slavery truly horrified us, we would be equally horrified by most of what our society considers normal practice in the fields of economics and international relations: the world money markets, trade 'agreements', IMF and World Bank policies, multinationals' business practices - the list goes on.

But we are not, on the whole, horrified by these things, for we have convinced ourselves that we no longer traffic in slaves, or tolerate slavery. What happens to people nowadays, as life becomes ever harder everywhere, is the fault, we think, of great impersonal economic forces, not *our* fault. We Westerners rely squarely on the present global economic system for our daily bread, our pensions, our house ownership, our affordable transport, our security. We cannot live for a single day in the manner to which we have become accustomed without depending on the impoverishment and dispossession and on the dehumanizing labour of the non-Western majority world.

The abolition of the slave trade is a case study in how we in the West have tried, again and again, to abolish the past with enlightened legislation, and of how we have failed, because we have refused to confront the heart of darkness within ourselves and within our economic system.

It was in primary school that I first began to learn how my society thinks about things. History lessons gave us the official view, the playground supplied the local commentary. From our textbooks and BBC schools' broadcasts, we drank the British establishment version of history neat, but never forgot we were Scots.

How could we - none of us spoke the plummy, upper-class English of the radio voices. (Well, one girl did, but we never understood why.) 'The English', to us, were both the ancient enemy and the resented ruling class, and for them we felt that mixture of awe and contempt that debilitates, yet also invigorates the oppressed and the provincialized worldwide. We did not distinguish between upper-, middle- and working-class English. Even as a student in Edinburgh it took me a while to begin to tell the regional English accents from the 'Oxbridge' ones, and to recognize different class behaviours and attitudes. As a Scottish friend commented years later, 'When I was at school, I thought all English people spoke like the Queen'.

However, in geography lessons, I remember gazing in fond pride at the vast pink spread of British Empire - or Commonwealth - that reached from India to Canada and from the Shetland Islands to New Zealand. And in history class, while we concentrated on the remarkable achievements of Scottish inventors and explorers, we also basked in the reflected glory of British exploits in the colonies, and against the Spanish, the French (the Scots' Auld Alliance partners against the English) and, of course, the Germans, who stopped being 'goodies' some time after they stopped being the Prussians, who helped us out at Waterloo.

I managed to follow all these twists and turns, more or less, without too much anxiety. But I remember my confusion and unease about the slave trade: was *that* an achievement, to be wondered at and celebrated, or a disgrace, to be forgotten and regretted? What exactly were we supposed to feel about that episode? Nothing seemed to be made clear about that large chunk of our history - about the plantations, and how people lived in the colonies, and how that related to how all these people lived now, in this century.

First and last, in primary school history lessons, we celebrated Britannia ruling the waves. How fortunate for the world, I felt, that we and not some temperamental foreigners with strange moustaches and customs, had taken charge of everything. Obviously, the main reason for our proud, complacent view of the British Empire was that we and our educational system were British. But this reason was not exactly stressed. Other cogent reasons for pride were put forward: Britain represented common sense and decency, as opposed to the cruelly despotic and backward regimes of our enemies. Britain represented the progressive, enlightened impulse in European history - first to have a parliament, first to industrialize, first to abolish the slave trade, first to grant its colonies independence. And even though I can now list these messages with irony, as signs of chauvinist bias, this does not mean I am completely free of the prejudices that were instilled so early.

However, even as a child I could sense some discrepancies - for before you can *abolish* something evil, you must first have been *doing* it, and before you *grant independence* to a colony, you must first have *taken its independence away*. I don't remember challenging the teacher on these points. Perhaps they seemed too basic to mention; or then again, perhaps I was afraid to stand out.

Children learn, to a great extent, by extrapolating how adults think from what they don't bother to say. They compare how the world seems to themselves with how grownups say and seem to think it is, and where there are differences between the perspectives, they usually take on the adult response as the valid one for everyday use, and gradually 'forget', or repress, their own original response as invalid, childish or naughty. Those who hold onto their initial responses tend to have a hard time, and to stand out as different.

If something assumed by the grownup world seems absurd to a child, as it often does, that is usually because something which actually *is* absurd, or self-contradictory, is considered normal by adults. Children feel the tensions between reality and ideology from an early age, but because what they want is to be loved and accepted - to belong, not to be right - they usually choose to keep quiet and keep learning, rather than taking on every absurdity single-handed, as it arises.

Thus culture is propagated to the next generation, both in its healthy and its unhealthy aspects. It seems likely that the more a culture has to hide or to disguise about itself, the more absurd its attitudes will initially appear to its own children, and the more its children will suffer emotionally through their need to be loved and accepted within such a wrong-headed and repressive culture.

In primary school, then, we learned how coffee, bananas and cotton were cultivated on big tropical plantations in the New World, using slave labour. It was explained to us that this trade in tropical crops was what had enabled Britain to become a world power. We were also told, rather incongruously among all this jingoism, that slavery was a bad thing and that Britain had been first to ban the trade in slaves. And that the thriving merchant cities of Glasgow, Dundee and Liverpool - the pride of industrial Britain - had grown up on the colonial trade. We were told that our wealth-bringing Empire was a great and beneficial thing, which had brought Progress to our colonies, and eventually enabled us to defeat Hitler and save the world from fascism.

(One year we all entered a schools' competition run by a well-known chocolate manufacturer, for which we drew and painted pictures of cocoa beans and bushes and black plantation workers, without any sense of whether or how things might have changed for these workers since they had been slaves on these plantations. As a reward for our efforts, we won prizes of flat, heavy tins of chocolate biscuits with a photograph of the neat, clean factory on the lid. Nothing at all was said about slavery or the Quaker-led campaign against the slave trade. Maybe nobody else made the connection.)

The slave trade and its abolition were dealt with together in our primary school textbooks as one topic. In this lesson we learned about the dreadful conditions on the slave ships, the suffering undergone by the terrified captives, kidnapped from their homes and separated forever from their families. We learned what proportion of the captives died, on average, before completing the crossing, and how long such a voyage could take.

I remember one hot afternoon, listening to a disturbing BBC schools radio broadcast about life aboard a slave ship. I remember the cruel, foul-mouthed sailors - but I don't remember any discussion afterwards. What seemed to get lost among all the horrific facts was the most personal and relevant point, that the people who inflicted these sufferings and treated others worse than cattle were not a separate race of benighted monsters but our own forebears. Our textbooks and our teachers avoided facing this basic fact of our history, and so we missed our first chance to examine the roots of racism in our culture.

Come to think of it, we never did have a radio programme about life on a plantation. Only now does it occur to me that perhaps the BBC avoided dramatizing this topic because the accents appropriate to the big house would be similar to their very own radio announcers. It might embarrass middle-class programme makers, and teachers, and raise uncomfortable issues (the very issues I have mentioned were never raised) - to hear slave-owning families talking in 'nice' English or Scottish accents. It was OK (unless we had been East Enders ourselves) to have Cockney sailors on the slaving ships as 'baddies'. But to have ladies and gentlemen treating Africans badly, and being shown up as racist wrongdoers - that might be a bit near the bone.

So class and race prejudice complement and uphold each other. In fact, they are interchangeable.

After learning about the slave ships, we heard a programme about the Quaker campaign against the slave trade. ('Educated' Northern English voices arguing passionately for liberty and equality.) The programme built up to the moment of truth, in 1833, when Britain, first among the slave-trading nations, saw the light of Christian compassion and human decency and abolished this lucrative trade in human beings. (Murmurs of grudging parliamentary agreement.)

Henceforth (stirring music) the British navy bravely policed the waves to prevent other more backward, less scrupulous nations from continuing to engage in this vicious practice. As a little girl, I was particularly moved and impressed by Britain's apparently selfless voluntary demonstration of international moral responsibility in this matter. I was still too innocent to suspect a less altruistic motivation for spending all that money controlling the slave traffic.

According to our history books, the abolition of the slave trade transformed us British into international guardian angels. From this lesson I extrapolated that the most important thing was to *be ahead of the rest*. Being first to realize you were doing a bad thing and quitting, *gained* you points, like being first in the class or in a race. Then if you went on to preach your new morality to others who were less enlightened, and/or to enforce it on them, any remaining stains of guilt were swapped for a halo of righteousness.

Lagging behind, on the other hand, was an affront to human Progress - the Arabs and the Portuguese who continued to traffic in slaves were depicted as brutal beasts, stubborn in their ignorance. There didn't seem to be any points for nations who did not participate in slavery at all - at least, I don't remember any such lessons.

The thing to do, apparently, was be ruthless, amass loads of wealth, and when you had built up a clear advantage, strike a moral posture from a great height.

If a mother is secretly proud of her cheeky, bossy child's intelligence, however much she appears to scold her/him, the child is encouraged to continue being rude and obnoxious into adulthood. I believe we have been taught to regard the inhuman, exploitative excesses in our history with the same proud indulgence, as signs of precociousness, rather than with shame and regret, seeing trouble ahead unless we change profoundly.

And so we Westerners go on committing those same moral blunders, and having them committed on our behalf and in our material interest, not realizing how low we have fallen, or how ethically out of touch we have become.

The story of how 'abolitionist' Britain rose to industrial power after 1833 on the backs of the slaves we had traded shows up the gulf between the way the West acts and the way we like to think of ourselves. We should bear this gulf in mind whenever we are tempted to preach to the South or to the East about human rights.

The word 'gulf' recently gained a new meaning to Western ears. The transparent double standards applied by the US/UK to the war against Iraq (what about Panama, Grenada, Lebanon and the West Bank?) suggest how frighteningly habitual lying has become to Western politicians 'for reasons of State'. There is always a moral explanation for Western aggression, or for the West's refusal to act. In fact, we Westerners have got so used to lying about our real political motives, that we often don't know what we really *should* be doing or thinking. We have become both cynical and confused.

The roots of this confusion, I believe, go down into a basic contradiction embodied in the abolition of the slave trade - a contradiction which still dogs our white Western relations with blacks - in the USA, in Africa, in the Caribbean and, for British readers first and foremost, of course, in Britain. Most Westerners have not yet faced up to this contradiction and so we are still held unknowingly in its grasp.

The problem is that while Britain changed its moral-political posture and its legislation on the slave trade in 1833, the slave economy itself was unaffected, profits continued to roll into Britain from the plantation industries; and the lives and attitudes of British people - at home, in British outposts abroad, in the merchant and Royal Navy, and on the plantations - continued unexamined and unchanged.

Britain's industrial expansion of the mid-nineteenth century was firmly based on racial as well as economic exploitation - first on slavery, then on imperialism and its successor, colonialism. During this long era of expanding power and influence, British society had evolved the rule of political convenience: 'If it makes money, do it; if you get into trouble, outlaw and condemn the practice, but keep the money coming in and keep on doing the same thing under a new name'.

As a child, I could not imagine grownups doing such dishonest, hypocritical things, for I knew that lying, or deliberately misleading people was 'bad'. Although a child cannot help equating 'good for me now' with 'good' *per se* (any more than most school teachers or governments can), the infantile impulse to short-term advantage clashes both with children's own innate sense of logic and justice, and with the slowly-evolved social values we call moral or ethical. 'Traditional' social morality has developed through long ages of human culture and so sees further than 'good for us now' to 'good for our community in the long run'.

The gradual but accelerating breakdown of traditional, long-run morality in favour of shorter and shorter-term profit or 'pleasure' is one of the most dangerous features of our modern way of life, and one of the things which shocks and worries the peoples who have to share the earth with us more and more intimately.

We are not the first civilization to lose our heads in this way: it is a common sign of a culture in decline. The more cutoff the elite becomes from the basic livelihood concerns that keep ordinary people thinking communally and realistically, the more likely such moral infantilism becomes at the 'top'.

Ironically, a society's very ability to support such a potentially crazy and irresponsible elite is regarded as the hallmark of 'civilization', they way we in the West use the term. And worse still, the expansion of this affluent elite to include the average Western citizen has been hailed as the triumph of capitalism, and cited as proof of the capitalist system's right to penetrate and supersede every other culture it encounters - on the basis of its superior ability to deliver the goodies.

The world is in a precarious situation when so much power rests in the hands of the international middle classes, whose perspectives and priorities are inherited from the much smaller national elites which preceded them. For, to put things crudely, the morality of exploiters is likely to be exploitative. It is also bound to be distorted, since it has to give an acceptable account of its crimes that does not upset either its members or the ruling order.

To consume the fruits of slavery and colonialism and keep reaching for more, while pretending innocence and disapproval of the crimes that have produced the fruits, is to do worse than Adam and Eve in the Garden of Eden. It means *denying the sin that gave us our power*, suppressing the unpleasant side of our Progress, our history, and so cutting ourselves off from the full truth about ourselves and about those we have abused.

In Judaeo-Christian spiritual language, to deny our sin is to cut ourselves off from God and from the possibility both of repentance and of forgiveness. In psychological terms, we make ourselves ill - neurotic - by suppressing a painful memory instead of consciously facing up to it and coming to terms with it. But suppressed or not, the truth is not easily quelled, and our shared social attitudes express our true history loudly and clearly. It is both logical and inevitable that our society - our whole modern European culture - is blighted and twisted by racism; and that we are hopelessly confused about how to get rid of it.

Yet *the history of white racism is only as old and as deep as the history of white abuse of blacks and other peoples.* Before we started that, we had no need of racism. Systematic abuse of another people generates racism as too much alcohol generates cirrhosis of the liver.

All things considered then, is it not amazing that, as early as 1833, the British government allowed itself to be persuaded that the slave trade was a disgraceful business, and should be banned? After all, we were not about to change our attitudes or our behaviour towards Africans, as the rest of the nineteenth and the twentieth centuries plainly show. Judging by the language and tone generally used by whites to refer to blacks till well into the 1960s - and still in extensive private use - we had not realized then, as we still have not realized, that by treating black people like inferiors, and even saleable commodities, we were degrading ourselves; or that until we acknowledged their equivalent humanity to our own we ourselves would not be fully human.

If, as a society, we have not really seen - or been changed by - the moral light held up by the Quakers and their fellow abolitionists, why did abolition come to pass at that early time when there were still plenty of theological as well as economic justifications for slavery around in our culture? There must have been other reasons than the moral ones. There were.

The *economic* case for abolishing the slave trade was argued in Parliament using language which bears its own witness to the inhumanity of what was going on in our culture, in the world and in white minds. The fact was that by 1833, the slave trade was no longer economically necessary, from Britain's point of view: for the slaves already transported to the New World and working on plantations could be relied upon to have children. Only the word used for having children was 'breed', and the method of insemination used on black women in slavery was very often white rape.

This last piece of information may be shocking to contemporary ears, or even dismissed as propaganda: the stating of it in Parliament would have been shocking in 1833 too. But the truth of it would have been assumed by a contemporary male audience, and passed over without mention.

For the rape of female slaves by their masters in the New World was paralleled in Britain, and throughout Europe, by the rape and sexual exploitation of servants and working girls and women by their male employers and by young men from the upper orders. We usually tend to assume that such acts were exceptions rather than the rule. I thought so too until I went to the USA.

I was sitting on a tram in New Orleans in 1981, watching the faces of the people as they got on. It was only twelve years or so since blacks had been allowed to sit at the front of trams and buses. Apart from one or two lily-white old ladies, po-faced under their sunhats, I was the only white on this tram. Yet there was scarcely a really black face to be seen, a face which held an African look. Most people were light or medium-skinned, many with freckles, all kinds of variations. Racially - except, of course, for the lily-white ladies and myself - this was obviously a melting pot.

Yet I knew, from my brief experience of life in Louisiana, that there was scarcely any mixed marriage here, and barely any social meeting between blacks and whites. And I could see for myself that everyone on this tram, barring myself and the old white ladies, was 'black', culturally speaking at least. I could see this by everything about them, from the tone and accent of their voices to their gestures, facial expressions and body movements - all completely different from white American sounds and movements.

Suddenly, the meaning of this strange evidence hit me: for the past however many hundred years, this white-dominated society had been 'protecting its racial purity' by casting out every child born with a drop of black blood in its veins, no matter who its parents were. The realization is still fresh in my mind. This unacknowledged mass rape of African Americans by our white ancestors and the rejection of the children must be one of the meanest and deadliest forms of immorality known to humanity. Systematic lies and hypocrisy uphold the continuing fiction of 'white society' in the USA.

The rape of their mothers is indelibly imprinted on black American consciousness. It should be imprinted on ours too, not glossed over or denied. How much of the tight-lipped hardness of those old white New Orleans ladies came from suppressing the facts staring them in the face every day of their lives? How must it have felt to know your husband, your father, your sons, had unmentionable sex with women out the back, and children by them whom you would treat as property, and quite possibly sell to a stranger?

How must the forefathers of these white ladies have lived - not devils or war-crazed commandos but decent, ordinary settlers - people like our own fathers, uncles and brothers? They must have kept their wives and children in the big house, dressing them up in buttons and bows, lending their all-white children to black nannies to be looked after, while their mixed-race children lived as slaves in the 'boys' quarters'!

White men, alone of all the race-gender combinations, could come and go freely - sexually and socially. White women were kept in gilded cages: no wonder white women still fear and flee from these cages. No wonder it is so hard to be a woman confidently in this culture, without being either prim, angry or vampish. No wonder middle-class Western women are severely compromised when we make out that gender and not class or race is the main factor dividing the oppressor from the oppressed - and no wonder much Western feminism makes black women sick.

This terrible underlying race-gender scenario also explains why black men, even after all the oppression and humiliation they have suffered at white hands, still present such a threat to the white male ego; why lynching was felt to be too good for a black man who had sex with a white woman.

Black women took care of all the children in the divided society of the old South. Black men, whose partners, sisters and daughters were so abused before their eyes - were called 'boys' by white people. During my stay in independent Malawi and Kenya, they were still called 'boys', if they worked in the garden or in the house of whites. Old habits die hard. Being a grandfather doesn't make you a man, if you are black in a white-run society: settler society treats black men as minors all their lives and black women as unpaid prostitutes and breeding stock. This is our white, Western history, our practice.

The crime that blacks cannot swallow is our white denial of parenthood. They cannot grasp how we could bring ourselves to do *to our own children* what we could do to them, to another people. How could white men let *their own children* be treated on a par with their slaves? How could white women allow their husbands' children to be so treated? Something has gone deeply wrong in our hearts when our racism, or our economic advantage, or a combination of both, can take precedence over our social obligation and our natural impulse to care for our children.

But there is another factor at work in our culture, besides racism and economics, that would have impelled these men to disown their children. And that, with crashing irony, is their (our) self-image as shining lights of godliness.

This ingredient in whites' rejection of their mixed race children is *respectability*. The slaveowners who lived in the big 'plantation homes' regarded their innocent mixed-race children as reminders of sin, and of their lower, 'bestial' nature - which they projected onto the black women they abused. *The victims of brutality were blamed so the perpetrators could avoid facing the consequences of their actions.* White women must have collaborated in this charade.

The concern with appearances and with respectability is the crux of what is wrong with us Westerners even yet, and it affects our children. For children are not respectable. They are natural and direct. But many Western grownups still see them as bundles of potentially evil urges - for nature, according to our philosophy, is sinful - and in need of firm discipline.

Our traditional middle-class Western denial of our children's needs leads in turn to enmity, declared or undeclared, between the generations, and this enmity has fuelled our cultural pendulum swings of the last two hundred years. One generation gleefully overturns what the last one built up - yet nothing really changes, because for most people, the reaction remains subconscious or semiconscious. We do not realize what has been done to us, or why, and we cannot return to our innocence, before we were unjustly punished for being children in a respectable culture.

Our race of self-appointed preachers and teachers is often unable to act with even normal human kindness and decency towards its own offspring. We know this, but so rarely ask why, in a way that reaches beyond individual family stories, into our wider background.

Africans and African Americans are angered by white treatment of them, but not particularly shocked, since they understand that it stems from our racial and cultural arrogance. But they are deeply shocked by our cruelty to our own kind.

I believe the virulence of white racism and much of our middle-class culture's psychological rigidity and unhappiness have grown out of buried memories of evildoing hidden in our psyches. We have tried to put our unpalatable history behind us by forgetting it, but it doesn't work.

Evil tends to spread itself around, and evil unacknowledged spreads most effectively of all. The veil of respectability provides evil with the perfect camouflage to walk freely through the world unnamed, unchallenged and beyond reproach. If, instead of hiding from our past, we try instead to expose and own up to our shameful actions, these crimes may gradually cease to twist us subconsciously.

I mentioned the interchangeablity of class attitudes and racism in connection with the BBC schools' broadcasts on the slave trade which I heard as a child. This link between race and class resurfaces in the issue of rape and unacknowledged paternity through Europeans who took our past and our social habits with us to the New World, and re-enacted them in a new social setting.

Class and race indeed come to the same thing, in terms of the attitudes of the powerful towards the disempowered. I mentioned the age-old social habit among higher-class European men to sexually abuse women and girls from the lower classes. The double oppression of poor European women, in class-based European society, became the triple oppression of black women, in racist colonial society.

None of this immorality can be kept safely at arms length. It comes home, and it taints our most intimate relationships. In particular, it taints our experience of sex.

In order to live with what they were doing, the slaveowners had to abuse their own minds to invent excuses for themselves. So they projected the split in their own sexual behaviour onto the human world they were desecrating.

Blacks were seen either as 'animals' or as 'children of the devil', given to all forms of vice and licentiousness. White wives and daughters were raised 'above sex', purified of physical pleasure, and turned into the female eunuchs first described by Germaine Greer at the end of the 1960s.

In this distorted view of the world, not only blacks, but children and animals are twisted into evil shapes. The diseased authoritarianism which has been exercised by many respectable fathers in our society is surely connected with such projections of inner corruption onto the world beyond the ego.

Desire left the respectable marriage bed, and sexual excitement became inseparable from illicit and often abusive 'pleasure' - physical enactments of exploitation and degradation. The integrity of sexual fulfilment was broken, and we were left with either joyless procreation and respectability, or enticing but shameful encounters.

'Hard' pornography caters to the shameful side of the split, while 'soft' porn, in advertising, romances and popular film culture seek to appeal to both sides of the confused and divided white psyche. So we find in these media messages a mixture of soft-focus romance (disembodied desire) and implied or explicit sexual abuse - the celebration and sexual connotation of male aggression and rape, female humiliation and submission - or sometimes, an image of a pseudo-male, sexually predatory female.

The steamy dreams of the respectable young lady imprisoned in her boudoir reach out for the touch of real life which she knows is evil and for the lower orders only. The respectable man who has 'sown his wild oats' in brothels and slave quarters brings his sexual memories and associations to the marriage bed, where he now needs them to stimulate him for his dreary duty.

It is difficult to do an archaeological dig in the psyche to ascertain just when and why certain habits became lodged in it. Christianity has been blamed for the West's shame and guilt about sex, and that story goes back a lot longer than the period focused on here.

Besides, early Christian theology was steeped in Greek and Roman thought and experience, and both of these imperial societies knew the sexual eccentricities (or abuses) of privilege.

Perhaps it would be true to say that any privileged social group in a patriarchal society is liable to have its sexual imagination twisted: in that powerful men will keep wives for themselves alone, to ensure the continuation of their line and property; while taking other women and girls (and men and boys) as they please for unofficial liaisons. A double standard is set up which inevitably passes into the psyche of the women of their own class who are expected to put up with this infidelity while remaining sexually faithful themselves.

Inasmuch as women help to maintain the 'rights' and illusions of their men, in order to benefit indirectly from their power - or just to be accepted as members of their class - they collaborate in the dominant values and are therefore co-perpetrators as well as co-sufferers in the disorders that develop.

Whatever the precise historical reasons, white middle-class sex, love and marriage have for generations been perverted by the effect of unjust power relations. (It seems that Islamic society and the Muslim psyche have also suffered in this respect.) I will not try to explore these issues in more detail here. But it is important to remember, when we are thinking or reading about emotional and psychological problems, that we are dealing with the psychic effects of our whole history - our personal history first, but through that the history of our community, class and culture. We are woven into a web of past events. Even if we feel isolated and cut off from our families and our roots, we still belong in the web, and our very thoughts and feelings express the current movements of the web in the winds of change.

White colonial society denied blacks human dignity on all sides. They were not allowed to speak their own language, nor to retain their own customs; nor were they allowed to marry, or to worship with whites, although they were becoming Christian.

This cruelty was not inflicted sadistically. It was mere grim necessity. For whites to maintain their psychological integrity in racist society, blacks *must* be stripped of their humanity. Otherwise the whole system would be revealed as a self-serving sham and an obscene structure of lies.

But deeper and more scarring than genetic lies is the moral lie, and here too reality - or truth - will have its say.

Westerners suffer a particular psychological tension which I have already mentioned when we participate in systematic injustice, because our moral identity is founded on the Hebrew and Christian Bible, in which the voices of the prophets never tire of railing against oppression and worldly pride and wealth. With these voices ringing in their ears, and the Beatitudes by their bedsides, how could our ancestors mistreat another people with impunity? They could not, and neither can modern Westerners.

The fact that what the slave owners were doing was morally and psychologically untenable *in terms of their own culture*, was proved by the way the Africans brought to the New World responded to the whites' own Bible. They heard Jesus and the prophets giving clear messages of hope and liberation for the downtrodden and warnings to the arrogant.

When a culture has once proclaimed the equality before God of all human life, it becomes much more difficult and dangerous for it to trample on that sacred ground. Here again we find ourselves up against the inbuilt contradictions of Progress: for the very moral and philosophical 'achievements' of Judaism and Christianity - the insights that all people are equally precious and that the poor are especially blessed - are inseparable from the tendency to believe ourselves (Jews or Christians) superior to those who do not share our cultural heritage!

Thus, every 'advance' and refinement of thought and feeling can initiate a coarsening of moral sensibility, a deepening emotional stupidity, whenever we feel ourselves raised above the 'common herd' of the 'general public'. There is a levelling humour in this irony that smilingly checks, among other things, the writer's impulse to soar.

By 1833 then, because of the number of children being born into slavery on the plantations, *the price of slaves was dropping*, and it was clear what had to be done. The British government appeared to yield to abolitionist pressure and outlawed the slave trade. To safeguard the slaveholders' interests and peg the price of slaves, there had to be a total embargo on transatlantic slaving. Hence the noble British naval effort to enforce the ban.

Moral motivation was loudly trumpeted and economic factors kept carefully backstage. In fact, what happened was that, not for the last time, sensibility had followed economic surplus. *We became as squeamish as we could afford to be*, or rather as squeamish as it was *profitable* to be.

New-found scruples which cost nothing, and indeed have hidden material motives, are nothing like re-found moral integrity, which always costs. And self-serving moral fanfares leave no quiet space for real, humbling change within a society apparently reforming itself. As Jesus said of the Pharisees who prayed for everyone to see, 'They have their reward already'.

It may seem unhelpfully negative to keep the real versus apparent motives for something so obviously necessary and welcome as abolishing the slave trade. But recognizing the full historical truth about our much-vaunted Western Progress is essential for understanding where we find ourselves at present. We are still faced with issues demanding solutions which can be opportunities for real renewal and about-turn (repentance) - or just more public relations exercises.

The abolition of the slave trade clearly did deserve to be hailed as a check to institutionalized inhumanity. We are surely right to feel relieved that Britain withdrew from that particular obscenity at that particular time. But honesty demands that we admit this piece of legislation was not exactly what it has been cracked up to be. It was not a straightforward, outright victory for humanity over inhumanity, or for conscience over exploitation and economic pragmatism. Far from it.

During the campaign for abolition, these two forces did meet and did join battle, but neither conquered the other. What emerged was a new stage in the long synthesis between Western conscience and pragmatism, between Western Christianity and exploitation. In 1833, 'enlightened' Christian conscience, as embodied in the British government, made do with banning the slave trade, and made its peace with the continued and (for us) hugely profitable existence of plantation slavery. The abolitionists themselves were surely not cynical or even pragmatic about the continuation of slavery. They probably felt as strongly about that as they had about the trade itself, but there was less they could do to stop it.

The plantation system carries on today all over the world where tea, coffee, sugar, tobacco, bananas and cotton are produced and consumed. That includes every house I have ever lived in.

For decades after abolition of the slave trade, slavery continued unchanged on the American plantations, but there were no British government boycotts of the cash crops they produced. On the contrary, the following decades saw a steady rise in trade, profit levels and in associated industrialization. This we learned in primary school. In other words, slavery continued to fuel our growing affluence.

The contradictions of the abolition are echoed in every anti-racist struggle. When I was in the USA in the early 1980s, I found the American Civil War still a very sore point among Southern whites. 'The Civil War wasn't about freeing the blacks', they would tell a white visitor at the first opportunity. 'That story was Yankee propaganda: *Lincoln kept slaves himself*! It was an economic war. The South was underpricing the North, so the Yankees had to smash slavery and smash the Southern economy to get cheap labour for their Northern factories and mills'. And as for racism itself: 'The Yankees don't like blacks any more than we do down here - but at least we're open about it'.

My aim in naming these contradictions in Western history isn't to apportion blame, or even to analyse the reasons for compromise. Both these tasks have been done often and well enough. I simply want to look squarely at what actually happened, at what we have done as a society, and in a spirit of owning up, to try to appreciate what that might mean for our own inherited habits of thinking and feeling, as members of this heavily compromised society. I want to unwrap the bundles of this white man's burden we have been carrying about the world these long years, to see what exactly is hidden inside them.

None of this implies dismissal or contempt for those who have lived before us and made our history - though there is certainly anger, and sadness. We cannot look down on our ancestors and maintain dignity ourselves. Somehow we must learn to think critically and fearlessly while maintaining respect for others and for earlier generations. Self-righteousness will close the door on real understanding, so we must unmask received opinion without sneering at anyone.

Unmasking the ironies of Western self-righteousness does not deflate the authenticity or significance of activist effort. Rather, it deflates the complacency and self-deception of our society at large, and more especially of the powerful in our society, when they seek to absorb and gain moral credibility from the lonely and painful work done by those who protest against oppression.

At first these people are branded as dangerous subversives, then as cranks and fanatics. Then a time comes when the truth of their message can no longer be resisted, and history itself forces our society's hand, by means of economics and/or political power play: and all at once the message of liberation is embraced as a self-evident truth, and the words and gestures of the cranks and subversives are suddenly assimilated into our ever-expanding cultural repertoire of progressive claims, as if by magic.

These reforms - or moral facelifts - usually happen without a word of thanks to the radicals for their long struggles on behalf of our whole society, much less an apology for the contempt and dismissal previously meted out to them. And needless to say, they happen without any apology to those we have made to suffer by our freshly recanted crimes. We Westerners never humble ourselves before our victims - we simply take another brave step into our glorious future.

5

The Colonial-Industrial Excuse

Cultural roots - Early shock and protests -
Marxist acquiescence - 'Economic development' -
Three realms of suffering - The escape valve of emigration -
Progress defended - Laissez-faire immorality -
Democratic deficit - Cultural costs

THE LONG ERA OF EXPLORATION AND DISCOVERY led into the colonial-industrial era, which continued until the 1960s saw the formal release of most European colonies into independence, and
the final surge of hopeful, Progress-minded industrialization in
the West. The facts of colonialism and industrialization which I
discuss in this chapter are widely known, and we Westerners now
disapprove of much that was earlier condoned in the name of
Progress. But I believe we are still trapped in the habits of self-
justification formed in this era, and that we need to look more
steadily than is usually done at what our past behaviour as a culture reveals about our Western assumptions.

In this chapter, as throughout this book, I look at the *inner* story,
rather than the outer events of colonialism and industrialization:
what have these huge socio-economic processes done, to us Westerners and to the others who have been affected by them?

In this era the Western concept of Progress really came of age.
It was used to justify every excess, much as the concept of salvation had been used in medieval times to justify persecution, torture and the murder of Jews, witches and heretics, by those who
wished to do these things.

Colonialism and industrialization have relied on each other
from the start and are inseparable. The West couldn't have

afforded to industrialize, had it not been subjugating and colonizing large areas of the world. Without the plantations, the trading stations and the taxes, there would have been no luxury goods for our big houses, or raw materials for our factories. And without the 'undeveloped' continents, including North and South America and Australasia - our so-called 'New World' - what would have happened to the European victims of industrialization? Where would they have gone?

Without industrialization, on the other hand, the West would not have had the material wealth or the military and technological edge to impress and dominate the rest of the world, which had never seen such gadgetry. We used trade to increase our advantage over other people, finding we could swap trinkets, guns and whisky for exotic luxuries like silk and spices (so more Westerners could imitate the aristocracy) and useful things like food - and even, as we have seen, for people.

As 'the market' is nowadays cited to explain and excuse social damage and suffering, so in the early days of our modern Western life, *Progress* was the watchword. During the Highland Clearances of the late eighteenth and early nineteenth centuries, absentee landlords forced hundreds of thousands of people to leave their homes to make way for sheep, and felt no qualms: the fact that sheep would generate more income for the landlord was argument enough that this was the way 'forward'.

If I were from Lancashire, I would probably have cited the mills and the way rural communities and self-reliant craftspeople were forced into inhuman factory conditions and overcrowded slums. Examples are endless.

What happened in the colonial-industrial era was prepared in the previous eras of our history, looked at in chapters two and three. The class structure of European society facilitated extreme dissociation in the powerful. So Highlanders could be regarded with as little respect or concern as was felt for Africans chained and suffocating below deck on a slaving ship.

Indeed, Scots too were shipped West like Africans, or south to New Zealand, to get them off British soil. But if *they* made it safely to North America or Australasia, they were usually left to make their own way, allowed to claim land and, if they could, to rebuild European civilization on a 'heathen' shore.

The feudal class system had accustomed the majority of Europeans to look longingly upwards at how the powerful lived; and this common desire to be wealthy like Europe's elite provided the hook by which Progress could be sold to the 'masses'. The trick is still working, here and in the rest of the world, where people look up, both at their own affluent class, and to the West where, they assume, *everyone* is living the good life.

The age of discovery had set a new cultural imperative against the medieval one of accepting your position in the scheme of things. Henceforth, educated Europeans would be encouraged to think for themselves, to enquire, discriminate and generally 'go beyond' what their forefathers had done, thought or achieved.

This apparently laudable new tendency, combined with a lingering Western horror of medieval authoritarianism, led to a long, culturally disorienting acquiescence in whatever innovations have passed for Progress, whether or not they are morally defensible. In other words, even as we bore high the banner of Progress and wrote Victorian hymns to civilization, *we lost our way*.

The post-medieval emphasis on individual initiative and critical enquiry in Western culture was grafted onto an older consciousness that was still hierarchical, and owed a lot to the 'heroic' myths of the Celts and Germanic peoples. This helps to explain the Western fascination with the great genius, explorer or statesman who towers above the rest of humanity. For the medieval strain in Western culture still prescribes that there must be an elite of some sort, whether by birth, brains, expertise, or just pure wealth.

I believe we in Britain were most aware of the specifically *human* costs of Progress right at the start of the Industrial Revolution, when the effects of modernization were hitting British people as well as Africans and Native Americans for the first time. The eviction and impoverishment of rural people, and the resultant crowding into filthy factory towns could not be overlooked or swept away under carpets from Persia. Living and working conditions in these places were seen to be inhuman, by any standards, and they took a public toll of degradation, disease and death which shocked most contemporary observers.

In the early days of industrialization, people had not yet become inured to 'modern' forms of degradation. They could see that what the enclosing landlords and the mill and mine owners were doing flew in the face of human decency and was destroying the livelihood, wellbeing and dignity of the majority of people in large areas of England, Scotland and Wales. So basic questions *were* asked about the new order both by educated and uneducated, by the powerful and by the relatively powerless.[1]

But these inconvenient criticisms and analyses were largely ignored - or discussed, and laid aside. Adam Smith in his book *The Wealth of Nations*, gave academic respectability to what I believe to be moral abdication and regression in a theory which foreshadowed the modern Western reduction of human life to economic or quasi-economic functions. It was left to individual industrialists to pursue their profits more humanely if they so wished, and some did - for example, Robert Owen at New Mills in Lanarkshire, and the Quaker firms in the Midlands of England.

The protests of the powerless, however, were not ignored. They were ruthlessly put down and branded as mindless and dangerous outbreaks of mob unrest. In our school history books, the Luddites, who smashed factory machinery in protest at what mechanization was doing to people, were mentioned merely as backward objects of ridicule. The weavers were represented as doomed victims of inevitable Progress. Meanwhile Samuel Butler's critical utopia *Erewhon* describes a society where technical innovation has been banned for the sake of physical and social health.[2] Such alternative visions were never mentioned in our history classroom.

Since those early days of pamphlets and protest, the debate about Progress has grown ever tamer and more technical, and economics and economic rationalization have repeatedly triumphed over reason, scruple and compassion. The idea of renouncing or reversing the processes of industrialization for the sake of human happiness, or out of basic respect for the people whose lives are otherwise destroyed, seems never to have been seriously entertained.

Because of this consistent refusal to question the pursuit of profit-led Progress, our Western criteria for thinking about human life have become materialistic and dehumanized. The quest for profit has dried up our view of the world, and of who we are.

Even Karl Marx never radically challenged this motivation. In fact, I believe he was judged dangerous to early capitalist culture precisely because *he was not radical enough to be ridiculed.* For he *accepted* the idea of industrialization as Progress. The materialist view of life which Marx preached so enthusiastically was already implicit in the practice, though not yet in the ideology, of the God-fearing industrialists and bourgeoisie of his time. These early entrepreneurs did not yet realize that their brave new Progress, given its head, would soon enough render their Christianity culturally irrelevant.

For the early industrialists and colonialists were, of course, only radical economically. In most other ways they were arch-conservatives. These pious Victorian and pre-Victorian patriarchs would not have been at all pleased to witness the inexorable cultural working-out of their economic preference for the new in such areas as churchgoing, marriage and sexual morality.

Marx limited his critique of industrialization to the question of who got rich and powerful, and who got dispossessed. In what turned out to be a serious misjudgement, he believed industrial-style Progress could be organized to liberate and benefit the majority, if the ruling group could be overthrown and a new regime established, on behalf of that majority.

Since the onset of industrialization, then, fundamental challenges to profit-led Progress or 'economic development' which question its very motivation and morality, have simply been swept aside. In defence of the indefensible, it has been suggested - or promised - that at some time in the future, *everyone* will come to share in the accumulated profits of the undertaking.

This is perhaps a good place to look critically at the phrase 'economic development', this term which is used so freely in our culture, as if everyone knew what it entailed, and approved.

'Economic development' refers to *the development of wealth-accumulating techniques*. Politicians and economists prefer to talk of 'wealth generation' rather than 'accumulation' - because 'generation' implies that by a mysterious process *something is created out of nothing*, or next to nothing; or that something's true potential is realized, much as a great tree is generated from a tiny seed. But the distinction between 'accumulating' and 'generating' also implies a contrast between the miser's and the businessman's approaches to getting rich: the second is supposed to benefit lots of people.

Economic development is purported to be a dynamic, self-perpetuating process, whereby money goes round and round, making more and more money. On the other hand, the miser's hoarding produces a dead-end effect characterized in Jesus' parable about the lazy steward who buried the talents entrusted to him, when he should have invested them 'productively' in business.

The ironic thing is that nowadays, once you have accumulated a few thousand in hard currency, you can act the lazy steward *and* get the glory, by 'letting your money work for you'. All you have to do is invest it at interest, or buy something you can later sell for more money.

I suppose it is fair enough to talk of wealth being 'generated', in the sense that heat, smoke, light and ash are generated by burning wood. The parallel is just. For *economic development means the transformation of land, minerals, and most of all, of people's lives - their work and their rest - into money.*

But this transformation of life into money is a one-way process which, like fire, needs to consume more and more so-called 'natural and human resources' in order to maintain its momentum, and to maintain our Western, money-based 'standard of living'. In fact, referring to nature and ourselves as 'resources' is a good indication of our 'burn-it-up' approach to the world.

Every transaction in the process of 'economic development' is a form of privatization of the means to survival, which were originally given to us all free of charge.

In the industrial revolution, there were relatively few winners and very many losers. Following the Africans kidnapped, transported and enslaved, there were now millions more Africans and Indians and others who lost their autonomy in their own land as European colonialism tightened its grip across the world. Then there were the millions of rural Europeans ejected from their land, forced into factories or into exile across the sea. And the third realm of suffering was among the peoples - and the animals - of America and Australasia whose sacred land was grabbed while they themselves were attacked, betrayed and treated like vermin by Westerners.

The genocidal encounters in North America were filtered romantically into European consciousness by way of the mythologized history of the Wild West. 'Cowboys and Indians' was still a favourite game in my childhood, and those who have played it must be familiar with our culture's traditional gloss of that era.

Ignorance is no defence. Westerners have always known what was happening, at home and abroad in the name of Progress - but we have chosen to look the other way. If we listen to the words of *Rule Britannia* we can see that in the height of our imperial arrogance, Britons well understood the humiliation inflicted on slaves, and never never *never* wanted any of it inflicted on themselves.

Another reason we were able to overlook the true nature of our colonial-industrial Progress for so long has been *the escape valve of emigration* - the magic wand that transformed defeat and dispossession into conquest and new colonial wealth for so many

Europeans. I believe the true, rapacious and destructive nature of Progress would have been much harder to ignore, had not the huge nineteenth- and twentieth-century expansion of white society throughout the Americas, Australasia and Southern Africa helped to take the pressure off the home base. Emigration spread the benefits of modernization throughout white settler and home society, and spread its devastation throughout the societies we encountered everywhere else. *In other words, we transferred the costs of modernization to other societies, and kept the benefits for ourselves.*

So we were able to point to a general rise in affluence in 'our own' countries (including North America and Australasia) and, completely overlooking the decimation of the peoples whose land we had invaded and settled, imagine we had somehow 'created' (or 'generated') wealth out of poverty! Thus the good name of Progress was propped up for Western cultural consciousness, while other peoples bore the brunt of our expanding appetites, our urges for *Lebensraum*, power and wealth.

As we grabbed their land and forced them to work for us on and under it, we labelled these other peoples backward, uncivilized savages. Had the losers in Britain all stayed here, and been the only ones to be branded like this by the winners, perhaps we would have seen through these insults long ago.

As it is, British working-class consciousness retains a constant awareness of the rip-off perpetrated on ordinary people by the powerful and privileged - for the British-Irish working class suffered the worst of industrialization's destructive effects at home. Yet working-class Brits are notoriously willing to resort to racism. Also, although the Irish are our racial and geographical neighbours, they have suffered abuse and cruelty through the centuries at British hands, and many on the mainland still feel distinctly superior to them - not to speak of Ulster Protestants.

The notion of Progress demands the notion of 'backwardness' to offset it, just as the notion of Enlightenment needs the metaphor of mental darkness for ignorance to let it shine. It is surely a help to a 'progressive' culture if most of the people who are designated as 'backward' live somewhere else and look and behave differently: this helps to keep the home society more united in 'progressive' superiority, and to overlook the gulfs between their own social classes. But for a society already used to severe class distinctions, geographical distance is not absolutely necessary to preserving feelings of superiority.

Emigration, then, helped to maintain the West's myth of Progress by providing an escape route for the European casualties of enclosure, clearance, famine and industrialization. And colonialism helped to maintain the myth by providing us with cultural contrasts (between ourselves and Native Americans, or ourselves and Africans, for example) which we took to be proof of our superiority. In these ways, our class-ridden society was bonded together by a unanimous contempt for other cultures.

The so-called Third World has no such spacious backstage facilities - which is why the contrasts of affluence and degradation are so blatant and unavoidable all over Asia, Africa and South America.

Given the undeniable costs to human life in Britain, Africa and in the 'New World' exacted by industrial-colonial Progress, it is worth asking what on earth was said in its defence by the political advocates and by the philosophers of the early industrial age. The question remains essentially the same today: what *can* be said - what *is* said, in defence of 'economic development', given the worldwide suffering it entails?

There are two kinds of defences of Progress - materialist ('Look at the things we have managed to produce!' 'Look at improved disease control, medical treatment and so on!') and philosophical: in the last century, 'God has given us mastery over nature', nowadays, 'It's human nature to be curious and inventive' and 'we've always found a solution, we'll do it again'. And the old chestnut: '*You can't turn the clock back!*'

But although the individual arguments for Progress-as-economic development merit attention, the central issue remains, for me, the choice of *direction* the West has made. For it seems that, as a culture, we have chosen to turn our backs on our past and our faces towards the unknown and increasingly dangerous future which our style of Progress promises. It feels almost as if we Westerners would prefer *anything* new to anything we have already known.

We don't quite come out and say it but this underlying agenda becomes harder to overlook as our Progress comes to make less and less sense, as we lose our hard-won material security to unemployment and ill-health, and our very survival becomes threatened by our 'standard of living'.

The first defence of modern industrial Progress has always been the very fact that it is Progress! Clearly, this is not an argument, but a tautology which has meaning only for the people who accept the assumptions contained in it. A Western anthropologist would immediately spot such circularity in another culture's reasoning.

To break into this circularity, we would first have to ask: 'What exactly does this tribe mean by Progress?' To which a simple answer might be: 'Progress means *improvement* or betterment'.

The next question would be: 'Why does this tribe regard mechanization and the accumulation of profit as Progress, or improvement, in the face of all the evidence of human suffering caused by these cultural practices, among themselves and neighbouring tribes, evidence known to them?'

Possible answers might be: 'Because these practices ensure that powerful groups within the tribe retain and increase their power. They also provide an outlet for the energies of ambitious individuals to improve their status, in a way which does not threaten the social structure. The innovations of Progress free tribe members from work they perceive as hard, boring and repetitive. They give the tribe power over other peoples (this is rarely admitted explicitly even among the members of the tribe). On the cultural side, this people believes that its enquiring and innovative spirit represents its highest faculty. Thus, these economic processes are in a sense gifts from God. Therefore to criticize or reject what Progress brings is taboo.'

I believe the last answers come closest to the nub of the issue. Progress has become bound up with Western cultural identity, and this is the knot we Westerners must unravel, to get to the roots of our arrogance, our racism and our irrational faith in 'more Progress'. Observers from other cultures could help us here: but, unlike Westerners abroad, most non-Westerners are too polite to criticize us on our own home territory, when they have been our guests.

T hose who are involved with any kind of counselling know that our psychological defences have to be strong to shield us from hurt in our childhoods and ensure our emotional survival into adulthood. In later life, it can be very difficult and even dangerous to deconstruct these defences and face the pain of the past.

So it may be too dangerous, or at least too threatening for many people to question their cultural commitment to Progress. After all, what would we be without it, as individuals, and as a culture? What would be left of us?

I believe it *is* possible to renounce the arrogant claims of Progress and still be a Westerner. But the way to do it must be found by going along it.

I traced the start of the modern European spirit of enquiry to the age of exploration, the great escape from feudal Church and State. But the great escape has, sadly, turned into the great excuse. Progress cannot and must not, we feel, be impeded, because - well, because it is Progress! It is the way of our 'civilization'. It is what we are good at and where we are going - it is *who we are*. We do things simply because we have figured out *how* to do them - from nuclear technology to genetic engineering.

We in the West pride ourselves on our intellectual vigour, our ability to discover things for ourselves, and to apply new knowledge gained to 'mastering' nature and making life easier for ourselves. But we are helpless in the face of our discoveries - for as long as there is profit to be made from them, our culture will pursue them. 'If we don't do it, somebody else will'.

This abject submission to the 'inevitability' of Progress will be the undoing of us.

The second defence of Progress (though less reputable these days) is that the lives disrupted, degraded and lost as a result of the West's Great Leap Forward were mainly the lives of 'less advanced' people, and hence worth less than ours. Although we dare not say this out loud any more, this belief is still well lodged in the Western psyche - as the choices and omissions in our news coverage make plain.

We have not valued the cultures we have conquered and suppressed, or rendered obsolete, assuming our own was better, more civilized, more worthy of the name 'humanity'.

And so the *admitted* human costs of the industrial age have been treated as regrettable, but unavoidable hardships involved in conquering a new continent in the name of civilization. If this Western arrogance now strikes some of us as shameful, then at least some real progress has been made in two hundred-odd years.

As we look more deeply into our Western identity, trying to understand what we mean by Progress and why we cling to it so firmly, it is instructive to look at the terminology employed in the early days of the industrial revolution. The phrase used to advocate Progress with no holds barred was laissez faire - or 'let them get on with it'. In those days, the Tory Party was the one which wanted political intervention in economic affairs, while the Whigs, representatives of the new entrepreneur class, wanted a hands-off approach, to let business have its head.

The cry of laissez faire suggests an indulgent parent's response when an adolescent is suspected of out-of-order behaviour, and the more authoritarian parent is about to put a stop to it.

Indeed the nineteenth-century entrepreneurs *were* up to things that were, at the time, known to be irresponsible and destructive to human life and inherited values - *but they made money*. Therefore, the liberal (indulgent) ideology ran, they should be allowed to get on with it. Turn a blind eye to how it's done - the main things is, *the economy grows*. This is now a tired, familiar line of argument in the West. Then, it was shockingly revolutionary.

In the history classroom of my teenage years, the arguments about protection versus free trade had an arcane ring - as they still do to most Westerners, I suspect. I never remember really grasping that the fundamental issues underlying these Whig/Tory differences were moral issues of human decency or the lack of it.

The one instance where the moral confrontation underlying the economic arguments did become clear was over the famine in Ireland in the 1840s that followed the failure of the potato harvest, when the British government refused to send famine relief and tried instead to profit from the horrific situation by demanding the 'market price' for corn. They deliberately tried to starve the Irish out. Millions of Irish people died, hundreds of thousands emigrated from Ireland, and none of this will be forgotten by the Irish any more than the Jews will forget their more recent persecution and near extermination.

The crimes of history are felt first hand, *as personal injuries* and are passed down through families and communities in anecdote, attitude, song and silence. Conventional history books rarely manage to convey this inner story, at least not primarily, although these books inevitably reflect *someone's* inherited internal history.

Most modern Westerners would say that the laissez-faire argument has won hands down, for look at how wealthy and comfortable we are now, thanks to free trade and the temporary hardships of untrammelled economic growth. These arguments put forward by the New Right have a grim logic which seems closer to the truth than the left's pious yet evasive conviction that industrial-style Progress and economic growth can co-exist with equality and justice.

It is hard for Westerners now to imagine a time when business was not king. But the early merchants and industrialists and their defenders felt themselves to be cultural pioneers, Galileos and

Vasco da Gamas of a new age, who had some kind of calling to lead Western society onward and upward. Society was being overhauled according to new rules of 'the marketplace', and, thanks to the dawn of this new liberty, tomorrow would be brighter than yesterday.

In this atmosphere, the cry for a free hand for business was a shout of liberation, and government controls on the economy reminded many of the repressive weight of the old, elitist, corrupt and resented power structures of Church and State.

Marx put a progressive gloss on protectionism, arguing the need to curb the rule of capital and bend it to the service of the people. But few Westerners have ever been willing to entrust their new-found economic, political and psychological freedom to a new, albeit godless priesthood of ideologues. Because our fear of medieval constraints is still so lively, it has always been easy for Western leaders to use the Communist bogey to scare the 'free world'.

In all three ideologies, medieval Christianity, laissez-faire liberalism and revolutionary Marxism, the *happy ending* format so beloved by the West is preserved. People as distant in time and space as the early European and North American industrialists, the Russian Bolsheviks and the British New Right (and New Labour) have shared an attachment to 'a better tomorrow'. Old values, old patterns of life and old communities have been seen by all of them as less worthy of nurture than new towns, new industries, and new patterns of life. Old has been considered if not bad, then certainly dispensable; and new has been considered if not good, then certainly better than what went before.

W hat are we running from? And what are we running towards? The first of these questions was famously formulated by a Native American leader, Chief Seattle, as he observed white behaviour. These are not rhetorical questions. This book is an attempt to answer them.[3]

I believe our economics-obsessed society is still directed by the bourgeois impulse *to flee from feudal restriction and humiliation*, and to make its own way in the world on its own terms. And I believe *we are running towards catastrophe* on an indeterminate number of fronts - social, ecological and psycho-spiritual: an industrial-size catastrophe.

T here is a lot more to our Western conviction of cultural superiority than our possession of brute power and affluence. We feel we are superior in more subtle, cultural ways too - politically, as well as intellectually and spiritually. We are very proud, for example, of our *struggle for democracy*, the political struggle which Marx analysed so clearly. Woven into our economic history, this movement amounted to the rising middle classes demanding a say in government from the landed classes who traditionally ran Western society. In other words, 'Votes for better-off white men, whether or not they happen to be aristocrats' - which was exactly what they achieved.

Less wealthy white men had to wait a lot longer, though not as long as women, well-off or not, who were only enfranchised in the late 1920s in Britain.

We have already seen how the rise of the Western middle classes was based on the conquest, subjugation and exploitation of other peoples and their lands. But to appreciate what this bald statement means in human terms, we must appreciate that the political and social advances on which we in the West so pride ourselves were won at the expense of others: namely the societies who lost their priceless birthrights of dignity, power and freedom, autonomy and self-sufficiency to our expanding empire.

As we look at our whole Western history, first in Europe, and then in the Western diaspora, it seems as if Westerners needed some firm ground to press down on in order to take the massive step up from feudal subordination to modern democracy. As we struggled to rid ourselves of our medieval sense of inferiority and disempowerment, we have passed on our pain and trouble to others. Our gains have been their losses, politically and psychologically as much as economically.

Our Western cultural prejudices hide this history from us so that Westerners still manage to feel a glow of self-satisfaction about our democratic system and all our institutions. And when we look at other societies, we tend to feel exasperation rather than shame about their huge and mounting economic and political problems. Standing at the top of the ladder of privilege, we have the gall to exhort peoples we have robbed and denigrated to pull themselves up by their own bootstraps 'like we did'! Or we may generously offer them a hand up - an aid programme, or an electoral commission - expecting them to trust the hand that is joined to the foot that stamped them down.

But for the peoples of Africa, India, the Caribbean and elsewhere, there is nothing to press down on in order to regain *their* lost security and dignity, except their own oppressed majorities. Westerners are not offering to come down a few rungs - to loosen our stranglehold on their economies or on the world's political affairs. Rather, more and more weight is being put on the weakest by economic restructuring, interest repayments and the whole gamut of international currency arrangements and stock markets. The same old floorboards, the so-called 'poorest of the poor', and ultimately, the long-suffering earth, have to bear all of this weight.

We in the affluent West just don't seem able to perceive - or willing to admit - the crucial and blatant connections between our present power and our former colonies' present powerlessness, between our bulging supermarket shelves and their deepening hunger. We *know* so much about how the world has got into its present condition of instability but we choose, it seems, not to *understand* what is going on.

I believe the reason for our selective Western blindness to these connections lies in our wish to see Western history as Progress. The more we have done, as a society, a class, a culture, which we are unwilling to consciously admit, the more our minds will suppress, sublimate and rationalize for us just so that we can carry on from day to day. *Mental survival (however warped the world view that survives) is the mind's contribution to our continuation as a species.*

We will not be able to think clearly, as individuals or as a society, until we face up to what we have done and continue to do as a society squarely, without excuses - and ready to change. The more our society goes on repressing the historical truth which is being transmitted involuntarily to our younger generation in everything our society does and stands for, the more hurt, confused and alienated our young people will remain.

Whole encyclopaedias of human history and knowledge have been distorted or destroyed, and suffering caused which will never be catalogued in our Western archives. Catalogues exist in the cultures of the survivors, and those survivors can be consulted. But this has to be done, on the whole, face to face. There are few books which tell the stories. I can't write with the voice of a black American, but try Toni Morrison's *Beloved*. I can't write with the voice of a slave, or an ex-slave, but read the autobiographical *Equiano's Travels*.[4]

The process of colonial-industrial accumulation is not over yet. The accumulation of money and of misery goes on today, all over the world, still bearing high the banner of 'economic development'.

The crimes of the frontier and the debasement of other cultures also continue today. 'Service industries' - prostitution, gambling, sale of alcohol and drugs - grow up around tourist centres and military bases and in every world capital, wherever there is money to be made by selling what you have - or what you are - to those who have money.

I suspect that the cost of all this to modern Western society and culture has been equivalent in weight and pain to the destruction and suffering caused by our economic Progress. I do not write this glibly, to make light of the agony undergone by others, nor to block out their agony with self-pity. If it seems an enormous claim (and it is), we should not underestimate the depths of the human psyche or its capacity to absorb and transmute suffering.

Each human being is born a complete and balanced world of feeling and character, fit to be raised in any culture or in several. Our years from birth to adulthood are a concentrated effort to take in all our culture(s) tell us of themselves, so that we can form a coherent adult identity. First we learn from our family, then from our schoolmates, our social class, nation, and in our fast-changing Western youth culture, from our peer group, our 'generation'. And all that our culture can hand on to us is what its people have been and done, or had done to them, and what they feel and think in the light of these events.

One of the many features of traditional African culture that impressed me in Zimbabwe was the *conscious* way it was passed on. ' "This is who you are", the elders seemed to tell the children constantly: to greet everyone properly, to lower your eyes respectfully, to help with the work cheerfully, to go to funerals no matter how far you have to travel - this is how and who we are, and so this is how and who you are, for you belong to us'.

Of course, there are aspects of Zimbabwean culture which I never heard taught, because they were kept within the family, or within the culture: ancestral praise-songs, all-night ceremonies of song and dance, beer-brewing for the ancestors, spirit possessions, healings, storytelling, arbitration of disputes.

Africans often asked me, 'How do you learn *your* culture?' All I could come up with was table manners, bits about hospitality, and quite a lot of Christian stories and theology. Of course, I have learned far more than I am conscious of, but most of it was not taught to me explicitly or deliberately. Most of what I have learned about who I am seemed to be enacted almost involuntarily, out of family idiosyncrasy, class or national prejudice, school habits and so on.

Norms and expectations that are in the air, but never articulated in so many words, have a way of entering straight into our subconscious, so that we are not even aware of having learned these things. The less our Western culture chooses to *say*, or is *able* to say, about its way of being, and the more it resorts to such sub-liminal teaching of its children, the less well-equipped these children will be to act freely and confidently as adults, *knowing what they are doing and why*; and the more they will find themselves tripping over internal wires they didn't even know were there.

The Western psyche has turned into a minefield. No wonder there is a growing demand for bomb disposal experts - counsellors, psychotherapists and self-help groups.

Class is another area where things are rarely made explicit, especially in middle-class and upper-class homes.

Working-class children in the UK learn two cultures - their own, and the dominant middle class one; just as rural African school-children learn their own culture at home and a new post-colonial one at school and in town. Members of the ruling culture are less likely to learn two sets of rules: their own is usually enough to get by.

So Western culture hands on to its children all it has been and done, for good and for ill. Some of this, as I have said, is handed on directly and consciously, as stories, lessons, rules; other things are passed down subconsciously, through silences, refusals and psychological attitudes learned by example.

Between the conscious and the subconscious lies the huge area of indirect, semiconscious teaching through jokes, commonly-held beliefs and prejudices, and whispered 'illicit' revelations.

In all of this avid and involuntary learning and teaching, nothing significant to our history is lost to our cultural memory - regardless of what we would prefer to retain or to forget, for the sake of our conscious self-image. Because of the way culture is taught and learned, I believe that everything Western society has taken from others is 'paid for' in Westerners' psychic inheritance.

The costs to Western culture, like the suffering meted out to others, appear as negative quantities, partial losses and distortions of given human qualities and forms of understanding. Since we Westerners now live more or less within these parameters, they are more difficult to delineate than the sufferings of the victims of industrialization and colonialism.

But because of our inherent appetite for health and balance, most people are able to appreciate more attractive and healthy qualities and atmospheres when we encounter them within or outside our own accustomed cultural framework. And so it is possible to attempt an outline of what we may have lost through our history.

The first cost to Western society of the enslavement and degradation of other peoples was the brutalization of those who owned and dealt in slaves or who came into other kinds of exploitative contact with other peoples. These effects gradually filtered throughout Western culture and were confirmed and boosted by the experience of colonial power.

The longer-term cultural costs have included the blunting of middle-class Western sensitivities and the twisting of our dealings with our own subconscious minds, with the less powerful groups within our own society and with every other culture on earth.

It must be said here that women and children do not remain 'innocent' in such a tainted social atmosphere: they internalize their society's dominant attitudes and perpetrate them upon themselves and each other, as well as suffering under them. It seems to be in the nature of evil and oppression to seek to turn its victims into collaborators.

The cost of Western rape of other cultures has included the reduction of respect to politeness - and then to plain disrespect and abusiveness - in our own; a rising tide of violence and amorality, and of confusion about what to do about it; and a loss of vitality, spontaneity and joy that is immediately apparent to visitors from other parts of the world in Western faces and behaviour - and even apparent to Westerners ourselves, when we come home again from those places.

Part of the cost has long been paid in estrangement and loneliness, divided consciousness and even insanity, by people in Western society who have tried to resist the destructive flow of these distorted values.

Yet none of these colossal social and psychic costs has acted as a deterrent to the 'forces of Progress'. Indeed, even when the symptoms of social deterioration and breakdown have been noted, few have traced the connection between the West's present social ills and our past and present antisocial practices. If with all the benefit of hindsight, this causal link is still virtually invisible to the naked Western eye, it is scarcely surprising that the early industrialists and plantation owners failed to foresee the likely consequences of their brave new Progress.

Ever since Europe found its intellectual feet in the age of discovery and got its first scent of freedom from feudalism, there really has been no turning back for Westerners. We have felt a cultural imperative to forge ahead, break new ground, and to compete incessantly - with our own past and with each other. To misquote the hymn, we Westerners know no rest, and most of us no longer *have* a Thee to find our rest in.

But although we have tirelessly explored, dissected, examined and experimented, theorized and revised our theories, and generally dazzled ourselves with our own brilliance, we have also become extremely adept at using our intellects to construct rationalizing defences of our own behaviour.

We have spun webs of self-justifying falsehoods to excuse our own behaviour, however disrespectful, unacceptable and harmful this behaviour has been to others. As we have become more and more emotionally damaged by the effects of our brutal history, our appreciation of life has waned, and our academic arguments have become less and less relevant to everyday life, and to everyone else.

Yet *still* we believe we are Progressing! After a long and exciting courtship in the age of discovery, at the start of the colonial-industrial era the West met Progress at the altar and committed itself for richer, for poorer, in sickness and in health - and, I fear, barring an unforeseen, sanity-restoring estrangement, till death us do part.

Introduction to Part II

The Way We Are Now

*East/West, North/South - Economized values -
The measurable and the immeasurable - Colonizing our cousins*

THE NEXT THREE CHAPTERS OF THIS BOOK look at different aspects of what is going on in the world now, at the turn of the millennia, and at our Western attitudes to these events. I have tried to show how, culturally as well as individually, our expectations and responses are conditioned by our past.

So, if chapters one to five dealt with the past as a way of understanding the present, the rest of the book, it could be said, deals with the present in the light of that past.

Chapter six shows how the recently collapsed opposition between capitalism and socialism hid common cultural roots in 'educated' Western philosophy, attitudes and practice. This common heritage helps to explain why alone among the cultures of the world, both Western capitalism and Marxist socialism have dispensed with God and resorted to materialism. By materialism, I mean respect for and reliance on the material world to the exclusion of the world of the spirit, in which all other cultures put their trust.

This attitude of ours, which seems at first sight such a strange and sudden break with our pious missionary past, is in fact the natural destination of Western cultural impulses that have predominated for a very long time.

Chapter seven looks at the West in the world, and the way our past colours and determines our behaviour towards other cultures. In this chapter I will try to enable readers to step out of Western shoes for a moment and get a glimpse of ourselves as others see us.

Chapter eight takes Southern Africa as a microcosm of the neo-colonial two-thirds world.

In Southern Africa, though there is socialist talk and a capitalist economy, there is very little cultural common ground with the European history of these institutions. The contradictions of Southern Africa encapsulate many of the problems of a world caught between traditional value systems and ways of life and a 'modern' Western-dominated culture that seems more and more inescapable.

For these reasons, in thinking and writing about Southern Africa, Westerners (including South African and Scottish Westerners) come up against our racist prejudices and our cultural superiority syndrome.

South Africa's struggle for 'freedom', and to define 'freedom', throw up questions which will have to be faced eventually, in South Africa, in the former Soviet bloc and everywhere else. What do we mean by 'human rights'; by 'justice', by 'a decent standard of living'?

Can capitalism provide all these things for all the peoples of the world and if not, why not? Can Socialism? What is the difference between these two options; what *should* the difference be; and how much more of all this ideological wrangling and materialist aspiration can the earth and its peoples afford?

The tremendous events in Eastern Europe, the release of Nelson Mandela and the political liberation of South Africa have all taken place since much of this book was written. These events have opened up Western political thinking to areas of discussion which environmental anxiety and Green politics were already highlighting.

Many radicals are dismayed by the way the East has opened itself to Western business penetration. To express their grief, they talk the language of the marketplace, because the left has become accustomed to speaking in economic terms to voice its social and ethical feelings: the left laments the loss of economic security for women, rising rents and food prices, the threat of unemployment, removal of free childcare facilities.

But though we can list all these economic indicators of free market measures, what is really being threatened, and what the left grieves for, cannot - and should not - be quantified in money terms.

When I visited Dresden for the first time in 1992, my hostess told me that in the days before the 'changes' she used to take her children to the park in the afternoons, and her husband, who was a government office worker, would join them there after work. They would all play together for an hour before walking home to their high-rise flat.

Now, she told me, though he had been lucky to find a new job (his old one had disappeared, along with a lot of other people's, at reunification), she never sees him before seven or eight in the evening. 'There is much more pressure on everyone now. Under the old regime, with all its faults, there was time to relax, and we had a good family life. I feel sorry for the children now, and for those who are just becoming parents'.

This couple, through their church discussion group, had been part of the movement which helped to prepare the ground for the East's self-liberation. However they were not consulted about reunification, which was imposed from the top, suddenly, without discussion, and they are saddened by the way things have gone.

People all over Eastern Europe in the 1990s are having to offer up the sense they have hitherto preserved that everyone in their society has a place, and a right to be valued and cared for. Parts of this humane social atmosphere were certainly the result of deliberate socialist policy; but a great deal of it was probably due to omission rather than commission. The Soviet-dominated East, with its lumbering bureaucratic machinery and unrealistic, hated Five-Year Plans just couldn't speed up the wheels of industry and tighten up economic performance as capitalism was managing to do in the West. In other words, failure of 'economic development' was good news for family life and human contentment!

The West *looked* very good to the East on TV - they could see the stuff on the supermarket shelves, see the clothes and cars, and they knew the phones worked, but perhaps they didn't - and couldn't - fully realize how living in the West *felt*. It is the same for us Scots watching Hollywood films. Los Angeles may look glamorous to us on screen: but I wonder how many of us would feel comfortable living there, or bringing up our children there.

I believe that those Westerners who take time to notice what is happening now in the former Soviet bloc can learn something salutary from this social destruction. It teaches us that societies which may look as if they stand to gain materially by unprotected exposure to Western business actually stand to lose a great deal, in human terms, whatever they gain or lose economically.

It should, therefore, teach us to look twice at our normal categories of 'poor' and 'backward', as we tend to apply them when dealing with less economically cutthroat cultures than our own. If this realization were taken to heart, I believe it could herald a new understanding of what matters more than Progress.

In the early days and weeks of the opening up in the East, I think most Westerners felt genuine relief on behalf of the courageous protesters and enthusiasm for the new freedoms being demanded and won by people who had been kept down and kept quiet for so long. The problems that have been generated since by Western economic predominance there should not stop us celebrating the priceless new openness we now enjoy with the East.

Being grateful is not the same thing as gloating that 'we were right all along', as our political leaders encourage us to do. We can be sorry and sceptical about the headlong rush for our lifestyle; we can try to oppose, or at least opt out of, efforts to make money out of the East - but we can still be glad for them - and for ourselves, as their cultural cousins, that they have cast off their discredited and oppressive regimes.

The value of this new freedom is hard to put into words, and it has little to do with the freedom to make money. It has to do with human dignity, with not having to tell lies to get ahead, or keep your mouth shut to keep your job. We in the West are far from completely free in this regard, but we have liberties we can and should be glad of.

Apart from political liberties, most of what our media observes in the East can be summed up in money terms. We are trained to look at the world economically, so we don't, on the whole, read stories like my Dresden friends' in our newspapers.

One phenomenon, however, which we cannot deal with using our materialist vocabulary, and which the West has noticed emerging in the East since 1989, is racism. We can try to analyse Eastern European racism in economic terms: it has surface-level roots as self-protectionist xenophobia - jobs for *our* boys - and it has much deeper socio-economic roots in our shared European history.

But the evil of racism, like the good of civil liberties, defies a purely economic analysis. Whatever its economic 'causes', racism is not a question of money, but a psycho-spiritual condition, a twisting of the mind and heart. Racism and fascism, like freedom of speech, cannot be dealt with satisfactorily without reference to non-economic, moral-spiritual categories of human experience.

Nevertheless, 'progressive' Westerners have become accustomed to 'explaining' things like racism, fascism and freedom in economic terms with a sense that we are trying to further objective understanding, as well as the socialist values of equality, fraternity and internationalism. But this way of thinking and talking has actually aided and abetted the Western *capitalist* habit of reducing life to narrow, materialist categories. While the right talks of buying and selling and entrepreneurialism, the left has talked about social conditioning and basic necessities. The two frames of reference meet, and find their most sophisticated expression yet, in the new exact sciences of 'what every human wants': the applied psychology and sociology of management consultancy, marketing and advertising which run the global economy.

This reduction of life to money and what it can buy is the latest in a long chain of cultural choices we have made. But when we subject people and events to these materialist categories, we wilfully and disrespectfully ignore vast areas of life which other cultures acknowledge and value - and which our own culture, traditionally, also held dear.

It seems to me that we Westerners still have a strong need to include these non-material areas in our life, but that we no longer have the language to express either our need or its satisfaction.

Speaking from my own experience as an activist and a British 'volunteer' abroad (I was paid Zim $600 a month, a very fine income in Zimbabwe, so I was not a 'volunteer' in the sense that I understand this term), left-wing analysis often seems to camouflage the real reasons why people involve themselves in, for example, Central American solidarity campaigns and fair trading, while 'development' vocabulary masks the real reasons for going to work in Africa.

These real reasons, I believe, are not abstract or ideological but emotional and spiritual. They are the people and communities and ways of life we encounter through our involvement in these activities, ways of life and points of view that inspire us and contrast refreshingly with our own backgrounds. These are what draw us in, stimulate, reward and involve us, and present us with subtle, complex challenges to our middle-class Western values.

Returning now to intangibles like racism, fascism and freedom: while the left deals with these in materialist terms, less political Western minds try to 'explain' them in terms of individual needs and psychological histories.

However, many Western commentators seem blind to these connections. Indeed, the individual psychological approach can even obscure them, since it often arises out of the contemporary Western cultural impulses to individualism and fragmentation: 'This is *my* very own theory' and 'This is *my* (or his/her) deep personal, unique, confusing-or-meaningful-or- random experience which is interesting *in itself* and has *no* wider ramifications, or at least none which can be scientifically proven. Thank you.'

The psychological approach is believed to further in-depth understanding of human motivation - but it often does so by virtually ignoring the far-reaching web of relationships through which we become and remain human. The Malawians have a saying which means: 'People are two. One is an animal.'

Like the left, most psychologists steer clear of the moral-spiritual sphere, however close to it their enquiries may bring them. Their modern, Western-trained minds feel more at ease with scientifically observable and measurable data, with 'plain facts', than with empathy and the intangible. In our culture, the immeasurable has become suspect.

However, the immeasurable within ourselves can have massive and measurable ill effects, and I believe that the fascist and racist tendencies in our European and Western culture should force us to confront our own immeasurable depths. Righteous outrage of decent citizens is not an adequate or even an appropriate response to militant racism. We need, rather, to ask serious questions about who we are, and what it means, in our culture, to be human.

Zimbabwean township children used to yell '*Murungu!*' (European!) at me as I walked through their virtually blacks-only areas. Once, I heard a parent check a child by saying, 'I *munhu*' - 'It is a *person*'.

Instead of asking for psychological and sociological information on racist attackers or asking futile questions about the existence of evil (in others), we should be asking what has happened to respect for personhood in our culture. How have we become so dehumanized as a culture that this contempt and hatred for people of different cultural and racial backgrounds has taken root so firmly throughout white society - from Australia to Texas, from London to both parts of reunified Germany and the ex-Soviet Union?

My own hope has been that what is happening now in Eastern Europe - culturally and economically - might be for the West a parable of our own colonial-industrial history that could prompt us to review what we have done to ourselves and to others over the last 500 years. This hope seems more forlorn now than when the changes came about, for our media pays very little attention to what is going on in Eastern Europe and in the ex-Soviet Union, unless there is bloodshed.

Yet the parallels between these struggling countries and the two-thirds world, in their relations with the West, have been pointed out in many places. 'Weak' economies are targeted by Western business, and under the banner of 'developing the infrastructure' or 'providing jobs and investment', we move in and make a killing, finding cheaper labour, bringing in our own highly-paid 'experts' and demolishing local ways of doing things with our 'superior' methods and technology.

I had hoped that we Westerners might find it easier to identify with Eastern Europeans than we had ever done with Africans or Indians, since they are more closely related to ourselves. There is nothing intrinsically wrong with feeling more empathy for our own people than for others.

Most peoples tend, naturally enough, to prefer their own company to that of other peoples, and this preference for the familiar doesn't in itself make anyone racist. But when a group seeks and gains power over other groups, these natural preferences become a source of sickness; and when the dominant start rationalizing their abuse and exploitation of the dominated, the minds of the dominant become infected and twisted.

I believe we would be better off, and psychologically safer, admitting a healthy if irrational bias for our own kind, than pretending we have no preferences between races, or else weaving self-glorifying myths about our own civilized superiority or 'racial purity' around our natural gut-level enjoyment and trust of the familiar.

If we would only pay attention to what is happening, we Westerners could watch chapters of our own history being re-enacted *now* in the Eastern half of our continent, and learn more about what is gained and lost through our style of Progress. We would have a chance to re-evaluate the non-economic categories of human experience that we have gradually lost sight of in the course of our rise to economic dominance, qualities we found it so easy to overlook and undervalue in the non-European cultures we have patronizingly defined as 'developing'.

6

The Triumph of Economics

*Christianity to Consumerity - Marx, prophet without God -
Feudal revolutions - No more Mr Nice Guy - Work, drudgery
and social values - 'Security equals socialism' - Cultural
impoverishment - Reclaiming the non-economic sphere*

TWENTIETH-CENTURY INDUSTRIAL CULTURE East and West, socialist and capitalist, has largely dispensed with God. This may seem
ironic, given how recently we carried our Victorian Christianity
to the ends of the earth.

The irony goes deeper still, since our forefathers' fearless confidence to preach the Gospel in foreign places, among such different peoples, was aided by their unwavering conviction that as 'civilized' Christian Europeans they were superior to any 'heathen'
race. Yet this sense of superiority was itself founded on the same
enquiring attitudes and scientific principles that would lead, within
a couple of generations, to the marginalization of religious faith
within European culture, West and East.

Some pockets of religion have indeed survived within Western
culture: but significantly, the parts of Christianity that survive
most visibly - like American-influenced evangelism, or the rump
of faithful churchgoers, young and old - have made their peace
with materialism as a way of life and have no quarrel with it.

Brands of Christianity, like monasticism, which demand non-
materialist values for everyday use, have experienced a severe fall-
ing-away and have had to make room for Buddhist and Hindu
sects who can advocate such a view of life with more cultural
consistency, given their non-Western backgrounds.

In place of Christianity, our new Western Gospel is consumerism. The main observance of this religion is shopping, and its cathedrals and cloisters are the supermarkets, malls and pedestrian precincts which now dominate our modern town centres. In these culturally sacred places, millions of Westerners walk, celebrate, look respectfully at beautiful images, and seek comfort for their hearts, as much as for their bodies. For this ritual they work, and from these temples, if they do not work, they feel excluded.

Christianity - our religious tradition - is dead on its feet in the West because the way we organize ourselves as a culture no longer proceeds from a spiritual basis. Karl Marx told us it never had, and many of us believed him.

After all, this man Marx had a towering intellect, he was a pioneer of the modern mind - he and Freud are our intellectual grandfathers. Of course we took his word for it when he assured us his work was 'objective', that he had no personal axe to grind, that what he told us was the plain, unadulterated truth. But his moral passion was quite exciting too, and fitted well with our cultural enthusiasm for being right. And how much he opened up with his sharp analytical scalpel for his students to gaze upon - the whole groundwork of sociology, the critique of bourgeois ideology, the roots of injustice.

His wife, on the other hand, must presumably have lived by the values of an 'earlier' - or rather, of an older era in order to find the strength and perseverance to live in a foreign country far from her own family and friends, and to look after her husband and their children while he pored over his papers. She probably had a more vivid sense of life's meaning and weight by living it, from hand to mouth, than the man who spent his days looking for meaning in the British Library, and dispensing the meaning he found in speeches, books and pamphlets.

She must have been aware of the emotional and material cost of her husband's dispassionate 'objectivity' about the workings of capitalism - since his theoretical work and his activism kept him from attending to the wellbeing of his own immediate family, the family who had accompanied him into exile. She may have wondered how someone so sensitive to the sufferings and economic insecurity of whole classes of people could bear to behold the suffering and economic insecurity of his wife and children. Did he simply overlook them or did she not permit herself to wonder any such thing?

'Shhh ... Papa's working'

The Western intellect is a very mixed blessing. For while it helps us to accumulate, assemble and analyse knowledge about the material world we inhabit, and about the economic and power relations between people, it also encourages us to construct mental ramparts to prevent us being distracted from our intellectual labour. These ramparts can stop us seeing - and more importantly, feeling - what is going on all around us. As we rely more and more on our own intellects, and on the intellectually-arrived-at conclusions of others, we can become more and more out of touch with real life, with other people, and with our other sources of experience and knowledge. The absent-minded professor and the great artist who is personally ruthless or insensitive are caricatures based on unhappy true stories.

The argument of this book leads to the conclusion, among others, that we Westerners will not be able to trust our intellects as long as we refuse to face up to the whole truth about what our society has done and continues to do. For *our minds will protect us from the pain we choose not to feel.* We will remain in our ivory towers and behind our mental security fences until we are ready to humble ourselves and give up some of our power and wealth.

Since Marx's day, Western culture has been greatly impoverished even as we have got massively richer. 'The family' has shrunk from a network of perhaps twenty to fifty people living fairly close together, to one set of parents and their children, or one couple, or a carer and her/his sick relative, or a single individual.

And the communities, in which several families used to co-exist, fight, gossip, marry and befriend each other, are now gone, or are faint echoes of what they used to be. 'Thank God', some will say, recalling oppressive childhoods - but we are the poorer for it, socially, spiritually and psychologically. We have lost the everyday feel of coming and going through each other's lives, and so we have lost the joy and point of it all.

In the nineteenth century, scientific materialism proudly bore the banner of Western intellectual Progress, and this tradition has spawned disciplines like economics, sociology and behavioural psychology which still seek to apply the principles and methodology of science to human affairs.

At the same time, the older Western paradigms of spiritual Progress and the warrior hero encouraged us to see these nineteenth-century intellectual pioneers as our cultural champions, who would fight the dragons of ignorance and fear for us and help to fulfil our expectations of a happy ending in universal justice, understanding - and affluence.

Marx's own discipline, scientific socialism, saw itself as the herald of heaven on earth, as well as an avenging angel against the forces of evil. Marx's version of the Western Progress myth allowed Marxists to blame 'capitalism, colonialism and imperialism' for the destructive effects of socio-economic change (or Progress). With evil thus ideologically branded and dispatched into 'isms', middle-class socialists could carry on with their professional lives feeling innocent of the crimes that supported their standard of living.

But such self-righteous political analysis has ended up serving exactly the same economic master as its 'enemy', capitalism. For dispossession, degradation and starvation are not just temporary side-effects of economic development which will fade away once capitalism is replaced by socialism (the left-wing illusion), or once it has completed and perfected itself (the right-wing illusion). These forms of suffering are economic development's inevitable and ever-deepening *end result*. Marxism, and all our progressive analysis of capitalism's evils, have merely helped to postpone the realization that *we are laying waste the earth and its people in the name of Progress.*

Our mental ramparts of Them and Us, and our habits of projecting all wrongdoing onto our chosen enemies, have blinded many on the left to devastating crimes. Several generations of purges, repressions and betrayals were overlooked for ideological reasons, just as the murderous violence of Pol Pot in Cambodia has been overlooked by the international community.[1]

Now finally, after Thatcher and Tiananmen Square, and after the collapse of real existing socialism in the Soviet bloc, the left has lost its moral confidence. But instead of facing the unpalatable truth about materialist Progress *per se*, the Labour Party in Britain is turning to advertising executives, marketing strategists and big-time entrepreneurs asking, 'What must I do to be successful, or at least to inherit the government of the country?'

In the 1990s, the triumph of capitalist-style economics seems complete. However, perhaps now is precisely the time for us in the West to finally realize the bankruptcy of our materialism. I must admit it seems more likely we will hide from the truth until we start to suffocate or drown, or until it is time to build more bunkers and go to war again - but we could use this breathing space, and this new open atmosphere, to draw obvious and necessary conclusions about the way we are headed, and begin radically changing our behaviour before changes are forced on us by catastrophe.

This is a good time for re-evaluation, because now that Enemy Number One has fallen into our arms, the right-wing in the West can free itself from its fears about Moscow-funded subversion. The real enemies within our society are our apparently insatiable greed and uncontrollable economic expansionism, and the social chaos caused by these, within and around our society.

The left too needs to re-evaluate its analysis, now that the European Marxist illusion of ideologically-guaranteed social justice has been laid to rest. It is easy to sneer after the giant has been killed, especially by his own supposed supporters, but the giant was not all militarism and malice. Like our Western society and government, Eastern bloc society and government contained an ineffable mixture of cynicism and faith, of social vision and self-interest.

The West has 'won' the Cold War partly because of the urge for freedom and Mikhail Gorbachev's amenability to it; but largely also because of the urge for affluence: because capitalism is more efficient than socialism at turning life into money and because socialism made a fool of itself by trying to beat the West at its own game.

The end of Soviet anti-Western hegemony over a large minority of the world's countries has changed things radically in the world, so much so that we will still be learning about the implications of the changes for many years to come. But one thing it has revealed already is that East and West were not so far apart in their experience and thinking as had been believed. The 'total incompatibility' and utter enmity assumed to exist, between 1945 and 1989, melted away in weeks and we have felt real, spontaneous joy in having our lines of communication with these people opened up again.

The sudden disappearance of supposed differences confirms many people's suspicions that our mutual Cold War fears were fanned by the powerful within each bloc, in order to keep themselves in jobs. But the other, usually unmentioned side of this insight is that we Western Europeans really do belong to one cultural family with Eastern Europeans - and that the political differences that have divided us for a few decades are nothing against what unites us.

Perhaps we can now begin to appreciate how socialism and capitalism, which for several decades seemed to be utterly inimical and countervailing 'global' forces, have in fact grown out of the same minority culture (ours) - and are, like feuding brothers, closely related.

Family members tend to know the worst and the best of each other, from the inside. The socialist (or ex-socialist) East, and the left in the West, have accurately criticized Western economic immorality, giving us an essential framework for understanding our modern socio-economic history. By contrast, the intellectual atmosphere in the USA suffers drastically from having suppressed and expelled Marxism in the McCarthy era - to a European, American political culture feels lobotomized.

However, what the Eastern socialists and the Western left failed to do was to convince most Westerners - and even themselves - that they had viable alternative ideas about how to achieve their declared goals of justice, equality and Progress. As it was, to keep their citizens on the right (left) track, socialist states resorted to a measure of social control (repression) which we in the West, left and right, would not willingly have stood for.

Many East Germans however, in the early days of the opening up, flocked across to the West not just for freedom but for jobs and goodies, which brings us back to the 'declared goals' of socialism: how different are these really from the declared goals of capitalism? The political means have been different, of course, and the social priorities are different. The rhetoric is completely different. But the desired ends are perhaps very similar indeed: a vision of plenty, well enough distributed to keep everyone more or less happy, in a clean, modern, industrialized society. It is a materialist vision of human satisfaction, embraced by both capitalism and socialism. This vision is the cultural product of a single intellectual and economic history - the history of modern Western 'Man'.

This history forked politically in our century, partly thanks to a few scrupulous nineteenth-century minds, who, although they did not question the ideal of material Progress, were too sickened by the inhumanity and injustice of early capitalism not to protest. From this point on, social criticism and social morality in the West became steadily more secularized. The Church was gradually replaced by the party, or the union.

Except for the working-class revivalist movement in the towns, Christianity began to lose its cultural moorings in industrial society. Churchgoing became and remained a middle-class habit, and our culture - particularly middle-class culture - began to lose its spiritual integrity and authenticity. We did not practise what we preached. This process began well before the heyday of world mission.

As the spiritual dimension disappeared from social criticism in the West, so it disappeared also from the dominant materialist culture of growth and consumption. The tiny remnant of Christianity in late twentieth-century Western society is still drifting, disconnected and riven with dissension, trying to find its way back to relevance.

White, North American evangelical Christianity survives anachronistically, like Northern Irish and South African Reformed churchgoing. The Americans, single-mindedly avoiding the social issues insistently raised by Jesus, the prophets and the gospel writers, have ended up with a kind of fundamentalist faith in private enterprise and 'every soul for itself' which reflects the economics-run atmosphere of contemporary US society.

Meanwhile, although great efforts and dollar expenditures are made to ensure that American values and the American way of life are preached in Africa and South America, Christianity there is still communal, socially integrated and vibrant, at least among ordinary people - reflecting the atmospheres of their more convivial societies.

Marx and Engels, the pioneers of Western liberation theology minus God, used the intellectual tools of their time, the mechanistic, determinist, 'scientific' framework - to analyse the social and economic features of capitalism. Like the prophets, they wanted to see the world changed, to see the kingdom of righteousness instituted on earth; and like the prophets they were ambivalent about how much this could be left to God (historical necessity) and how much would be up to us (revolutionary struggle).

Their activist impulse to liberate humanity from degradation and exploitation had to be reconciled with a detached, scientific approach to the laws of labour and capital. For only from such an 'objective' approach could a nineteenth-century Western intellect derive confidence in the 'rightness' of the proposed solution.

As we have seen, this fundamental contradiction of Marxism is closely related to Western theological self-entanglements over freewill versus predestination. It also links up with our cultural habit of accounting for our actions and intentions in terms of an overarching Progress which is somehow both given and achieved.

Other contradictions have emerged in the subsequent history of socialist revolutions, this time between Marxist thought and actual historical events.

Marx and Engels, of course, based their analysis and their hopes for change on the newly-industrializing societies in Western Europe which were still in the throes of transformation from agricultural to factory economies. But the working-class movement which they hoped would be the vanguard of revolution had its mind on other things. It was preoccupied, first of all, with the struggle to maintain workers' solidarity in the face of the employers' enormous powers to deprive them of their livelihood altogether; then, to achieve material security for its members within the new, emerging economic system - to wrest a share of the quickly-expanding national wealth, and to establish limits to its own vulnerability to exploitation.

The language of rights and of protection prevailed over the language of revolution. Feminist historians (mainly middle class) have claimed that much nineteenth-century trade union activism around female and child labour was directed towards shoring up men's domestic and economic authority, by restricting or removing women's economic independence of men. This observation does not have to be made with bitterness, turning all men into oppressors and all women into victims: it is understandable that men who were having their self-reliance and dignity removed from 'above' would seek to maximize their control over the human beings within their power. It is slightly invidious for socially privileged commentators to side with the wives and children of such oppressed men.

For would-be revolutionary intellectuals, such very non-revolutionary complexities of working-class reality must always have been highly frustrating. Middle-class activists are in an entirely different situation from the class whose 'objective, historical' interests they are trying to espouse: their Marxist perspective is not a function of their class background (neither indeed was Marx's), but is rather a rational expression of an often deeply emotional rejection of their own background.

As long as the 'revolutionary vanguard' looks to the dispossessed merely to help them carry out the programme they the vanguard have drawn up, the oppressive relations between powerful and powerless cannot be changed.

In the light of these considerations, it is telling to remind ourselves of the kind of societies which were in fact revolutionized through Marxist doctrine: not the industrialized ones which spawned the theory and which the theory was designed to transform, but vast feudal empires where harsh repression had been a norm of government for centuries, unmitigated by 'bourgeois revolution'. These societies, from a Western European, Marxist point of view, were at a 'previous stage' of 'development' to capitalism.

In both the Soviet and the Chinese revolutions, radical members of the educated elite led the action in the name of the workers and peasants. And so they found themselves in the classic self-contradiction that faces Marxist governments of 'underdeveloped' countries - trying to force the pace of 'modernization' in imitation of capitalist societies, in order to get to the stage where Marx 'foresaw' the socialist transformation of capitalism!

Rather than regarding these ironies as big historical mistakes, or flukes that cloud the issues, I believe these strange events have many lessons to teach us. They show us history's irrepressible capacity to dodge prediction, to subvert our efforts to direct it, and to use our contributions in unforeseen - often thankfully fruitful - ways. For surely we must celebrate the liberation of Russia from the tsars, and of China from the Japanese and the puppet government of Chiang Kai-shek, as well as the uprisings of peoples in Africa and South East Asia against the colonial powers.

Besides calling us to laugh at ourselves and admit that we and our theories are not the makers of history after all, these events also suggest that the Western society which generated Marxist ideology was the very one which, because of its increasing individualism and privilege, would less easily tolerate the authoritarian social control required to realize such a Utopian vision.

In other words, it is one thing to castigate capitalism and point out its massive inbuilt injustices; but how many Western Marxists have ever considered living 'under socialism' instead, and under the circumstances prevailing in those places - Cuba, China, Hungary, Albania - where a form of Marxism has become the government line? Very few indeed is the answer, and for many pressing and valid cultural reasons!

However, many Marxists refuse to acknowledge the ironies inherent in world socialism's history and insist on trying to explain all the events according to the orthodox Marxist categories of class struggle, even if that means ignoring or abolishing ninety per cent of the people - the peasantry - and talking as if the handful of urban workers represented 'the people'. The language of 'scientific socialism' lends itself to this kind of abstracted superimposition on societies completely unrelated to its industrial categories.

(In Zimbabwe, this doctrine is preached by 'radical' academics and government functionaries in Harare, who don't even pretend to abide by it - or sometimes to understand it - themselves. Such icing-layer Marxism easily turns into a new form of elitist oppression.)

Appreciating the European middle-class roots of Marxism is decisive, I believe, for understanding the dynamic that prevails between a Marxist government and its citizens, or within a Marxist political party or group. To say that Marxism's intellectual roots are embedded in Western European rationalism and materialism is to call Marxist theory the product of a cultural elite. For not everyone in Western Europe was deeply affected by Enlightenment values and habits of thought: the more privileged and educated you were, the more affected you were likely to be. The elite origins of Marxist ideology have expressed themselves in the doctrinaire, control-oriented atmosphere of Marxist circles, particularly where these are undiluted by grassroots strands from other cultures and classes - such as working-class solidarity, Southern African Christianity or South American liberation theology.

Within European Marxism, unity and solidarity are working-class values that sprang from the experience of proletarianism, and probably from peasant life before that. Communalism also - trying to live and work in groups - and the early Marxist critique of alienation, are anti-elitist in tendency. Yet these generous impulses are hemmed in by qualities which Marxist atheists have inherited from long ages of Christian dogmatism, without seeing the irony of what they are doing: an authoritarian dualism of left/right, or progressive/reactionary; and an intensely doctrinaire 'more progressive than thou' syndrome.

Such heavy-handed emphasis on being ideologically correct, the tendency to intolerance and humourless self-righteousness in political matters, have developed out of centuries of cultural and class history. The very structure of such thinking expresses a long inheritance of privilege and reliance on coercive authority rather than consensus.

The elite roots of Marxist theory sometimes betray themselves in disturbing ways. Several white Marxists I knew in Zimbabwe lamented the early end of the war of liberation, because they said, 'a longer struggle would have meant a more radical population'. It certainly might have, but these people would have been made more radical through grief and bitterness. A more honest description of what a longer war would have achieved would have been a more dead, maimed, bereaved and more psychologically-damaged population.

Whatever the Utopian pretext, it is both unacceptable and, in a most unpleasant way, culturally revealing to wish for more death and destruction than has in fact occurred. I have never heard a black Zimbabwean - or indeed any South African - voice such sentiments.

In the late 1980s, many (white) South African Marxists and their European supporters were very excited by the prospect of a socialist South Africa after liberation. They had grounds for confidence, since the South is well industrialized, and since the extreme and blatant deprivation of workers has persisted so long that the people have become more radical and class conscious than any other proletariat in the twentieth century.

I feel there was a sense of occasion and possibility - a buzz - in these discussions about South Africa which was very like the euphoria among a drama company after a successful production. Only here, this 'high' came *before* the event, and the people speaking were not the actors - perhaps not even the stagehands. But the feeling was: 'This time we can do it! All the circumstances are right'.

There is a mean streak in this way of looking at history - a callous, manipulative, opportunistic tendency that also emerges in the writings and the actions of Lenin and of Bertolt Brecht. To celebrate suffering and indignity as an enabling factor for revolutionary activism is surely getting things the wrong way round. It suggests a deadness of heart that augurs badly for any people to be ruled by such minds.

Marxism's tangled roots in rationalist Enlightenment idealism and in mechanistic nineteenth-century materialism are also, of course, the roots of our present-day capitalist culture. It is therefore, no surprise that the Soviet and Chinese definition of 'what everybody really wants' turned out to be not so far from our own Western consumerist aspirations.

I don't believe this is because human nature is basically capitalist, or that other cultures are bound to imitate ours because we are 'ahead' of them: I believe it is because a specific Western-based culture has been systematically spread across vast areas of the world via revolutionary authoritarianism (socialist centralism), while it was being spread elsewhere by colonial subjugation and commercial penetration (capitalism).

The last fifty to seventy years in the socialist bloc have been a crash course in Western European materlialism for the peoples of the East - though Mao's reflections, with their earth-bound mysticism and different philosophical traditions for a time provided a thick Eastern filter for those ideas.

The socialist struggles of the huge ex-empires of China and the Soviet Union have been, in a sense, doomed efforts to compete with the West on egalitarian principles, rather than attempts to opt out of the West's economic purposes altogether. East and West, all along, have been opponents in the same game.

Not surprisingly, the West has scored much higher, since it carried on playing by the old rules, with its head start, and the whole 'free world' at its disposal. The East not only had to start in the economic equivalent of the early Middle Ages, it has also been crippled by bureaucratic inertia and greed and by socialist ideals and rhetoric designed to tame capitalism in places where in fact no capitalism was present, and the whole 'modernization' project was quite new and alien.

Meanwhile, the left in the West has steadily castigated capitalism with rigorous and convincing criticisms; and yet most professing socialists have been gladly accepting the ever-expanding loot brought home by the system of global capitalist exploitation - and often asking for more.

This contradiction is not even admitted to be one, for the left puts just as much emphasis on productivity, economic growth and efficiency as the right - and assumes (in spite of all the evidence) that a socialist economy 'democratically' run can be, and ought to be, just as economically 'productive' as a capitalist one.

To question whether such economic growth is either moral or necessary is to break the taboo on Progress, our culture's ever-present underlying *raison d' être*, its only remaining metaphysical belief. The Greens must break that taboo, and not succumb to the language of environmental management - more control, more technical fixes, more new biodegradable products, more 'green' advertising, more documentaries. We urgently need not more but less. Our concept of linear Progress needs to be bent round into a circle, and our attitude needs to be changed from reckless, onward-rushing, eyes-on-the-horizon optimism (or arrogance) into a humbler, eyes-on-the-ground respect for the world and for our neighbours.

We are still very far from this realization, though I believe the end of the Cold War can help us towards reaching it by showing us the unity behind our European intellectual diversity.

Since the 1980s we have not been able to pretend any longer that our economics-led Progress is nice and humane at heart, as we had laboriously persuaded ourselves it might be. It is not about ensuring a decent standard of living for everybody. Capitalism did not start out that way, and it has not changed its nature in the meantime, however much we might like to believe otherwise.

The straightforward, unapologetic declaration of unpleasant facts about our economic system was the main ideological strength of Thatcher's politics: 'No More Mr Nice Guy' was the tone of the 1980s. While very few British people I know ever admitted to voting for her, hardly a single African I spoke to criticized Thatcher on her economic opinions. Her frankness and strength of will won her worldwide admiration and respect, outside the charmed circles of Western affluence.

I have wondered about this phenomenon of Thatcher's international popularity, and it seems to me that it reveals something about our modern Western political sensibilities and hypocrisy, as well as about the spread of capitalist values throughout the world.

For while the British people kept voting Thatcher into power in the privacy of the ballot box, her brash, 'might is right - greed is good' rhetoric sounded shocking and obscene to liberal and left middle-class ears. Whereas Africans were not shocked but rather pleasantly surprised by her frankness - for they have fewer illusions about the nature of capitalism. They know that business is about gaining advantage over your fellows.

We in the heartland of capitalism had suppressed this knowledge. Cushioned by forty years of steadily rising affluence and welfare state, along with the apparent end of colonialism, we have been happy to forget the deafening, dangerous machinery that manufactures our wealth. We had become proud and complacent enough to dub it 'the unacceptable face of capitalism' forgetting that, unacceptable or not, this is capitalism's true face, and the face of our economic culture. Rather than contemplate this unpleasant truth, we sat back in the comfy seats, glad we could hardly hear the purr of the engine, and didn't have to breathe the exhaust fumes.

Africans, on the other hand, are not yet ideologically embedded in our Western myth of Progress and all its self-justifications. They can therefore perceive the machinery of 'economic development' without evasion.

Yet even the realistic Africans were unrealistically disappointed when Thatcher's ruthlessness extended to the struggle in South Africa. They could spot her bias towards South Africa's big business profiteers through her rhetoric about saving jobs for ordinary South Africans. But Thatcher's lack of concern for South African liberation was quite consistent with the rest of her stated position, that profitability precedes and supersedes all else. Her political frankness was not unrelated to the overt racism of whites in Southern and East Africa and in the Southern States of the USA.

It seems as if everyone - Europeans and Africans - would like to see a capitalism without the bits we don't like, a fumigated capitalism without degradation or bigotry - capitalism without an unacceptable face. Perfect economics would be profit without pain - exploitation without exploitation.

'Does it surprise you that people want the same things?' my friend said to me on the hotel verandah. What could I say - more particularly, what could I say as a white person in Africa? Instead of saying and staying, I am writing, and I have come home to write.

The truth about capitalism is much harder to avoid in Africa or India, or in South America, than for example in Devon, or Amsterdam, or in California or Oregon, where selfishness has acquired a liberal gloss and surplus subsidizes radical and alternative lifestyles. But I believe that the collapse of socialism in Eastern Europe and the Soviet Union, and the 'gloves off' economic policies taking over everywhere, confront us once again with the real nature of economics-led Progress, alias capitalism.

The current orthodoxy, like the old liberal orthodoxy 150 years ago, when capitalism was getting its kick-start, is that the market is the best arbiter of human affairs. The role of government in this 'hands off - laissez faire' view, is to represent and support the entrepreneur class and the investing classes (the rich), in the belief (or with the justification) that more profit means more Progress, and so ultimately (eventually, maybe, don't rush us) more benefit for all.

Only this time round, the eventual benefits are less serenely promised and less believed in, and the tone is grimmer. If the gloves are off, so is the optimistic mask - and the unmasked expression revealed is somewhere between threat and panic - the expression of a desperado who knows the game is up, but is going to go out shooting.

I find it interesting that it took a woman to unmask modern capitalism - though many women would rather forget this fact. Margaret Thatcher is generally felt to be a 'hard' and 'heartless' woman, lacking in precisely those qualities which are supposed to characterize women. I would agree that there seems to be something missing in her emotional make-up, as a person rather than specifically as a woman.

Women, in Western culture, are supposed to nurture and suffer, while men are expected to be bold and to venture. Men are forgiven a great deal of insensitivity, women are not. And also, in our male-led culture, men have grown adept at remaining lovable while they pursue their rapacious purposes.

It is much harder for a woman to present herself as a cuddly capitalist: the doublethink necessary to the philanthropic businessman comes less naturally to her, and she has to break through so many stereotypes to present herself politically at all, that whatever she says, she will be perceived as a potential threat, or a joke, or both. At any rate, when Margaret Thatcher decided to espouse the cause of capitalism, its true, shocking ruthlessness stood revealed - hopefully, once and for all.

Another cultural reason why Africans were not shocked or alienated by Thatcher's crude and cutthroat political style throws light on an important area of difference between 'Northern' values - capitalist or socialist -and the values of other, less materialist cultures. For *Africa expects strength in its women*, strength both physical and spiritual. In Africa, motherhood has not been sentimentalized, and women's work has not been marginalized. African women have not been rendered merely decorative by their culture as middle-class Western culture has sought to do. So Margaret Thatcher's forthrightness was not in itself surprising or noteworthy to Africans. Quips about handbags and 'Iron Ladies' are meaningless in such a context of assumed female strength. Many Westerners find it difficult to perceive the *powerfulness* of African women. We prefer to pity them for their 'triple oppression' - of poverty, gender and race - all of which is true enough. We find things to deplore and campaign about - like genital mutilation - and fail to notice the ways in which we Westerners actively belittle African women.

Aid agencies, for example, wail about all the 'drudgery' done by Africa's women and pound us with statistics to make us feel sorry for them, but they fail to register or to publicize the dignity and good humour with which this work is done, or the freedom and respect that are accorded to such work in these communities.

'Drudgery', indeed, is a culturally-specific English word, and a class-based concept coined by an elite to describe work which the powerful would rather not do. It is interesting that the noun for 'work' in Shona (bhasa) is a European import - related to the Afrikaans word *baas*, or white boss. There could be no clearer demonstration that the concept of work as humiliating drudgery that has to be got through is a Western one. There are plenty of verbs in Shona to describe work, but usually mention is made of specific activities - building, ploughing, weeding, whittling, cleaning - rather than lumping them all together as 'work'.

Our Western/Northern attitude to work is one instance of how our materialism has trapped us in dry and unrewarding patterns of life. Work in a rural society is not only hard, but also enjoyable, physically and socially. Work commands respect and praise, it brings people together. Big jobs like building or harvest are done co-operatively and punctuated by big parties with lots of merrymaking.

Work, for us Westerners, has become reduced to a means of earning money with which to live. Generally, people don't celebrate the earning of money - though such celebration may be the origin of the predominantly working-class male custom in the West of going out and getting blind drunk most weekends.

Necessary, life-sustaining work which is not financially rewarded has become so devalued in our society that we call it 'drudgery' and expect people (usually women) to feel humiliated and trivialized by it rather than respected for it. Our values have been turned upside down by materialism.

The way we regard work is an issue of basic *social values*. Every culture has and transmits these communal values through the way it brings up its children, and they make up the feel of life for the members of the culture. As Western culture has become more and more embroiled in materialism and all it entails, we have gradually lost touch, both with our own cultural roots and with the values of other cultures.

Traditionally, work and rest have a daily and a seasonal rhythm. In industrial society we have almost lost our sense of rhythm, and not surprisingly, many people substitute the treadmill for a healthy balance of work and rest. But almost incredibly, work has preserved its other main quality - I refer to paid work, of course, since money is our source of value now. In spite of generations of relentlessly repetitive jobs in factories, mills and mines, work subjected to the rhythms of machines and the wills of profit-minded employers - paid work in the West still retains its ability to confer dignity and a sense of belonging to the culture.

Yet most of us have little experience of what our everyday work should be: satisfying, meaningful, expressing our true human nature as physical creatures in a physical world. Denied this experience at work, many find it in their gardens, or jogging, or in the 'leisure' centre. For many of us, meaning has been consigned to outside working hours!

We human beings are capable of such skill, subtlety and precision, it is a shame and a waste that the working lives of the majority in the West address so few of our capacities and are so unimaginative, if not downright destructive of contentment and health.

It is also a shame that a growing minority's lack of such trivial and degrading work should be a source of shame and despair to them, and that there seems to be so little alternative.

A very different attitude to work is expressed in the following story, which I heard at a conference about these issues a few years ago. A Mexican carpenter, asked to make six carved chairs like the one in his workshop, gave the Yankee tourist a price that was well above six times the individual price. 'But you should give me a discount if I buy six', the man protested. 'And who is going to pay me for my boredom?', countered the carpenter.

Our enslavement to the idea of Progress and to our own technological achievements has led us Westerners to put the man-made 'laws' of economics, or 'the market' above our own better judgement, our social morality and our enjoyment of life. We have alienated ourselves from our own deepest needs, and we have called this process of alienation Progress.

We have also deluded ourselves about the importance of this Progress to our survival. We think we owe our livelihoods to economics and technology. But in fact, we owe our very lives to the basic social values which our economics-obsessed culture treats with contempt. Our mothers looked after us as we grew up largely out of such non-economic values; and no matter how rich or well-insured or heavily policed we are, Westerners (particularly middle-class Westerners) would not be able to rest easily in our beds, or rely on our bank accounts, were it not for the impeccable social values of the poor, both here and everywhere else. Their decency, generosity and restraint allow us to feel safe, even when we walk around their countries as tourists, carrying cameras worth a year's cash income to them.

We Westerners tend to take for granted our relative immunity from disease and from the casual depredations of poverty and crime to which the poor everywhere are exposed. We seriously underestimate how much we are indebted for our safety to the morality of the poor.

Socialists and other revolutionaries who deplore this decency and forbearance as craven timidity and/or lack of political consciousness show a culpable insensitivity to their own humanity and to the essential nature of culture. The same insensitivity has enabled generations of pious entrepreneurs to treat their employees like disposable tissues.

In Britain since 1979, thousands of people who have worked long years for their employers have, in the name of increased efficiency, been presented with new conditions of employment, or been dismissed without prior warning, without thanks or acknowledgment of their service. Each person affected has experienced these acts of economic ruthlessness as a betrayal of trust, a personal, yet collectively sanctioned injury; and we will never know the cost of this wave of economic brutality in depressions, breakdowns, illnesses, broken marriages, damaged children and early deaths.

The general hardening of the atmosphere in Britain can be felt by all of us in the wake of the Thatcher years, however ineffectual and wishy-washy her successors manage to be. There is no escaping the triumph of economics. Yet, to me it seems quite remarkable that after nearly two centuries of enterprise culture, people of this country still have the capacity to be shocked by the impact of commercial values on human relations.

Our growing Western unwillingness to take seriously anything other than material values, profit or loss, budgets and forecasts, has rendered us increasingly inarticulate about what is being lost in our culture. However sanity, decency and kindness do survive, as I rediscover almost every time I get on a bus. Even in the most money-minded atmospheres, we still find the precious, unremunerated qualities of loyalty, affection, good humour and honesty which run quite counter to the values of the economics-style 'market'.

This is good news. But we shouldn't be complacent. Economic pressures put a strain on our culture's humane, life-sustaining qualities, and it is becoming harder and harder for many people to avoid these pressures, even those who have waged or salaried employment.

There is a deliberate policy abroad to expose everyone more and more to the vagaries of the market, since 'market forces' ideologues believe that *security equals socialism* and that it encourages evils like sloth and inefficiency.

Labour has more or less bought this analysis. And what else is there for them to do, unless they reject the whole materialist paradigm, to which socialism, like capitalism, is committed? Our Western media and the majority of the Soviet bloc's former citizens would agree that socialism has been vanquished not primarily because it threatened capitalism, but primarily because it failed to compete successfully in the material stakes for industrial affluence. Both the political brutalities and the social achievements of Soviet socialism have paled into insignificance beside the scarlet blush of its economic embarrassment.

But from the perspective put forward in this book, socialism does not look like a completely unmitigated failure. For all its futile, unprofitable materialism, its doctrinaire soullessness and corruption, and in spite of its unspeakable crimes of repression, the basic principles that everyone should have a decent home and work to do enabled more people, most of the time, to go on living in a fairly relaxed, convivial atmosphere, in spite of their material hardships and their political frustrations. If socialism did not exactly *build* social values, it certainly omitted to render them obsolete, as Western culture has done.

The shock these people are now experiencing is many times greater than the shock suffered by the victims of the New Right in Britain. The Eastern Europeans are presently going through the same process that Western Europeans have had fifty years to adjust to - and Americans a good deal longer. To be treated like economic ciphers, to have to elbow others aside, push yourself forward, grab your chance or settle for failure: this is not what they have been used to ; and it does not represent progress, in any but the narrowest , most self-justifying sense - the sense that calls for an ironic capital letter.

We should watch what is happening in these countries just now: for it gives us an idea of what has happened to our own Western sense of ourselves as a result of the triumph of economics in our culture. People can be sickened at heart, corrupted and compromised by what they have to do to keep their jobs, or to keep afloat in business, in the same way that they can be sickened, corrupted and compromised by fear and self-interest under a repressive regime.

Westerners have been aware, in general, of the political pressures on Eastern Europeans during the decades of Soviet power. I wonder if we appreciate the securities we in the West lost long ago, which they are only now losing. Social demoralization is hard to reverse.

I believe we affluent Westerners are severely deprived, compared with most other cultures in the world. We have lost our safe place as infants in a relaxed, secure community. Our parents are isolated and under stress, and unless we are very fortunate, we grow up bored, hurt and insecure, to face more boredom, stress and isolation in our adult lives - and possibly, a depressing old age.

Besides our psychological hardships, we have almost lost the arts of storytelling and communal singing, the language of myth and of magic, and also the language of faith, our only remaining spiritual tongue. Surely the clearest proof of the cultural continuity between capitalism and socialism is the parallel loss of faith under both systems: one by banning and oppression, the other by neglect and omission.

We have lost most of our religious festivals, our wakes and mourning rites, our springtime and harvest celebrations. Most Westerners no longer dance. We have lost our joy in large families and our experience of living among three or four generations of our kin.

Thus we have lost a great deal of the common ground we used to share with people in other cultures: and this makes it difficult for us to communicate with them. Though we may feel materially and educationally privileged, we are also impoverished and inarticulate in comparison to people who have grown up in more traditional, less disrupted surroundings. We tend to be more emotionally fragile as well as less psychologically robust.

The triumph of economics is the defeat of a great deal else.

The discipline of economics does not deal in human values but in monetary ones. Traditional economics, Western style, deals with human beings as if they were solely economic beings, engaged in making deals and ensuring mutual interest to the exclusion of all else. Understandably, economics has no language for the non-economic parts of life, the vast majority of life.

Green economists are now trying to extend the language of economics to include factors that were previously taken for granted in economic equations - essentials like clean water, clean air and other ecological factors, but also human qualities like social values: honesty, loyalty, willingness to co-operate and so on.

Though this is a useful challenge to the arrogance and wastefulness of traditional economics, there is a danger in this path too. By expanding economics to embrace everything that matters, by dreaming up schemes to cost the earth (or the 'environment') on our balance sheets, we pander to the already inflated image that economics has in our lives. When we propose that housework and childrearing should be paid, we are extending the economic umbrella, whereas I feel we should be folding it up now and again, and getting economics back into a healthier perspective.

We can limit the economic claims on our lives, by wanting less, consuming less, and earning less; by having more time for other things and other people; by finding cheaper pastimes - by discovering and pursuing pleasures which don't cost money.

There is much to reclaim, for the areas not recognized by economics have been treated as archaic mumbo jumbo and left to decay. Christianity has not been able to keep up with the pace of change, and has gradually died of irrelevance. On the whole, traditional scriptures can't cope with modern economics, though the Koranic veto on interest is a relevant and radical measure, and the Buddhist rejection of all violence and manufacture of the means to violence is direct and unambiguous.

The arrogant Judaeo-Christian model of Man as nature's crown and master has licensed Western efforts to dominate, control and exploit the life system we are part of. It is late in the day now for Christians to start talking in ecological terms about 'the integrity of Creation' - but better late than never. However, given the clear and consistent thrust of our whole religious tradition, and the desperate straits that most conventional churches are now in, I can understand how this last-minute 'progressive' Christian conversion to holistic wisdom must appear to less politically concerned and more 'fundamentalist' Christians as just another example of a dying establishment Church's eagerness to keep up with the Greens of the secular world.

Theology, and more importantly, inspired religious writing, still have not begun to get to grips with modern economics and what it is doing to the world.

Someone recently reminded me that a 'progress' in European history, before the modern era, referred to a more or less circular route travelled by the royal court around a medieval kingdom, so that the king could collect his taxes and obtain his livelihood for himself and his retinue from the hospitality and payments in kind of his countryfolk - in short, so the aristocracy could live off the people, one area at a time, in an annual cycle.

We could imagine our Western Progress of the last 500 years as expanding the route to encircle the globe. Now we are almost back to where we started. The problem is, our appetites have also been steadily expanding, and the areas we have visited have had no chance to replenish themselves, in order to feed us again. So we are about to run out of food.

Our industrialization has reached the point of deindustrializing Western society; our missionary zeal has imploded into agnosticism, and we are now the world's first non-believing culture; our former sense of purpose has given way to a widespread sense of futility and lack of direction. Socialism and capitalism, the two warring hosts of Northern industrial society, have joined forces under the banner of materialist pragmatism - 'What Every Human Wants'.

It is surely time to recognize that our Progress, rather than resembling a high-speed train rushing into a better future, is more like the ancient symbol of the snake swallowing its own tail.

Since there is no such thing in life as an absolute increase without sacrificing something valuable in return, the circular model seems a more realistic image for Progress than our usual linear one.

Cyclical symbols are also a large part of our cultural inheritance. And just as, in our Christian story, the world's reconciliation to God had to be preceded by the world's utter rejection and defeat of God in Jesus; so perhaps the West's surrender of world control and our return to the circle of humanity, as one culture among many, have to be preceded by the utter (apparent) triumph of our false values, of economics and materialism, over the human values that co-operate with nature in keeping us alive together on the earth. Values like, for example, respect, tolerance, humility, generosity and conviviality.

Sooner or later, we will find ourselves back where we started. And this, in itself, will be no bad thing. But it still feels like heresy to say so!

Racism and Development

*Dissecting development - Our racist inheritance - Western
dream merchants - Models of Western superiority -
Cultural blunders and the ruling class club - Learning to listen -
How does it feel to be underdeveloped? - Finding my voice -
Tackling our racism*

THE WORDS 'RACISM' AND 'DEVELOPMENT' evoke opposite responses: racism bad; development good. I have yoked the two together here to highlight a particular irony. For in fact, the critical concept of racism is not anything but racist in itself. On the other hand, the woolly notion of 'development', as we Westerners apply it to other cultures, is indeed firmly rooted in Western racism.

If the concept of racism suggests a measure of self-awareness and self-criticism in Western culture (as do the words sexism, capitalism, colonialism and so on), the word 'development' represents a different aspect of our culture - namely, the tendency to self-justification and self-deception. Like such words as Progress and civilization, 'development' describes something we Westerners think we have achieved, and are now willing to bestow on other cultures, using ourselves as the model for their - well, development.

The economic growth we in the West have experienced over the past couple of hundred years has been at the expense of the countries we have exploited, and the economies of our ex-colonies are now, not surprisingly, in a perpetual state of collapse. But the advantage grabbing and retaining characteristic of economic growth is masked by the word 'development' which suggests a natural, organic process of growth.

This word is a prime example of our Western tendency to euphemize and to universalize our own history as if every other

culture should - and could - do what we have done. Such characteristic Western reasoning is faulty on several counts.

Firstly, we conveniently overlook the fact that while we are ex-
horting our ex-colonies to 'develop', and handing them token aid
grants, we are also extracting crippling interest payments from
their tiny economies. Without our power-induced racism Westerners would not dare to confront the devastating impoverishment of our ex-colonies with such bland hypocrisy.

Secondly, when we point with exasperation at the booming
economies of South East Asia, and say to Africa or India, '*They've*
managed to pull themselves up by their own bootstraps - why
can't you?', we are actually saying, 'Why won't *you* regiment your
populations into factories, make them work fourteen or sixteen
hour days, ban unions, and do whatever it takes to achieve such results?'

What we forget - and what we can scarcely imagine - is that not
every culture has these impulses for discipline and deferred gratification. Not everyone is prepared to give up their familiar, enjoyable pace of life and their social priorities in order to get rich.
Certainly everyone, or nearly everyone, wants to be rich - but
many would rather not live the way we Westerners need to live in
order to get and to stay rich.

I believe we keep promulgating the myth of a culturally neutral
'economic development' because we prefer not to face the unflat-
tering comparison between our own and other peoples' cultural choices.

Certainly, most Westerners do not want to *appear* arrogant
or racist, and many of us believe we do not *feel* arrogant or racist.
So when our language starts to betray us, we change it. We have
already become embarrassed by some of our postwar terminology: 'underdeveloped' and even ' developing' are no longer felt
to be acceptable descriptions for the 'countries of the South', as
we now prefer to call them. Yet 'development' itself has survived,
so far, almost intact.

Many would regard our impulse to keep overhauling our vocabulary as proof that our culture is indeed 'progressing'. The
alterations certainly do reflect political changes, and a lively Western conscience, at least about the way we label things.

Words like 'empire' and 'civilization' which used to evoke swell-
ing pride, or expressions of unthinking contempt like nigger, wog,
native or heathen have gradually been re-evaluated, judged to reflect badly on us, and dropped. Our eagerness to 'get it right' has
led to a belief that we can *legislate* our prejudices out of existence.

But it doesn't work. Or at least, it is not *enough*. All these linguistic tricks do not mean that we have really changed at all, at heart. The clever, resentful phrase 'politically correct' sums up our true attitude to the perpetual face-lifting our culture under-goes: it mocks the efforts of those who wish to drag us by the scruff of our necks into a new consciousness that is non-racist, non-sexist, non-anythingist. *Private Eye* is probably much closer than *The Guardian* to the pulse of the *English* nation.

It seems to me that for many Westerners all these terminologi-cal changes merely add to the layers of hypocrisy and denial that we carry around with us. They stop us seeing ourselves and the world clearly. If we did, the sight might break our hearts and pre-vent us pursuing our self-interest any longer.

We will never rid ourselves of racism by changing the words we use, but only by changing the underlying *attitudes* that inform the words, and by *changing our practice*.

T he development concept and industry are, I believe, based on our Western refusal to see the connections between our ever-mounting wealth and extending political freedoms, and other peo-ples' ever-deepening poverty and the restriction of their political freedoms.

Yet the Marxist analysis of the past 100-odd years *has* helped to reveal these connections, and has succeeded in spreading its insights to the extent that many are now embarrassed by Western govern-ments' claims to represent freedom and democracy in an unfree and undemocratic world. It is widely recognized that our own economic and political Progress has been at the expense of other peoples' livelihood, that we have generated dependence and pov-erty cycles in the economies peripheral to ours; and even that political moderation in the West has presided over and profited from the removal of political moderation in other parts of the world: for example, in the worldwide enforcement of unpopular and punitive IMF measures, and in the brutal repression of lib-erty in Central and South America, to keep the continent safe for North American business.[1]

But knowledge is no match for faith. Even in the 1990s, 'develop-ment' programmes are still designed on the assumption that 'Third World' societies (societies reduced by us to this designation) can be 'helped up' by good advice, donations and loans from the West, their 'ex'-oppressors! Marxism, development ideology and neo-colonialism can work quite comfortably hand in hand, as they do in Zimbabwe, because all three ideologies accept the Western model of linear Progress, measured in economic and technological terms.

The ideology of development pretends to be a self-evident truth, but in fact it is merely a self-justifying construct. Since it is not an integrated whole, like a person or like real life, I believe it is helpful, not destructive, to dissect 'development' into its various levels and to keep reminding ourselves of its component parts.

The first layer is our *inherited cultural attitudes*, which is largely involuntarily: our unthinking disrespect for traditions and ways of life other than our own, our assumption of global leadership status.

The second layer is our *rationalization of these attitudes*, which leads us to construct great self-justifying ideologies of civilization, development, manifest destiny and the like. When we talk about other cultures, our very words express our largely implicit cultural superiority syndrome (CSS).

The third layer is when the above two factors combine with a wish not to appear arrogant or racist or imperialist, then we get all kinds of even more *convoluted ideology and terminology*.

The fourth strand, which most Western cultural commentators would put first, is *the economic story*: the plain facts of wealth and poverty, exploitation and deprivation, colonialism, neo-colonialism, aspirations for Western-style affluence, and so on. As the material grounds for our cultural superiority syndrome, they could indeed go first, but in this book I have argued that some measure of CSS preceded and impelled our world exploration and conquest, and that each step of discovery, conquest and commercial advantage-taking reinforced our arrogance, and in turn goaded us on to further exploits and atrocities.

The fifth strand in this study is a *personal confession*, acknowledging my own contradictions and struggle to find my own voice about these issues.

The last strand comprises *my suggestions for different ways of thinking, seeing and feeling*, once we detach ourselves from the linear model of Progress.

Nowadays most of us tend to admit that colonialism was a rapacious episode, and that we in the North did extremely well out of it, at the expense of the Rest. Some of us are uncomfortable about this, as we are embarrassed about our slaveholding ancestors and our racist relatives in Southern Africa and the USA. But even our guilt can feed the Progress-development myth.

Grassroots workers and office staff in aid agencies spend endless amounts of money and mental energy funding projects and programmes which they sense are doomed and misguided rather than admitting the awful reality that bleeds and sighs all around us: colonialism was not an episode - it was the beginning of the end. We will never be aid saviours to the poor; there will be no medals for knight errantry in the development crusade. For us there will be only resentment and frustration - at best, perhaps, self-recognition.

For ever since our society first met their societies, we have been not their saviours but their humiliators and exploiters; and we have educated them to self-contempt, in relation to our skills and power. And even if we act friendly and work hard, at the level of our survival versus theirs, nothing in the nature of our encounter has really changed. This is not your fault or mine: but I believe it is true.

It would probably be fair to say that most Westerners generally do not expect to learn from the 'less developed' or 'underprivileged'. Yet many 'development' workers feel most positive and confident precisely about what they have learned or received through living in another culture, rather than about what they have imparted in their 'development' work; and many continue to live in other countries because of their positive experiences there, rather than out of any deep conviction that what they are officially about is worthwhile. (No reproach is implied here).

The same hidden motives - relief at getting away from Western society for a while, and being among more joyful people - may also have inspired many of the initial bearers of the 'white man's burden', the missionaries, administrators and settlers of the colonial era.

Given our economic and cultural position in the world, it seems to me that conscious and overt *racism* is a more consistent and less neurotic state of mind for white Westerners than our efforts at political correctness.

For while we still assume the right to continue living in the style to which we have become accustomed, and even to guide the 'development' of the rest of the world, we cannot detach ourselves neatly from the crimes by which we attained our power. We do not want to own our racism because we can now see how ugly and inhuman such an attitude is. But racism is our society's inheritance, and if we really want to get rid of it, we have to get rid of exploitation and degradation - not export them to other places, spreading new forms of racism to the elites of the world, as we are doing.

When I was working in Africa, whites habitually talked to one another across blacks as if they weren't there, even talked *about* them. But when a black civil servant sounded off to me about illiterate peasants being the main stumbling block to the coun-

try's development because of their stupidity and superstitious-
ness, I was shocked. I would never be so crude, I thought, so
blatantly contemptuous - so how dare he?

There was once a poor man who made himself rich by stealing. For years, he preyed on his neighbours. Then, when he had
established himself as a wealthy burger, he joined a church and
started to preach about the sanctity of property and the virtues of
a law-abiding life. People laughed at him and called him a hypocrite.

But the parallel is not just, for while the rich whom the thief
robbed were perhaps the poor man's oppressors, the peoples whom
we robbed, enslaved and exterminated in our rise to power were
in no sense our oppressors.

Until we face the issues that underlie our development ideology, our suppressed guilt will keep driving us onwards in furious
economic and intellectual activity, trying to justify ourselves. And
this same guilt will numb us to the pain and humiliation of the losers.

It takes a lot of courage to lay our busy-ness aside and confront
the monsters of our own past, and the ugly states of mind they
have bequeathed us: besides our pride and sense of superiority,
our guilty fear of the Others, our victims (which white South Africans displayed so classically, up until liberation), and the distrust
and hatred born of that fear (which white America still displays).

I believe these deeply buried fears and hatreds contribute to our
surface indifference, our characteristic Western sense of helplessness about the suffering we hear and read about, and our inability
to identify with this suffering as our own. *But we are far from
helpless*, for much of the suffering is economically inflicted by
our own countries. And *these people are just like us*.

These unacknowledged feelings also fuel our insatiable appetites for material security, comfort, convenience and entertainment - our 'pleasure' buffers against reality. And so we complete
the vicious circle of oppression.

Though applied to history, the words Progress and development are habitually used with moral overtones. In this critique I
am insisting that we observe the distinction between the chronological and the moral: between the *procession* of time and events
which we measure in years and centuries, and the religiously-based
myth/ideal of a moral *progression* through time - a step-by-step
approach towards perfection, or in Old Testament terms, towards
God.

Most people concerned with 'development' issues in Africa would like the West to stand for rising living standards, better nutrition, clean water, immunized children, more education, longer life expectancy and so on - that is for increasing perfection of life measurable by UN-established criteria. This would be moral as well as chronological and technical Progress.

But in fact, in Africa, *the West means money, and the power conferred by money*, and Western-style Progress is embraced there because it represents glamour, status and respect - *not* survival, or life in its fullness. Meanwhile, tobacco and toothpaste hoardings trumpet the same message as the gleaming new aid vehicles that clog the traffic in Africa's capital cities, the message that the road towards a Western lifestyle is the road to heaven. Such Progress is not moral, but immoral.

Since Africa is presently suffering the rapaciousness of its own nouveau-riche classes for the first time, as Britain did in the nineteenth century, Africans, poor and rich tend to think of Westerners as hard-boiled successes. They don't tend to appreciate how alienated we whites have become from the roots of our own wealth, or how genuinely bewildered and helpless we feel in the face of the forces we have unleashed on the world.

When I lived in West Berlin in the 1970s, I remember my astonishment and even resentment at the wide-eyed innocence of the big, well-nourished, baseball-booted GIs stationed in the city, as they ambled about, 'benign imperialists', apparently oblivious to where they were or how they were seen by the Germans or ourselves, quite unaware they might be resented, perceived as an occupying force. For they were liberators, nice boys.

Even so, Africans watch Western 'development' workers distrustfully, even mockingly, disbelieving our naiveté, our well-meaning smiles. They feel our power over them, our power to make decisions, design programmes, grant budgets, and fly away home when our time with them is up - power that is so familiar to us that we are not even aware of it. It is hard for the disempowered to believe in the innocence of the powerful.

Unwittingly more accurate than government five-year plans and pious development agency propaganda, Western soft drink, cigarette and baby-milk advertising are good symbols for the impact of Western-style Progress on Africa and on the rest of the world.

The urge to buy a bottle of fizzy sugar water or to feed the baby infant formula - instead of breastmilk, are disastrous economically-generated desires which distract people from their own proper physical needs and abilities and from their local economy and culture, just as the urge to 'develop' into wage or salary-earning consumers sends rural Africans first to school and then to town. What you get when you buy a can of fizzy sugar water is a shot of sugar (back to the plantations) and a short-term ticket to the West - a brief sense of belonging to the 'international' youth culture which used to chant: 'I'd like to teach the world to sing/In perfect harmony'.

The soft drink and tobacco companies, like Hollywood and the West in general, are in the lucrative business of selling images of themselves, dreams of luxury and leisure paid for by the real work, real money and real lives spent (wasted) striving towards these unreal (that is, unattainable and not worth having anyway) goals. These companies, the West, and the development myth all sell or promote images of 'a better future for our children' while in fact their operations are doing these people and their children out of their very livelihoods. The baby milk companies are even more direct in their impact. All this Western dominance makes traditional economic practices less and less viable in a hundred different but interrelated ways.

These ways include: evicting people from public land to make way for private tobacco estates (Malawi); resisting radical land reform to protect the export-oriented cash crop sector (Zimbabwe) and so continuing colonial overcrowding and soil exhaustion on the marginal 'communal lands' where people are permitted to live and farm; enforced settlement of pastoralists (Tanzania), and destruction of their habitats by disastrous, high-budget 'improvement' programmes (Mali).

In the now notorious Green Revolution of the 1970s, which was supposed to wipe out starvation in Asia using modern seed technology, the better-off local farmers were soon able to buy out their poorer neighbours who couldn't afford the risks of the investment demanded by the new schemes. Of course, money makes more money.

These disastrous failures to help the poor - crushing ordinary people into the ground in the name of development - happens not because of some error in the fine tuning or in the planning stages of 'development' projects, or even because of white planners' cultural insensitivity, but because *growing inequity is intrinsic to the 'economic development' process which our Western intervention represents.*

We urgently need to face up to this unpleasant fact, before we have entirely consumed the poor of the earth in the name of 'drawing them into the cash economy'.

Besides the terrible material consequences of our misguided efforts at 'development', the ideological consequences are at least as destructive. For worldwide triumph of Western-style aspirations does not mean Progress, either in the sense of improved quality of life or of an advance in consciousness, for most people. Rather, it is an invitation to regard their own home - their parents and grandparents, and their whole cultural inheritance - as 'poor' and backward in contrast to the glossy billboard pictures of pseudo-Western happy families.

The messages of advertising everywhere are designed to lodge in us an unstillable dissatisfaction with what we have, and impel us to want and strive to acquire more and more things to soothe that discontent.

In the countries of the South, these messages also instil a fatal addiction to things which those countries do not have the resources to provide, but for which their Western-educated elites, backed by international credit and aid, will starve their people in the name of 'development'!

For most people in the two-thirds world, Progress and development mean mental, moral and material alienation: a spread of false consciousness and expropriated effort which is unprecedented in scope and scale.

Yet such is the force of economic factors, or such is human corruptibility, that this deadly consumerist virus is not yet widely discredited. Or at least, it is not widely enough discredited to halt its spread. Except for Islamic fundamentalism, there seems to be no alternative to our style of economic development or Progress which has any power to mobilize non-Western people en masse. So the insidious equation of 'richer' with 'better' goes on generating poverty and demoralization - not to speak of more pollution and ecological destruction.

Now, in the 1990s, after forty years of well-intentioned cultural and economic bulldozing, so-called 'Development Studies' is at last gradually trying to take off its Western blinkers. This is happening largely because a great many students of this discipline are now non-Westerners. However 'Development Studies' has not yet seen fit to change its name!

We in the West have put a great deal of intellectual effort into articulating the belief that we are called to lead the rest of humanity into the future. We have talked ourselves up, and we have talked others down, constructing models of Western superiority and non-Western inferiority.

Our interest in non-European cultures, while very limited, has usually focused on aspects of their societies which we find 'barbaric'. Where white treatment of other peoples has been indefensible, we have dwelled on horrific images of *their* 'barbaric' cruelty that make Western society appear enlightened, mild and principled by comparison with theirs - for example, whooping 'Red Indians' with scalps at their belts, or missionaries in the cooking pot, danced around by cannibalistic 'natives' with bones through their noses. We have beamed these images at each other and everybody else through comics, Hollywood films and bestseller novels.

More recently, our attention has been drawn to the agony of African teenage girls being circumcised, and to Indian brides who are burned on the pyres of their dead husbands. Whites in Southern Africa have revelled in bloodcurdling stories about black mischief - bewitchings, crimes of jealousy and so forth. The violence between the Zulu movement, Inkatha, and the ANC in South Africa even provided a grim sort of comfort for those who believed Africans were not fit to run their country.

Whatever the actual wrongs of other cultures, at least part of our Western motivation for exposing them is surely to polish up our image of ourselves as the world's most refined, enlightened, humane and liberated society.

W estern academic disciplines like history, science, psychology and anthropology all operate in a framework that posits - or often, implicitly assumes a kind of moving staircase of Progress, an ever-ascending escalator of 'development'. All humanity, we believe, is standing somewhere on this elevator.

The top step of the escalator represents 'the Present', which in the Western-biased view of history, does not mean 'now as experienced by everyone presently alive throughout the world'. Rather, it usually means 'the cutting edge of Western technology and consciousness' - the latest gadget or idea. This 'latest thing' is felt to be more relevant, more exciting, more accurate, sophisticated and desirable: and just simply *more* than what was the latest thing the day before yesterday, or ten or thirty years ago. Societies and social groups which do not participate in this 'cutting edge' are, of course, less of all the above and judged to be living, to a greater or lesser extent, in the 'past'.

In this connection it is interesting that although the West is compelled to respect Japanese innovations in technology and industry, we do not include Japanese culture, consciousness, ideas or perceptions in our concept of 'the cutting edge' of the Present:

rather, the Japanese imitate us culturally (and are mocked for their pains) or else they go their own way, ignored, deplored, or resented by us.

Looking at the world with Western eyes, time - human history- is called Progress and viewed from the top, from where *we* stand. This is the usual framework for teaching 'the history of ideas' (that is, Western ideas) which includes philosophy, languages and literature at our universities.

The moving staircase with us at the top, called *history* or the *humanities*, is connected to a complex system of converging conveyor belts with us at the centre, called *geography*, or *economics*, or *research and development* - or just *development*.

Latin American economists have described the process of global 'underdevelopment' in terms of the effect of the 'centre' or metropolis on the 'periphery', the outlying economic regions of the world. Just as the up-to-date, go-ahead West defines 'the present' and judges the rest of humanity to be lagging 'behind', so the dominant, ever-accelerating economy of the metropolis (London, New York, the national capital city) dictates the economic activities of 'dependent' (underdeveloped, 'Third World') regions and sucks them ever drier, while thrusting them ever outward (and 'backward') from itself, into deepening provincialization and marginalization.

Growing up in a small Scottish town taught me how such metropolitan domination lays waste the culture of the 'provinces' by drawing the energies and ambitions of the nation's young people to itself. As teenagers, we were convinced that life in our home town was boring, irrelevant and behind the times - whereas life in Edinburgh was more exciting and significant, and life in London must be really 'where it's at', in the 1960s jargon we were using.

These 'metropolitan' attitudes are by now so fundamental to life in Western - and increasingly, global - society that it is easy to mistake them for facts. But they are only circular and self-fulfilling dogmas, ideological props. Tell someone their 'provincial' or 'lower-class' background is inferior, prove it to them with your superior metropolitan hardware and sophistication, laugh at their old-fashioned innocence and morality and, if they are young and impressionable - or ambitious - enough, you may convert a potential critic into an abject fan hungry for the goodies at your disposal and for the respect to be awarded by your 'advanced' circle, alias 'the world'. Even the most radical economists and political theorists are susceptible to this temptation!

(The morning I wrote the preceding paragraph, in Edinburgh, I asked a woman from Leith whether she'd ever been to Orkney or Shetland. 'That's the last card in my pack', she said. 'I want to go to *future* places.')

The last model of Western superiority I want to mention here is the one I find the most pernicious, and the hardest to shake off. It is the evolutionary, or child development model of human culture and consciousness. This model is still very much in vogue, with Jungians, New Age writers, and many otherwise very insightful thinkers. What is confusing in these works is the intermingling of racist nonsense with perceptive intelligence.

According to this model, human culture passes through successive stages on its way to becoming 'fully developed', just as the individual human being does, on her/his way to becoming an adult. Traditional cultures, with their symbolic art and poetry, their magical beliefs and practices, their songs, dances and rituals, and their nonverbal riches, are likened to human childhood or infancy - the time of empathetic, emotional understanding before the age of reason.

Nation-building, emergence from 'superstition', written culture and especially the onset of the modern era in the West, are seen as human culture growing up. And guess who represents the fully-fledged adult condition of human life?

Western thinkers have concluded that if (by our own definition) the West is 'more developed' than other societies in terms of technology and global economic power and organization, Western *consciousness* must also be 'more developed' than other peoples' consciousness!

This fallacy is asserted, but more often assumed, in all sorts of academic and non-academic contexts. If we are honest, this is what most Westerners, deep down, believe. And this is what we teach the 'educated' classes of the world to believe, as well as the masses of people worldwide. This fallacy is the intellectual equivalent of the billboards which present life in the West as better and more desirable than local life. It is the spread of this belief in the superiority of Western ways of thinking as much as the spread of consumer items and affluent lifestyles that is meant by 'Westernization'.

It is hard to know where to begin deconstructing, or rather, debunking this ethnocentric misrepresentation, both of human culture and of what it is to be a full, adult human being. The Western experience of emotionally alienated, intellectual adulthood has already caused so much suffering and deprivation among the middle-class 'privileged'. The idea of laying aside childish things in order to 'grow up' is a foolish and joy-destroying notion: most Westerners can scarcely bring themselves to sing or dance after they pass the age of ten, let alone pray, cry or just shout in public.

And what is so 'fully developed' about losing the emotional awareness, the imagination and the nonverbal skills we were born with? They are some of our most precious - and useful - human gifts - yet our dominant culture doesn't know how to value them, or what role to give them. So they wither away, or are consigned to the esoteric areas of artistic creativity - or the occult.

The arrogance of our superiority complex vis-à-vis other cultures stands out clearly enough, as soon as it is put in so many words. I cannot accept the idea that Western consciousness is more developed than the consciousness of other cultures. On the contrary, it seems to me that the West's dominant culture has pruned away so much in order to develop the narrow parts of consciousness it values, that far from having a more advanced consciousness than members of other cultures, Westerners are deprived, from an early age, of the use of many mental and emotional faculties.

Also, even as an individual bully or oppressor is stunted and twisted by his abuse of people, so our Western consciousness - which includes our moral sensibilities - has been stunted and twisted by our crimes of conquest and consolidation of power. This both saddens me, and spurs me to write.

What we need now in the West, more than anything else, is to *recover* consciousness. We need to reintegrate our consciousness in order to communicate effectively with non-Western peoples, whose skills and awareness in many areas so often outstrips ours. Such 'personal growth' is, I believe, inseparable from intellectual and political growth.

The stunting of Western consciousness is especially evident in the area of race, cross-cultural and North/South relations. White racism is one of the ugliest signs of a social, moral and imaginative shrivelling in our culture, a degeneration which follows directly from what we as Westerners have done to other peoples. It represents a psychological and political regression which stunts and perverts all of us.

The black US writer, James Baldwin, remembering his childhood in Harlem, New York, wrote that once, after a nasty street encounter with white police, he asked his adored elder brother if whites were like them. His brother paused before he responded that the whites didn't think so.[2]

Most middle-class Westerners have learned, by now, to bridle our racism. It has not gone away, for we cannot simply undo part of our training, but we have learned to be guarded in our expressions. We know it is no longer politically correct to be racist. Many of us are downright, sincerely ashamed of this aspect of our cultural inheritance, and just want to shake it off. This makes us react badly to other people's overt racism.

In Zimbabwe, (still so recently Rhodesia) offensive behaviour towards a black Zimbabwean by an old white Rhodesian would provoke in most of my European peers feelings of furious indignation or even an outburst of moral outrage. Blacks themselves, however, whether they were the targets of the abuse or onlookers, were more likely to shrug the incident off philosophically, saying something like: 'Those old ones can't change any more. They will just have to die out'.

This patient and tolerant wisdom ('a dog does not bark forever', they say) has kept Africans, and African-Americans, not only alive but sane and humane through all their humiliations of the last few centuries.

Free of the Western obsession with being right and our urgent drive to get the world sorted out by the day after tomorrow at the latest, the African approach to life respects people as they are and allows things to take their course. I believe the West's return to sanity will be a return to a simpler, more stable style of living - and thus of thinking - which does not depend on incessant change to sustain our interest and sense of purpose.

Our Western impatience can lead to problems. For in our eagerness not to be racist, we often make cultural blunders which our residual - and now repressed and subconscious - racism stops us recognizing as such.

In Zimbabwe, people like myself were shocked and embarrassed by the elitist legacy of British colonial and apartheid rule. The destructive power play of arrogance and obsequiousness visible in every profession from education and medicine to politics and administration pointed straight back to our British forebears.

Many Western development workers, shaped by the 1960s and 1970s in the West, tried to avoid hierarchical patterns of behaviour in the only way we knew how, by treating everyone as equals, on our own terms. We meant well, but we didn't realize where we were, or what we were actually doing.

So, for example, the Zimbabwean staff members of a 'progressive' British aid agency just had to accept the chummy use of their first names by their British colleagues, however intrusive and belittling this might feel to them in terms of their own culture. For in Zimbabwe, to use an adult's first name after they have emerged from childhood into parenthood is an unheard-of mark of disrespect. From the time a woman becomes a mother, she will be called after her first child, '*Amai* Tendai', '*Amai* Rose' (*Mother of* Tendai, Rose) not because the child is more important than the parent, but on the contrary, out of the sense common to many cultures that respected beings should not be directly named.

I made mistakes too. When I had just arrived in Zimbabwe and started work at the rural school I'd been posted to, I made friends with a mother of six, Amai Gabriel. I remember trying to find out her given name, so I could use it as she used mine, as a sign of friendship. I had to dig with several questions before she told me: but using it never felt right, and I think (or I hope) I only did it once or twice.

I am embarrassed to confess this now, but I'm sure that then I had the vague idea that by using her first name I would be helping her 'emancipate' herself from a humiliating anonymity, and from thrall to her role as a mother. Understandably enough, I was transposing my own consciousness as a middle-class Western woman to my new friend's situation and our new relationship.

For women in the West, motherhood and household work have long been considered second-rate activities, merely private, not economic. For many generations, being a middle-class wife and mother has meant that your husband can afford to keep you at home. The women's movement has rejected that restriction and encouraged women to get out of the kitchen and back into the world.

What I failed to see at first, blinkered by my cultural spectacles, was how firmly Amai Gabriel was already established in the world. Admittedly, she is only on the edges of the 'modern' world, the cash economy: her husband was working for a pittance on a white-owned commercial farm, while she raised broilers for sale and has recently become an official pre-school tutor on Zim $50 monthly pay. But standing in her vegetable garden or sitting in her round kitchen house while a daughter prepared food, she was both central to and in the centre of the real world of farming and family acknowledged and revered by Zimbabweans.

The family, through the ancestors, reaches into the spirit world, and even those who have jobs in the corridors of modern power neglect it at their peril.

As I lived longer in that rural community, I began to feel that I was not in a cultural or psychological position to impart strength or self-confidence to other women there, but I should rather try to learn more of these qualities from the women around me, and from their culture, which had not spent hundreds of years breaking their dignity and authority, as mine had.

The misogyny of our Western religious tradition has no parallel in Zimbabwean traditional belief. There is no female circumcision in Zimbabwe. I would guess that over half the adult women are healers, mediums and/or midwives but it has not occurred to this society's patriarchal leaders that they need to suppress all traditional female wisdom.

Even after I had learned not to call Amai Gabriel by her given name, I still made mistakes. Once I had to draw up a draft questionnaire in Shona, to be used in teaching adult literacy. When I went through it with the health assistants who were involved in the scheme, one man told me to score out the question: What is your mother's name? There was an uncomfortable pause before he said, in explanation, 'This question is never asked'.

Looking back now, I see that his correction of me took courage. It showed that he had enough respect for the women he would be teaching not to ask them embarrassing or inappropriate questions; and enough political and cultural self-esteem to stand up to me on the issue, rather than letting it pass and omitting the question later, though it was on the form.

I should point out that although we were meeting in his country and culture, the situation was weighted in my favour, by the fact that we were using English, as the official national language, in our discussions; and by my role of 'visiting expert' to the institution where we met.

In the vast majority of cross-cultural encounters between Europeans and people in other cultures, the balance of power has been so tilted towards us that it has usually been difficult or impossible, or just not worth the trouble, for them to tell us anything that would require a change in our attitudes for us to accept. This is why I feel that *every time we Westerners are told something that stops us in our tracks, we ought to receive it gratefully and as an honour, for it is a rare gift of direct communication.*

If we are respectful in our cross-cultural dealings, we stand more chance of forming relationships that will take us closer to the other culture and help us to understand some of the things that are different about it. But we should tread with care: for even our well-meaning attempts at friendship and co-operation can offend and do damage if we are not sensitive to atmospheres.

When we are being enthusiastic and optimistic, Western writers, activists, politicians and scientists have a tendency to apply our aspirations and solutions to humanity as a whole, and to assume the right to speak for 'the world'. We write and talk as if other cultural norms and frames of reference paled into archaic, exotic insignificance beside our own. This is far from being a true representation of the world we live in.

The fact is that though non-Westerners may indeed want our riches and power, most do not want a lot of the things that set us Westerners apart from them. They do not want our social or psychological problems for a start - the isolation of our old people, the violence in our cities, the suicide rates and the drugs, to name a few. If we stop to think, it is obvious that these features of our society would not attract new members from more traditional societies - so obvious that we might wonder how we could have overlooked such a glaring fact.

Even in this area of cultural differences, well-intentioned Westerners find it hard to act sensibly because we are still reacting against the errors of our own ancestors. So, instead of stopping to take stock of the confusing truth, many just rush in the opposite direction from the one taken by their racist predecessors, thinking: if we do the opposite of them, we're bound to be right. Wrong.

Ever since Europeans started encountering other peoples in the age of discovery, we have been obsessed with the differences between ourselves and other peoples. During the colonial settler eras, these differences were used as justification for white racism - up to and including genocide.

Such abuses have made the issue of cultural identity and difference virtually taboo in 'progressive' circles for the past thirty years. Among the British and South African left, until very recently, no cultural differences between peoples were officially admitted to exist! At last, now, people of other cultures are insisting that we notice that they *are* different, and wish to remain different, from us.

Ignoring other people's cultures betrays exactly the same ingrained Western sense of superiority and disrespect that overt racists are now reviled for. Whereas the settlers and colonialists said (and many still say): 'Africans are not like us, so they must be inferior', the white left has insisted: 'We are all equal, so Africans must be just the same as us, or at least they can *become* the same, given a good enough start in life'.

Put as baldly as this, it is surely hard to say which of these positions on race is more false, or more offensive. The racist statement observes an evident fact - cultures are not identical - and then draws a twisted and evil conclusion. The leftist statement refuses to observe the fact at all, or else concedes the fact of difference only as a temporary *defect* in the other culture, to be removed by Progress! We can see that the second actually builds on the arrogance of the first. It is a typical, giveaway piece of self-satisfied ideology, another intellectual product of unrepentant Western culture.

The fact stands nonetheless: Africans and Europeans do think and act differently from one another in many ways, particularly in relation to social and economic activity. This, I believe, is one reason why Western business, financial and aid concerns (and the up-and-coming Japanese) control African economies. In spite of which, Africans, on the whole, don't *want* to think and act like Europeans, or Japanese! And in spite of which they and their cultural norms deserve equal respect to our own.

The confused position of many white anti-racists seems to be the obverse of the confused position adopted by men in the West who are afraid that women's liberation is trying to deny the differences between the genders. Whereas women are suspected of wanting to become just like men, so blacks are assumed to *want* to become just like whites - in order that women and blacks can be 'equal' to white men.

The genuine confusion of such men and such 'anti-racist' whites is the result of their genuine arrogance. They are so used to feeling superior to women or blacks, that the only way they can imagine these groups having equivalent value to themselves is if they are admitted to the ranks of the ruling class club, and conferred honorary white, or honorary male status. They cannot imagine that women and blacks might not want to join their club at all, but simply have their equality, and their distinct identities, recognized and respected.

The arrogance of ruling class club members remains intact, whether they rush 'progressively' to open the doors to outsiders, or rush to the door to put extra bolts on it. To people in this frame of mind, 'different' can only mean 'inferior to us', and 'equal' can only mean 'the same as us'.

Both groups miss the point that *the world is full of different ways of being which cannot be labelled 'superior' or 'inferior', or more or less 'developed'*. Which is more developed - a dolphin or an antelope? An orchid or a mahogany tree? Spanish or Swahili?

Surely it is self-evident that people should be accepted and respected as they are, on their own terms, and that they should not be required to become like Westerners before we will take them seriously. Yet ever since the advent of the colonial era, we in the West have moved steadily away from this normal, sane point of view and become more and more attached to the idea that *only by becoming like us can the rest of humanity 'achieve its full potential'*.

Since the Second World War, the ideology of development has been built on the ruins of the imperial ideology of 'Civilization'. Neither ideology is a relaxed or realistic way of thinking: in fact, both betray signs of obsession and neurosis. Like many unhealthy mental conditions, I believe these ideologies have their roots in our need to pretend the world is different from the way it really is, because we find the truth too challenging and threatening to our way of being. The road back to health and sanity for our culture leads through admitting the truths we have been suppressing, accepting the pain of our realizations, and confronting the challenges to our own lives and expectations that these realities present. We cannot let go of the ideology of 'development' completely until we let go of the peoples whose exploitation is justified by this ideology.

The fantasy of 'development' needs to be challenged by those who should know better than to subscribe to it - those who have spent years living among other peoples, witnessing and often benefiting personally from the joyful, energetic self-sufficiency of their cultures wherever these have not been undermined by privatization, plantation and industrialization.

It might be expected that 'radical' Europeans who opt to work abroad for a time would put themselves in the forefront of such debunking: but Marxism itself encourages dismissal of other cultures' social values, and superimposes its own, 'scientific' view of things. Knowing better than other peoples is a well-established European tradition, and in this respect, Marxists have not broken with 'bourgeois' Western thinking at all.

We Westerners have become accustomed to setting up the structures, designing the rules, and controlling the resources: we expect other peoples to play *our* games.

This process has worked brilliantly in non-economic areas: cricket, football, Christianity. The West Indians and the Asians can beat us at cricket; Africa and South America are now the booming areas for Christianity, in marked contrast to the modern West.

But economically, the cultural graft doesn't seem to have taken: or rather, if you will excuse a pun, the graft is often all too obvious. This is one of those observations which is normally considered taboo for left-wingers - a snide sign of racial prejudice and capitalist arrogance. In radical circles, such awkward facts as African government corruption are suppressed or heavily qualified by casting all blame for Africa's political and economic ills onto the international 'baddies', the multinationals, the IMF and so on.

And of course, dishonesty and corruption are also common in the West, not to speak of massive waste and irresponsibility. However, in relation to the relatively small size of African economies, these abuses have grown to overwhelming proportions, and constitute normal practice in many places. Official procedures and unofficial, but universally recognized practice diverge completely. The wealth and security of the elites are based on uses of power considered abuses in the terms of the colonially instituted administrations and the international corporations and agencies that run the show from abroad.

Traditional loyalties are maintained in the salaried sector through nepotism and regional favouritism. Others must pay above the odds to set the wheels of officialdom moving for them. The Africans do not play our political-economic games by our rules. (Though neither, if we are honest, do we.) Among themselves, Africans do not even pretend to.

Why are these facts so embarrassing to the Western left that we have to pretend they are pieces of racist propaganda? Denying part of the truth in order to maintain a sanitized version of reality leaves the field open to the right-wing, and makes it all the easier for them to mock the left as unrealistic dogmatists. Can we not face the reality that peoples are *different* from one another, have different styles and priorities and ways of living, different strengths and weaknesses - *and* free ourselves from racism?

I believe we can, but only once we are prepared to face the idea that *our way of doing things is no more intrinsically valuable or 'grownup' than any other way.*

I believe that Westerners are now gradually moving towards accepting that Western history is only one path among many, and is not, after all, the culmination of human development it has been cracked up to be. Our interest in other cultures is becoming less patronizing and more respectful, more aware of their strengths and of our own shortcomings.

But meanwhile, sadly and ironically, many of the 'educated' middle classes in the two-thirds world seem to be moving in the opposite direction, becoming more arrogantly anti-traditional and anti-peasant than we in the West would nowadays like to admit to being. And of course, the steamroller of 'international economic development' continues to trundle on, flattening rainforests, thatched homes and independent ways of life.

As other cultures become more battered, distorted and impoverished under the impact of 'development', they lose more and more of their dignity - in their own eyes and in ours - and so there is more and more for us to deplore, feel guilty about, and appeal for funds to alleviate. We see increasingly blatant social injustices, our attention is drawn by the media and by agencies to people's inability to feed themselves or even provide themselves with access to drinking water. We send famine relief and aid for refugees. It is such a dreadful situation. Who can grasp it and what can be done?

If only we would stop *helping ourselves* to the world's wealth, and regarding our unjustly-won privileges as our birthright, the people of Africa, India and elsewhere would need no help from us to live well. Unlike most Westerners, *they know* how to build houses for themselves, how to acquire their necessities of life, from fuel to food, without recourse to huge, profit-making conglomerates. They are very well prepared for survival. In fact they survive largely in spite of, rather than thanks to, our interventions in their lives.

But the sad irony of 'development education' is that those with most commitment to change things for the benefit of the oppressed become, like the rest of us, entangled with equivocating institutions which depend for their existence on the continued existence of oppression. For whenever we start out to name and remove injustice, it is only so long before our enquiries come back round to practical questions about ourselves and our own way of life.

This in itself leads to awkwardness. Although we Westerners believe we want to draw the world into our circle - the cash economy, universal health care, literacy and so on - Western development workers tend to talk *to* each other and *about* the people whose lives are supposedly to be enriched or extended as a result of our efforts.

I remember, for example, sitting in a group which included expatriate health workers and young, local people and hearing rural life expectancy and infant morality rates discussed without a single question or remark being directed to the locals present. They were not regarded as eligible to join in the conversation, though they and their families were the theme of it, and though they spoke good enough English to understand the conversation.

Whether it is due to social embarrassment or to language difficulties, middle-class Westerners usually seem to avoid talking to
the poor directly. This means that we rarely have an opportunity
to listen to what they have to say. Very few whites who work in
Africa get round to learning a local language to a level that would
make conversation possible beyond greetings and the price of veg-
etables. Those who do are much more likely to gain fresh insights
from broadening their cultural perspective, and even to see themselves as others see them.

Tanzania has encouraged its expatriate workers to learn kiSwahili
and they do. But in most other parts of Africa, Westerners imagine they don't need a local language since their 'educated' colleagues tend to speak English (or French) to them automatically,
and are eager to practise their language skills on a native speaker.

Learning a language is difficult and often humiliating. We have
to become babies again, and put up with being the focus of amused
and delighted attention, which can sometimes shade into ridicule.
We have to play the public role of beginners and learners, as well
as experts and teachers. But those of us who don't learn a local
language when we work in another country never really taste life
outside the club, and so never get the chance to realize how rich,
rewarding, and infinitely more enjoyable it can even be in some
respects than life inside the club.

We have become unused to seeing anything in other peoples'
ways of life but symptoms of poverty, disease, starvation and deprivation, and we keep ourselves so busy with these symptoms that
we fail to notice a sense of humour and of style, a store of knowledge and skills, or music and stories, an experience of life distinct
from our own.

Yet Western expatriate workers cannot avoid being aware of
the other culture's 'differentness', because it hits them every day
in the form of misunderstandings, disappointments and frustrations. It is hard to appreciate these differences positively when
they keep undermining and obstructing our work objectives.

If only we could see ourselves as others see us, as learning to
talk with them would help us to do. Yes - we do look powerful
and glamorous, endowed with wealth and choice. But at the same
time, we also look somehow 'cut off', isolated from family and
roots; we look anxious and inhibited in our social behaviour: 'You
are not free,' was the way African friends put it, where 'being
free' meant feeling confident, relaxed, and 'at home'.

Indeed, to them we look quite undignified as we rush, harassed,
from appointment to appointment - from home to work, to the

market, to a friend's. For in Africa, the proper dignity of adult-hood requires that an adult never appear to be in a hurry. (To teach their children this, some mothers tell their children that if they run, the policeman will arrest them.)

Those Westerners who are more relaxed about their jobs, and able to laugh about (and learn from) their frustrations, do seem to enjoy their foreign postings much more than those who remain attached to targets brought with them from home.

This excursion into Africa is also relevant for those who have not worked abroad. Our society here in the West also knows cul-tural differences between the powerful and the powerless, and the same communication barriers exist, with divisions drawn along all sorts of lines - professional, class lines, denominational, re-gional and so on.

We can recognize the same social tendency to avoid uncomfort-able clashes and incongruities by maintaining the circle, and hence excluding outsiders, even in groups where the lives of outsiders are the professed concern. Radical political circles, social services agencies and churchpeople could serve as examples.

We don't usually have literally to learn a new language in order to break the circle, in our home country - though in confronting racism against Asians in Britain it must be crucial. In other cases the image of language learning translates into the equally demand-ing but less celebrated task of *learning to listen*. Listening means suspending our usual jargon and frames of reference. It means humbling ourselves to hear a new angle on things without judg-ing or classifying the speakers from an imagined height.

Breaking the circle, stepping outside the ruling class club, is a liberating act - but like any big change in attitude, it is not a once-and-for-all event. The circle keeps trying to reform, the door of the club won't stand open. Throughout our lives we will have to keep breaking the circle, in different contexts, in order to admit reality and hear what people have to tell us.

Some readers may be muttering: it is *obvious* that we in the West are better off, have more choices, more chance of surviving childbirth and childhood, live longer ... Why should we get senti-mental about extended families, traditional medicine and other social arrangements which are kept going by poverty? These are not cultural *achievements*.

It may seem unrealistic, when assessing how 'advanced' socie-ties are, to expect emotional, ethical and other immeasurable criteria to count for anything. Western achievements in the areas of technology and economics are clearly and objectively measurable against those of other societies, whereas the more social and psychological qualities I have described are rather intangible. And the immeasurable has become suspect in our culture.

I believe the best response to these objections and arguments is try to *feel*, rather than merely see, the outsiders', the non-Westerners' point of view. If we imagined a different scenario, perhaps we could step out of our own shoes for a moment.

In some respects Japan now outdoes the West at what we have until recently prided ourselves on - industrial production and profit-making. If it was not us, but, for example, Japan who had grabbed the global initiative back in the early modern era - how would we Europeans feel then? Would we agree that this power gave *them* the right to run the world?

We might develop a more critical attitude to power if Japan started bossing the West around on the basis of its economic edge, superior efficiency and technology, as we have been bossing most of the rest of the world around for quite a long time. Let's go one step further and try to imagine how we in the West would have coped during the last fifty years, had Japan defeated Britain and the USA instead of the other way round.

Japan might well have gone on to dominate the West and the rest of the world, economically and culturally as well as militarily and politically, much as the US-led West has dominated the world since then. Imagine our defeated countries rebuilt in Japan's image through the 1950s and 1960s.

Imagine our people used as cheap labour pools and captive markets for banned Japanese drugs and pesticides, our beaches turned into seaweed factories to keep up with new 'international' (that is, Japanese) eating habits, our ports turned into brothels for Japanese seamen, young girls running away or being lured from home by big money to train as geishas for 'international' businessmen, and our cinemas filled with Japanese-style romance, heroics and brutality.

Had the Japanese gone on to vaunt their superior political and intellectual development to ours, would we have felt the insults added to the injuries, and seen through their complacent ideology? Probably we would have been forced to cultivate the survival skills of communality, co-operation, patience, tolerance and humility - the virtues that presently sustain the oppressed worldwide.

But we would also have suffered the spiritual miseries of the

oppressed - self-loathing and self-destruction, the impulse to identify with the oppressor and look down on others like ourselves.
Suffering may ennoble some, but it undermines and corrupts many more.

Imagine our feelings about the Eastern 'experts' sent 'out' to
'help us develop'! There would be hordes of well-paid consult-
ants and contract workers setting up multi-million yen projects,
and young, ignorant, bright-eyed 'volunteers' scooting around
Scotland and Devon on Hondas trying to uplift us to the level of
Japanese culture and standard of living - perhaps through 'appropriate technology' (that is, not hi-tech, which would be considered appropriate to Japan but not to us).

Innocently, matter-of-factly, they would bully and bribe us into
doing things their way, presenting our governments and town
councils and our activist groups with offers they couldn't refuse.
We would be no match for their money, their plans and their amazing, expensive equipment. And all the time they would see themselves as our saviours and benefactors, never noticing how they
trample on our dignity as they talk amongst themselves about us
in our own country, sighing about how we don't know how to
run our own affairs - never noticing that we have different ways
of organizing our lives from them, different ideas about what is
important and what is decent and good.

Economically, we would be left no choice but to play their games
as best we could for the sake of our families' survival - even if that
meant helping them to suck our own countries dry. *Our strength
would remain in our ability to see clearly what was being done to
us, and to feel the terrible cost of it. Our dignity would lie precisely in the things to which they were blind.*

Having considered how *we* might feel if we were on the receiving end of development ideology, perhaps we can now empa-
thize a little more with the complex and painful situation of the
rural students I taught in Zimbabwe.

Each student had apparently come to school in the hope of escaping their own culture of fieldwork and cattleherding, the culture that had given them the qualities I most admired in them -
their confident and graceful individuality. Each was hoping to enter
the culture of jobs and money. At least, this is what they cheerfully assured me.

Standing before them in my smartish teaching clothes, looking
into their shining alert faces, grouped under a tree or perched on
little piles of bricks in a furniture-free classroom, I felt I knew so
much about where they were headed, and could see how much
they stood to lose by the transition.

But no words of mine would arm them against the economic forces that shape the world we all live in, forces that had enabled me to stand there in front of them, a living example of their dream condition: educated, salaried, shod-free to travel and see the world. Certainly, no words of mine would deter them from having a go.

It was sometimes excruciating to feel myself the object of these young people's alienated aspirations: the very colour of my skin was a coveted symbol of wealth and power, and my every action personalized the heartless economic system that was destroying the independent livelihoods of their parents and grandparents.

I recently heard from a friend who was one of those students, complaining about the 'slave labour' conditions he was working under as a field hand. Because of poor exam results, and not having influential relatives, he has not yet managed to escape the bottom of the heap; and although he sees the objective injustice of his own and his family's situation, he also feels it as his own personal failure.

I am home again, well fed and housed and doing work I choose to be doing. And though I know the systematic nature of the economic injustice grinding him down while it cushions my life, I also feel bad that I have not managed to help them out of their insecurity. Indeed, in material terms, my students were right to envy my privileges and to take my criticisms of the good life in the West with a pinch of salt!

Yet I haven't come home because of the 'good life' - but because I prefer to live where I understand, at least more or less, what is in people's heads. That doesn't mean it's the same as what's in mine, but there is a direct, cultural relationship between my thoughts and those of most other people here in Scotland.

I found my voice as a writer through my intense discomfort as a British volunteer in Zimbabwe, and I am still looking for ways to challenge my own culture's wilful ignorance and inertia about our relations with Africa and with the rest of the world. 'What were these people doing before we came along to civilize them? Sitting around, scratching the earth with sticks - they were still living in the *Stone Age*'.

Though such classic Western arrogance may embarrass us, *what do we have to counter it with*? If you watch a contemporary TV programme about Africa, the only thing that comes across clearly, from a white Western commentator at any rate, is the total confusion over what to say, what to feel, what to think. How *do* we now assess the impact of Western interventions in African life and culture? How do we value African norms in relation to our Western ones? Has our mindset shifted much at all since the days of the 'colour bar'?

Do we see them as 'backward' or just as wronged? Because they are different from us, are they therefore doomed to extinction, or assimilation? Are we exploiters, or leaders or both? Our minds are full of contradictory statements about colonialism and 'development'.

The UN has recently coined the phrase 'human development', as distinct from GNP-measured 'economic development'. This is an attempt to improve on the misguided, destructive and now at last discredited World Bank big projects approach to development. Yet this new phrase holds a fresh insult - for it encourages the grotesquely racist notion that not just economies, but *people* are underdeveloped, and to be developed by our interventions!

Truth will out. Each attempted 'humanization' of the original, underlying and *unreversed* inhumanity - colonialism, slavery, enclosures of land, clearances - takes us one step further from reality. Changing the words we use confuses only us.

Perhaps this is why, even though I disagree with them, I sometimes feel on firmer ground when I am talking to unapologetic supporters of capitalism than I do when talking to its critics, exponents of 'development' or 'socialism'. Marketing or advertising executives, entrepreneurs, small business-people and commercial farmers know how capitalism works, and are not afraid to work it. They get angry with social idealists who think there will be more for everybody if we just kill the goose that lays the golden eggs.

Organizations like the UN, the FAO (Food and Agricultural Organization), the OECD (Organization for Economic and Cultural Development) and countless others, large and small, are busy even now pumping out more and more 'enlightened' versions of 'development' ideology, project reports, planning documents and so on. Many of the people doing this work are doing it because they believe in it to some extent, and think it's more helpful than working for Shell or for the military and/or for the money - which is usually very good. Some, especially those who have worked 'at the grassroots', on projects and so on, have stopped believing in the visions propagated by their organizations; some stopped believing in them before they landed a desk job.

The strain on these people is enormous. To cope with the demands of their jobs and to stay true to themselves - to remain loving and lovable - they need a very good sense of humour and a strong sense of out-of-the-office reality. Some people have these qualities in good measure, others don't - or not enough of them to save them from becoming in some ways indistinguishable from their right-wing opponents: defensive, inflexible, anxious and harassed, uptight and ambitious.

This all happens while they still think of themselves as radical and 'different' within their organizations - indeed, it happens because, instead of surrendering to the pain of their lives' contradictions and learning from them, laughing and/or changing, they are putting their energies into maintaining their untainted, but false, self-image.

This is a dangerous condition to be in, first for the people involved, who lose touch with reality (with who they really are), and thus lose touch with their opportunities for growing through their difficulties. But it is a dangerous condition also for their society, since their efforts encourage our habits of self-deception. Personally and professionally, for the two are really one, they are helping to generate more comforting lies and propaganda about global capitalism - or 'development'; in other words, to further fudge the issues.

Every time we hear another song of Progress sung over the air, or listen to another funny story that feeds our sense of cultural superiority, or read another sneering commentary on Third World chaos and incompetence, we will have to set it against the true story of West versus the Rest, the basic human facts as we know them, in our hearts.

We have to learn to recognize lies and half-lies, and learn to let the truth out to shame them. We must resist the seductive voices that try to smooth everything over and assure us it's all OK, its all being taken care of - just a bit more of the same will make everything all right. It won't.

We will need to gather more facts and fresh perspectives to strengthen our new understanding of who we are. We will need practice and we will need friends. But our aim will be steady and our bow-hold relaxed, *for we don't have to prove anything* - only to *admit everything*. The burden of proof is on those who seek to deny half of the past. We can accept the honourable and dishonourable sides of our inheritance, - the failures as well as the triumphs, the fallacies and dogmas as well as the discoveries, the narrowings, as well as the broadenings.

If we keep resisting the lies and admitting the truth, we will gradually become able to deal with our racism, and it will show us things we never imagined were inside us.

Tackling our development ideology is less personally threatening than facing up to our racism, since 'development' is a mere intellectual construct. I believe we can more or less rid ourselves of this construct, though we will never manage to live completely independently of its structures and 'achievements'. But the ideology of development has ways of insinuating itself back into our minds, and to stay clear of its influence takes constant vigilance and a steady refusal to succumb to self-congratulation.

For example: one of the many ironies about the approaching end of the earth's capacity to absorb our destruction and pollution of it, is that it catches the world's peoples at very different levels of responsibility for the crisis, and thus with very different attitudes to it.

After years of trying to persuade and force the world's majority to turn away from their inherited, ecologically sound and sustainable ('backward' and 'ignorant') ways of life, and to covet what we have, in the name of Progress, Western society is suddenly beginning to accommodate Green consciousness in anticipation of trouble ahead.

But meanwhile, the elites of poor countries have already grown accustomed to our style of living, and many of the rest are being encouraged to join the elite, by education, advertising and example - which are all linked up to the economic thumbscrews of IMF and 'development' logic. While the West starts to go green round the edges, the rest of the world is desperately trying to turn factory-grey like us.

It is tempting for Westerners to take this difference as more proof of how 'ahead' we are - to refer to 'different levels of consciousness about environmental issues', and 'the need for raising awareness' and so on. But this only amounts to more Western self-justification. For here at last, the imagined line of our Progress is clearly shown to be like a snake curled up with its tail in its mouth.

While we are only beginning to see an ecological light (or explosion) at the end of the technological tunnel, the world's majority still knows and practices much more sophisticated, tried and tested, environmentally sensible ways of life. And while we have just started to rediscover respect for the inherent wisdom of traditional ways of life, these people are still being actively taught to look down on them, and economically - or militarily - forced to relinquish them.

Perhaps we are about to learn in a new way, by watching others attempt to follow in our footsteps, what terrible losses of wisdom and perspective this path of Progress involves, and how it destroys the basis for human co-operation and mutual generosity - precious human qualities that have been nurtured and maintained over long ages of careful and difficult, but balanced living.

Whatever our political standpoint, whether we are green activists or diehard capitalists, we Westerners come to the end of our affluence ill-equipped both psychologically and practically for subsistence and communal, co-operative life. In relation to the poor of the earth and their cultures, we have a great deal more to learn than to teach. In the confusing clash of consciousnesses between left and right, North and South, one thing seems clear - that we in the rich world are in no position to preach to anyone but to each other and ourselves.

8

Southern Africa *Unmasking the Myth*

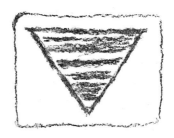

100 years of what? - Unmasking the myth - Britain in South Africa - Settlers rule OK - The right to land -The Boers' tragedy- Progressive hypocrisy - The culture taboo - Zulus - Urban poverty

IN SOUTHERN AFRICA, the West meets itself in a magic mirror, and we can learn a lot about ourselves by studying our distorted reflections there. Since the conversation on the hotel verandah described in the introduction, South Africans have achieved political liberation from the fifty-year old apartheid regime, and have won majority rule, finally ending the era of European political dominion in Africa. No-one predicted that this liberation would come so quickly, and few can have hoped that Nelson Mandela would live to lead his country into political freedom.

My observations about South Africa are based on stories told to me by South Africans or those who have lived and worked there. I am not trying to write as if I have been to the country, but to reflect on the issues that this country raises for us as Westerners.

Political liberation is no mean feat. In Zimbabwe in the early 1980s, the air of freedom was unmistakable. 'Progressive' South African friends felt invigorated by the atmosphere in Harare, which I could not properly appreciate, since I had not experienced the atmosphere south of the border - or in Harare when it was still Salisbury.

There is something absolute about such a release from institutionalized fear and tyranny into a basically democratic system, however embryonic, imperfect, neo-colonial or even chaotic. The quality of freedom is priceless. I say this from my tastes of fear and political repression in East Germany and Czechoslovakia in the 1970s, and in Malawi in the 1980s, but also thinking of the change in atmosphere when I have crossed the border from Derry into Donegal from the 1970s onwards.

Yet the political progress that South Africa and Zimbabwe have experienced in the last fifteen years is merely the long-postponed restitution of human rights which were first violated by Europeans - by a colonialist and by a settler state. And this restitution remains far from complete.

In the essential matter of livelihood and self-reliance, the people of Zimbabwe and South Africa are much *worse* off today than they were 100 years ago, or before the whites started moving north from the Cape; and their situation, in this sense, does not look hopeful.

The experience of Southern Africa over the last 100 years challenges the Western myth of Progress head-on. One century is a very short time in terms of human history. Yet in that short time, Europeans have taken over the best land in this huge, rich and relatively temperate part of Africa, and have driven the local population onto the barren and rocky ground. We have forced them to work down our mines and persuaded them to wear our clothes, sing our hymns and share our consumerist dreams.

Because the main era of white domination in South Africa has been so brief, and yet so overwhelmingly influential in shaping the present society and economy there, Southern Africa shows us microcosm of Europe's own Progress over the last 300 years, or since most Europeans lost their right to live on and farm the land they were born in.

The Afrikaners, or Dutch and French Huguenot settlers, have, of course, been in Cape Province for 300 years, but they spent most of that time farming alongside Africans, and though little love was lost between the two communities, the levels of technology available to each did not vary that much. No huge European advantage over Africans was established. The British also settled in the Cape, and brought slaves from India and Malaysia to work in construction and in the vineyards there. Generations of intermarriage between these slaves and the local people, black and white, have produced a multiracial, Afrikaans-speaking culture. (These people used to be referred to as Cape Coloured. This awkward formulation became the progressive term for the Cape Province's Afrikaans-speaking majority, of mixed racial descent. With the general discrediting of racist language, this term has been rephrased to 'so-called coloured'!)

The original antagonism in South Africa was between the Boer farmers and British settlers, traders and administrators. The Boers did not want to become citizens of a British colony, so they moved north, thereby pressing on the already jumpy Zulus, and setting off an aggressive and fear-spreading Zulu migration (like the Germanic migrations of Dark- Ages Europe) that moved northwards through central and East Africa, as far as present day Kenya and Uganda.

Then gold was discovered in the Transvaal, putting paid to the Boers' hopes of peacefully farming there, out of British imperialist range. We British defeated the Boers for control of South Africa in an extremely dirty war (during which we interned all the Afrikaner men, women and children we could find in the world's first concentration camps). Then we set about humiliating them in their own country for the next fifty years.

Afrikaans was banned in schools, as Scottish Gaelic had been and the Afrikaners were treated not much better than Africans. In fact, we much preferred the assertive, noble-looking Zulus to these shabby, taciturn farmers, who probably reminded British colonial types of their more surly rural tenants, or perhaps of best-forgotten poorer relatives and ancestors.

All this mistreatment of our fellow Europeans stoked the fires of resentment and injured dignity that burst into flames in the 1940s with the rise of the Nationalist Party. At last, the Afrikaners felt, they had managed to organize themselves politically, and had cast off the yoke of arrogant British colonial rule. Now they would run the country *their* way.

Of course they didn't have the elegant style of the cosmopolitan British, who had come to rule most of the world, or the fine gestures of the Americans, who saw themselves as freedom fighters even as they took the reins of world power out of British hands.

The Boers weren't gentle folk, or smooth-talking businessmen - they were old-fashioned settler-farmers. They hadn't exterminated native peoples as the white Americans had, only expropriated some of their best land and taken them on as farmhands. But they weren't about to hand over the country to the blacks, as the British were getting ready to hand over Ghana, Nigeria and Kenya to black nationalist leaders.

For not only were they old-fashioned, they *lived* in Africa and had nowhere else to call home. They didn't administer the country absent-mindedly from afar. To them Harold MacMillan's 'winds of change' were not invigorating sea breezes but terrifying gale-force squalls that threatened to toss them into the sea.

The Boers, caught in their odd ideological time-warp (from our Western point of view) became useful pariahs to the West. They ran the South African administration and kept order, while Brit-

ish and American money could get on with the business of repro-
ducing itself there, flowing in and out, unimpeded by scruples.

We British 'disapproved', of course. We sneered at the Afrikaners'
crudely racist legislation, and at their Old Testament justifications
for it. We British were busy reforming - or refining - our own
behaviour to disguise our racism (at least to ourselves). But we
were more than happy to share in the spoils of the Afrikaners'
booming gold-rush-and-cheap-labour economy.

Many British people emigrated to South Africa during the years
of apartheid, and Britain, carrying on the advantageous commercial traditions of the previous era, remained South Africa's number
one trading partner throughout this period.

The above-mentioned 'refinement' of Britain's institutionalized
racial oppression had been necessitated by the changing cultural
atmosphere in Europe in the years following the Second World
War. German fascism and the Allies' war against it had finally
blown the gaffe on overt white racism and explicit theories of
racial superiority. After Hitler, it was much harder to go on lord-
ing it over 'inferior' (darker-skinned) races while posing as a be-
nevolent, civilizing influence. Imperial Britain risked being accused of the same discredited racism we had fought so hard to
save the world from.

Besides, university-educated Africans and Indians were starting to identify with their downtrodden and rebellion-ready peoples - the natives were certainly getting restless.

Our growing British embarrassment about colonialism was as-
suaged by conceding political independence to our colonies, then
instantly embracing them in the newly dreamed-up British Commonwealth - to which (if they knew what was good for them)
they would be keen, and proud, to belong. This brilliant solution
cost mainland Britain nothing at all, although the British have
been moaning ever since about our loss of global influence. Our
economic ties with our ex-colonies (always highly advantageous)
were retained and the profits continued to roll in. We saved money
on administration - far more money than we reluctantly earmarked
for 'aid' and 'development' purposes, which made us feel altruistic.

The timeliness of political independence in the early 1960s allowed the British once again to see ourselves as progressive, liberal and ahead of the other European colonial powers in reading
the writing on the wall.

The Afrikaners on the other hand, *admired* Hitler's brownshirts.
How crass! *We* were not like that.

Parallels with the abolition of the slave trade abound. Once again, British people basked in a glow of self-congratulation as our ex-colonies celebrated their independence of us. As with the release of the slaves after the eventual abolition of slavery in the 1860s, we knew little and cared less what might lie ahead for these countries in an open, international economy dominated by ourselves.

The disastrous story of fifty years of Third World debt, famine and war is known to us all now, whether or not we care. Do we still think we can give the name Progress to the last one hundred years of Africa's history and experience?

As long as we believe that Progress is bound up with 'economic growth', with the development of international trade and foreign exchange reserves, with 'modern' facilities in transport, business, health care, education etc. then we will answer 'yes' to the above question.

But if we insist on seeing the Westernization and industrialization of Africa as Progress, then we are also bound to condone much of what the Afrikaners have done in South Africa, and what the colonial adventurer, Cecil Rhodes, did in Rhodesia. For Zimbabwe and South Africa now have far and away the best developed European-style infrastructure and industry in Africa - thanks to the racist white settlers.

We can't have it both ways. If we regard economic indicators as the main measure of Progress, on what basis can we say the settlers were wrong to keep the reins of power in their hands so long? On what basis can we argue for African self-rule at all?

'Denial of human rights and democratic freedoms' are high-sounding phrases, but our conventional Western arguments ring a little hollow. For the anti-apartheid or 'human rights' approach to political Progress for Africa, when followed through with hopes for economic development, becomes self-contradictory. However we may want to distance ourselves from our embarrassing cousins, the Boers, and from our rapacious, Christianizing and civilization-besotted forebears, the Victorians, we can't consistently deplore what the settlers did in South Africa *and* approve the economic agenda as the yardstick of success for Africa.

We fool ourselves when we think we can dispose of the unacceptable face of white racism, yet keep the rest of our cultural attitudes intact. If we *have* given up the idea that we are intrinsically superior to other peoples, why do we go on assuming that our path should be theirs, and that more industrial, European-style 'development' will improve their lives?

The settlers were consistent. They believed Europeans knew how to run things, and that, therefore the European way was best. Most whites who work in Zambia, Malawi and Kenya, as well as in Zimbabwe and South Africa themselves, feel that African independence leads inevitably to inefficiency, corruption and economic ruin. They believe the economy is better run by whites than by blacks, and in support of their argument, they point to the contrast between Zambia and Zimbabwe.

Zambia, they point out, is floundering in bankruptcy, black market and violent crime, after thirty-odd years of independence which started with a government policy of 'throwing out the whites'; while Zimbabwe's administration works relatively smoothly and its modern sector flourishes, after a much shorter spell of economically 'moderate' independence - that is, accommodating the whites - preceded by fifteen years of white settler rule.

'We set all this up', the Rhodesian settlers say, with a fierce proprietorial pride. They feel that Britain betrayed them, having sent many of them out to 'develop' the country, in the 1950s and 1960s. Liberation has not humbled or discredited them, in their own eyes, except where their projected fears of violent revenge have proved unfounded.

To seriously address these 'racist' arguments, I believe we need to go much further than putting Zambia's problems down to the falling price of copper on the world market, or blaming 'neo-colonialism' and the old boy network , even though such factors do play a big part in these problems. We need to find the courage to break with political correctness, and *admit the importance of cultural factors in the successful running of an industrial economy, and of a European-style nation state.*

We also need to question the very definition of Progress based, in Africa, on foreign influence, and question a definition of Progress *anywhere* which promotes 'economic development' at the expense of human dignity, freedom and self-reliant survival.

In terms of this discussion, the parameters of South Africa's liberation have not challenged the Western world at all - nor have they been meant to. For in theory, we already had racial equality in the West. Nothing wrong with *our* human or democratic rights. After all, we invented the terms.

Within such a Western-inspired framework, the struggle for human dignity in South Africa is likely to stop not far beyond the abolition of apartheid laws. Everything else will remain, as far as possible, in place.

More effort and money will go into keeping the economy running, keeping the whites happy and keeping the commercial farms and the mines in operation, than will go into redistribution of wealth, or provision of services to the majority. *Radical land reform* - giving South Africa back to South Africans - *will probably remain a political taboo.*

Even if a left-wing black government earnestly seeks to construct a socialist state on the basis of South Africa's mineral and industrial wealth - which looks less likely than it did ten years ago - such efforts will again vindicate the whites' economic activity over the past few decades, since they built up the means of production.

Given the scale of repression and violence in South Africa over the past fifty years, this criticism of the 'political rights' approach to Progress may seem in bad taste. However, I feel that without such a critical perspective, we cannot fully comprehend the problems that face South Africa, or Africa as a whole, or ourselves in the West.

When I was working in Zimbabwe, the Rhodesian settlers and the socialist volunteers from Europe felt they were on opposite sides of the barricades. Yet they had far more in common with each other - naturally enough - than with the people in whose land they were fighting their ideological battles. For they all accepted the Western model of Progress - industrial - educational and 'cultural'. They were all concerned with a future based on economic growth.

The Freedom Charter (the ANC's declaration of independence) which was drafted in 1953, could have been written in the USA, or in pre-welfare state Britain, for its aim is to claim the full material benefits of modern urban society for all South Africans. The ANC, in that era, clearly accepted an industrialized, urban 'standard of living' as the goal to be striven towards, and the Charter treats decent municipal housing, running water and electricity as basic human essentials, or 'rights'.

Yet nowhere in the Freedom Charter is there an affirmation that South Africans, like other Africans (and Europeans, for that matter) have *a basic right to their own land*. We Westerners find it very hard to think straight about land. Whereas the right to *property* has been debated and agonized over in our culture, the right to private land ownership has scarcely been queried. Yet if property is theft, private land ownership is much more patently theft. For property can be crafted, produced, built and traded. But land is not a human product. It is finite, and given to us all to live on, and from, by virtue of our being born here on the earth. Land belongs to no-one, and to everyone. This is why the land is held sacred in all traditional cultures. It is a humbling point of view particularly for modern Westerners.

Surely the right to a place to live, and land to live from, is a more natural, basic and inalienable human right than the right to a house, to drugs-based medicine and books-based education. But according to our Western social norms, which reach right back to the Roman Empire, the earth is a commodity, up for grabs, property of the rich and powerful, wherever they see a chance to take it over.

Our vaunted Progress has from the start been built on the expropriation and privatization of land, first of all in Europe, then in the Americas, in Australasia and Africa. So all our Western-initiated development tends to further the deadly process of land privatization and impoverishment, wherever we go. Without our violation of this most basic of human rights - the right to land - there would quite simply be no nation states, no supermarkets, no New York, no plantations, no United Nations to declare human rights, no *Progress*.

Many so-called 'human rights' are based on a Western model of society that reduces the various peoples of the world and their self-reliant cultures to the proletarianized population of a global welfare state. And this bleak vision is presented, not as a regrettable side-effect of industrialization but as an *ideal*!

This fundamental gap in our Western democratic principles when it comes to the issue of land is more obvious when it is perpetrated in Africa, a continent where the great majority of people still retain land rights and provide themselves with most, if not all of their needs by their own agricultural and other work. This is indeed one of the ways in which South Africa acts as a magic mirror for the West. As Jesus observed, it is always easier to spot specks of dust in others peoples' eyes than great planks of wood in our own.

Although we fail to acknowledge the sacred commonality of the earth, Westerners take the concept of human rights terribly seriously. To us, they are both a touchstone of timeless morality, and a proud achievement of our modern democratic political culture. Ever since the revolutions in North America and Europe which ushered in the modern era, our highest and holiest aspirations as a progressive society have been enshrined in the language of democratic rights. The reverent tone of displaced religion in the American Declaration of Independence leads magnificently into the ringing phrases of contemporary UN declarations.

The thing to remember about the American Declaration of Independence, however, is that though its claims sound like universal truths - intended to shame the British oppressor and hearten the ex-European American rebels - they were not applied to African Americans at all. In fact, for most of their history since these 'universal human rights' were coined in our culture, what we call human or democratic rights have been, properly speaking, white rights.

The word 'human' was added to the word 'rights' not to distinguish them from 'animal rights', but to make the point that not only whites (or men) were entitled to them. (It is troubling to consider that this basic, moral education of Europeans had to happen almost two thousand years after Europe's own official religion was opened up to 'all nations' from its own previously privileged Chosen People!)

The African view of 'human rights' is therefore very different from ours, for Africans remember what we did to them the day before yesterday, and how newborn these apparently absolute and inalienable Western rights really are, when it comes to our Western behaviour towards them. They know that the Afrikaners' main crime in Western eyes was in being forty years out of date, and out of step with the rest of the West.

For the institutional racism of apartheid which the West condemned in the 1970s and 1980s was normal British and French social practice in the 1940s and 1950s and was called the 'colour bar'. In the Southern States of the USA and in Australia, the 'colour bar' was preserved in state law until the late 1960s and early 1970s, and it is still social practice. Although it may no longer be legal to 'discriminate' against blacks, segregation is still social practice throughout these large areas of white settlement.

Ian Smith's government, after the Unilateral Declaration of Independence (UDI) in the late 1960s, took advice from the state government of Queensland on how to set up an apartheid legal system. (A friend of mine recently told me, with horror, 'My grandchildren in Australia think the aborigines are the dirt of the earth'.)

We Westerners take our political rights seriously, even reverently - because our culture has suffered several hundred years of feudal restriction and humiliation.

Africans have different histories to look back on: often, they can remember enjoying *more* freedom in the pre-colonial past than they have had since the arrival of Europeans. From an African cultural standpoint with its emphasis on common interests and consensus, the Western concept of 'rights' seems individualistic, demanding and morally infantile. This difference in our histories may help to explain how easily 'human rights' - which appears to Westerners to be sacred and universal - can be suspended in Africa, without causing instant uproar, when it suits those in power to suspend them.

The further back our sense of history reaches, the better we are able to grasp our position in the world, and how we got here. The accelerating pace and increasing superficiality of Western media culture conspire to trap us in a shorter and shorter timescale of awareness. So we strike heroic postures, in all seriousness, on issues like racism and democratic rights, where thirty years ago we were the culprits. We've forgotten already. But they haven't.

I heard an example from the Dresden woman who described the relaxed pace of family life in East Germany before reunification. She told me that their church discussion group had recently had a session on the worrying upsurge in racist attacks in Germany, and her husband had introduced it with a prayer that he himself might not succumb to racism.

We could do with a more humble and honest attitude, like his, towards the Afrikaners. After all, it is easier to have compassion for defeated bullies than for those still wielding guns and laws.

For forty-five years, the Boers resisted the tide of history. The more out-of-date and out of step their policies became, the more force they had to expend on repressing resistance, both inside and outside their borders - borders of the country, of the family and of the mind. They wreaked huge destruction - in Namibia, Zimbabwe and Mozambique as well as South Africa. But they also paid a huge price within their own culture and psyche.

With every uniformed attack on township youth and every torture of a detainee, the Afrikaner people have inflicted violence on themselves and their children, and brutalized their own culture. This is their tragedy. But it is also our own Western tragedy - as Europeans, ex-slavers, settlers, ex-colonialists and continuing directors of the world economy.

Westerners are both audience and co-authors of the Afrikaners' cultural tragedy. We should bear in mind that the 'international community' which condemned them more or less unanimously in the 1970s and 1980s was born only in the post-Second World War break-up of the European colonial system.

So, rather than righteously condemning them, as we did when they were still in power, or dismissing them from our minds now that they have forfeited that power, we ought to acknowledge the common ground between them and ourselves, and try to learn from this insight.

The English-speaking white South Africans whom I spoke to in Zimbabwe apparently found it quite comfortable to side with 'international public opinion' against their government. They liked to blame the Afrikaners for the country's bad reputation; to project all indefensible racism and injustice onto the 'backward Boers', whom they called jumped-up peasants and 'as thick as two planks'.

Later, in Malawi, I became friends with two Afrikaner women who were teaching at a mission near Lilongwe. They both rejected their government's political principles and practices, but they still smarted at the easy superiority of the Boer-bashing 'Anglos'; and though both are extremely articulate in English, they still feel unconfident in English-speaking circles, whether South African or 'international'.

Though these women have disagreed radically with their parents, they love them and are intimately involved with them. This contrasted with many 'progressive' young Germans I knew in the 1970s, who would have nothing to do with their 'fascist' parents, except perhaps to accept expensive gifts from them. The messy and confused integrity of my Afrikaner friends impressed me a lot, and endeared them to me. I respected their avoidance of neat, abstract solutions to their country's ills, the way they kept the door open to their own guilty roots, their pain.

The grandfather of one of my Afrikaner friends spent years in a British concentration camp in the Far East (we never hear about those!). There he carved a hardwood chest, which he decorated with trees and elephants, and brought home to South Africa, where it now graces the family's living room in Pretoria. One grandmother brought up her family of eight by baking *koeksisters* (pastries) for the tea parties of English madams. Of course, she had to use the back entrance. This is the Afrikaners' story, and the story of a people's pain deserves to be listened to: it is not usually invented out of thin air, and it can help to explain a lot. Pain is a form of warning. Pain ignored is dangerous, for everybody - for those suffering and for those ignoring the suffering.

I believe we Westerners have misused the Afrikaners. Though South Africa's liberation seemed such a clear-cut moral issue, we have detached ourselves from blame and pointed the finger at the Boers in a way that denies our real implication in what they did.

We have made them suffer for lagging behind, as we made them suffer for opposing us over the gold lying under Johannesburg.

Westerners are so committed to the idea of Progress that we are very quick to dissociate ourselves from abuses which can no longer be glossed over. So we drop the old terminology, revise the legislation, and move on to pastures new, the next plane of blame-lessness. But our quick moves leave behind those - usually less powerful and privileged - who cannot, or will not move so fast, those who cannot afford to change, even superficially.

Any improvement in our Western attitudes to other cultures represents a *return* to more decent and normal, less abusive behaviour, not some *onward* stride that puts Westerners even further ahead of everyone else!

So one of the ironies of our imagined Progress on race is that the people we 'leave behind' as we 'progress' are stranded like seaweed on a beach after the tide has turned, as incontrovertible evidence of the abusive lengths to which our culture has gone. They are our moral tidemark.

To fall to the bottom of the pile in a 'progressive' society like ours is to be lost, even to yourself. You lose everything - not only shelter, clothing, food, but dignity, self-respect, the sense of being human, which depends on being included.

White racism has found one of its most concentrated expressions ever in South Africa, and again, within white South African society it has been easy for better-off whites to adopt liberal attitudes and to deplore the rabid excesses of poorer whites, without acknowledging the massive privilege on which their liberalism is based. For black emancipation does not threaten the livelihoods of middle- and upper-class South African whites: most of them will always be needed and paid, as long as South Africa's modern economic system keeps running.

But for poor and ill-educated whites, liberation spells the bottom of the pile. Stripped of racial advantage, they will be without advantages altogether. Without the support networks and survival skills of black society, their material future may be grim and their cultural outlook, already blighted by bigotry, seems a bleak one.

Most of these people did not have the option of dodging off to the USA or to Australia or Argentina when their nightmare became reality and the blacks took over the government. Ordinary Afrikaners' jobs in the state bureaucracies - police, civil service, post office - are being Africanized with priority. No wonder they flocked, in the 1980s, to the neo-fascist rallies of Eugene Terreblanche, whose Huguenot name - 'good breeding, white earth' - perhaps held a faint promise that they might not yet be completely washed up. We were right to be frightened by the right-wing thugs of the Afrikaner Defence League but they should also have frightened us in the sense that 'There, but for fortune, go you or I'. When we read about their twisted world view and their racist outrages, we should not trust our own indignation. We should ask ourselves: 'How would I react if my own back was against that wall?'

I saw some of the burned-out remnants of the white South African underclass sleeping, drinking, fighting and begging in the streets of Bulawayo. Nowhere in Africa did I see blacks who had sunk to such a level of degradation.

Even the Mozambican refugee children, the destitute and crippled who begged in the streets of Malawi's main town, Blantyre, retained their grace and dignity, and the ability to smile and laugh. These white men, though not maimed or disabled like the Mozambicans and Malawians, were human wrecks compared with those others. The pitiless violence and awful loneliness of their social and mental world struck me with shocking force, in contrast with the easy-going, convivial atmosphere around them in the streets of Bulawayo. But at the same time I had to admit I had seen and heard it all before.

The broken, shambling gait, the distracted, inward-turned expressions, the slumped, semiconscious resignation; the desperate attempts at intimacy, the sharp, bitter humour and the sudden cursings and lacerated wailings - I had seen and heard all this at home in Scotland.

The parallels between South Africa and Britain are strong. Most of Scotland is 'owned' by a wealthy minority, many of them foreign, while most of those who used to farm this land have been 'proletarianized' or have left Scotland - emigrated.

If the Scottish Highlands had not been virtually cleared of crofters for sheep, but deforested and then turned into 'homelands' for Glasgow labourers' families to go on scratching a living on the edges of the 'modern' British economy, we would have a similar situation to the one facing South Africans now.

The South African government is running a full-scale first-world economy in a third-world part of the world - a country which was still, in African eyes at least, a colony until 1991. That is at once the settlers' achievement and their downfall, for no-one can ignore most of the people in their own country forever, especially if they are marked so clearly by skin colour.

There are obvious reasons why South Africa and Zimbabwe took so much longer to liberate than the countries where few whites had settled. It was easy for Britain to wash its hands of countries where few British were resident. Whites, on the other hand, who have emigrated to Africa and regard it as home, do not easily give up control of economy or government to people they consider unequipped to take over the reins.

Although the privatization of the best South African land in white hands parallels the kind of colonial oppression inflicted in Kenya and Tanzania, the proletarianization of Southern Africans through the mining-based industrialization of South Africa, and to a lesser extent Zimbabwe and Zambia, has been more like what happened in Britain.

Looked at in the light of these parallels, the 'New South Africa' is pregnant with challenging ironies for the West, for there Africa and Europe meet in a head-on encounter with an unprecedented balance of power and mutual influence between blacks and whites. Zimbabwe would be the only apparent precedent for this kind of encounter. But Zimbabwe is like a village version of South Africa - neither industrialization nor its brutalizing social effects had deeply changed people's values there, and traditional African beliefs remain relatively untouched by either missionary or settler. Indeed, apartheid under Ian Smith and the struggle against it actually enhanced again the power and dignity of ancestral beliefs, which helped to mobilize the rural people against the white regime.

In South Africa, on the other hand, a large proportion of the country's black population have never known anything but township life, while millions of Afrikaans-speaking 'So-called Coloureds' do not have roots in African tradition. The white population in South Africa is much larger - six million, to Rhodesia's one-quarter million, half of whom left before or at independence (though many have since drifted back). Most white South Africans are not going anywhere else - many are too poor to emigrate, and for the Afrikaners, this is home.

Every black Zimbabwean has a rural 'home area' to which they go regularly, especially as children, to learn about what they still regard as real life and true values: farming, and the traditional customs, the family history and obligations which are inseparable from that life. I do not know to what extent ordinary black South Africans still identify with their traditional history and with the land, but I would guess, from the parallel with Zimbabwe, that the bond is much stronger than left-wing political propaganda would suggest, or than most urban activists would admit.

The notorious 'homelands' policy of the Nationalist government was designed to try to neutralize the threat to white land ownership of this ancestral bond with the land by transplanting people far away from the parts of the country which were wanted for commercial agriculture. But people's cultural memories are not easily erased: as the Afrikaners know only too well, they make a crucial difference to the way people feel, think and act.

In attitudes to culture there is a strange polarity, or there has been, between Westerners and our cousins, the Afrikaners - it is as if our common cultural inheritance was cut in two. *They* were left holding the cultural awareness, and a lot of the overt racism; and *we* were left holding the Progress banner. Because traditional cultures have been so weakened in Europe, Australasia and North America, most Westerners act as there were no significant differences between different groups of people. Trying to transcend our racism, we approached the coming of black power in South Africa with a benign and dogged ingenuousness. It would be a straightforward transfer of political and administrative responsibility from the minority to the majority. Of course the South African economy would carry on growing and doing just as well after liberation as before. This was, at least, the official position. Any scepticism was kept in the privacy of the boardroom or the club.

In fact, the coming of black power to South Africa means a fundamental change in the cultural atmosphere in the corridors of power - a change of values, norms and world views. This change had already made a huge difference to the way things happened in Zimbabwe, when I lived there, and similarly huge changes are now happening in South Africa.

Anxious to rehabilitate ourselves after centuries of institutionalized racism, which we know we can no longer get away with, we Westerners are afraid that if we are honest, we will come out with something racist, like: 'They'll never run the country properly!' So we fix a polite grin on our faces and say, 'We're sure you'll make a very good job of it'.

The trouble is, we still have the same old notion of what 'running the country properly' implies - and it means our way. So Western political idealists are stuck with insincerity, false hopes, and inevitable disillusionment. We cannot help feeling frustrated and condescending towards people who don't run their businesses and administration as we would, and we can't see that this doesn't imply incompetence, simply *different priorities in life.*

A Zimbabwean lorry driver who had spent twenty years living and working in South Africa, told me that his idea of a sensible changeover in South Africa would allow the whites to go on running the economy while the blacks took over political power. 'You people are good at planning for future generations; a man like me thinks of himself and his family. I want to buy a sack of maize meal at the end of the month, and then I can rest happy'.

(Carrying out his proposal would turn South African whites into a rich but politically powerless business class, like the Asians in Malawi. Their political power would stretch only as far as their ability to bribe the powerful - a comedown which would remove white moral confidence at a stroke.)

The thing about belonging to a 'progressive' culture is that we Westerners can never 'rest happy' like the truck driver with his sack of maize. But being committed to Progress *can* also be our saving grace, if it keeps prompting us to find ways back to being more true to ourselves, by unmasking our false Progress. We can make real progress by healing ourselves of immoral and alienating habits that fake Progress has bred in us.

W orking in Zimbabwe a mere four years after independence, I found a great deal of anger among the white Rhodesians about the hypocrisy of 'progressive' white opinion including the British government.

Attitudes to the Rhodesians among the British, Irish, German and Canadian volunteers ranged from irritated disapproval to loathing tinged with contempt. They were nicknamed 'Whenwe's' for their habit of harking back to the days 'when *we* ran this country'. However, I felt that the left-wing teachers and health workers in my volunteer group were less straightforward about our own role in the country, and about the Rhodesians' role in its recent history, than the 'Whenwes' were about themselves.

For while my volunteer group lambasted the settlers for being racist white exploiters, and criticized Zimbabwe's half-hearted socialist government from the left for compromising with capitalism, we made the most of the excellent roads, supermarket foods, and holiday facilities that the settlers had thoughtfully installed for us. We didn't, on the whole, seem embarrassed by the contradictions between preaching land reform and grassroots democracy in Zimbabwe and enjoying the 'conveniences' of the colonialist era - indeed, relying on them for our daily 'necessities'.

The Rhodesians, however, remember that the British government *encouraged* them or their parents to emigrate there, in the

1940s and 1950s, to settle and 'develop' the country. Many RAF veterans were given large tracts of good farming land as demobilization payments.

Many more came out as business and tradespeople, to help themselves by helping to build up the infrastructure and economy. The Rhodesians, understandably, regard Britain's about-turn on black rule as a cowardly betrayal by their own relatives; and their resentment seemed to me a more honest response to the reality they found themselves in than the political 'correctness' of my own radical volunteer group.

My colleagues had removed 'racism' from their vision of 'development'. By doing so, they denied the organic connection between what the settlers had done *economically* and what they had done politically and culturally - the first was seen as a blessing ('At least they've got cold beer!'); the other two were rejected as racist, reactionary, Neanderthal - those sorts of words.

Yet the new ideology of 'development' *still* assumed the 'backwardness' of local culture: only, instead of denigrating Africans en masse, we concentrated on education and modernization in order to hasten equality - and bring local 'expertise' and 'services' up to scratch. Not surprisingly, the only blacks most of our group felt comfortable with were fellow professionals.

I suppose that this perspective on what they were doing in the country helps to explain why most of my colleagues were not ashamed to hold Marxist discussions in game parks only accessible by private transport, from which the local people had long been chased out, and where they are still not allowed to hunt or fish. For both settlers and socialists seem to agree that African wildlife should be protected from African people so that those with cars can go and see it when we want.

Without such an all-embracing acceptance of modernization, I felt alienated and unhappy attending meetings in pseudo-traditional chalets where the sheets were changed daily and the dishes washed by gracious, silent, barefoot (black) servants. Our expatriate life was full of such incongruities.

Over the six years I stayed in Africa, I became less sensitive to these things, thank goodness, and more able to function socially without offending my white peers. But for the first year or two I was staggered by the glaring injustices of 'normal' expatriate life, and it was a double shock to find myself alone in my alienation. When I expressed - or betrayed - my feelings, my colleagues of course felt criticized, and gave me a wide berth.

The sharpness of their reactions to my reactions gave me a bitter taste of social isolation, confusion and pain. However, it was a valuable experience, for it taught me that integrity is difficult as well as necessary; and it started me thinking seriously about the awkward, often shameful facts of cultural continuity in a so-called post-colonial world.

I have to say that in spite of the awkwardness of the situation, nearly all the people concerned remained individually respectful and affectionate to me throughout our differences. Only the 'group vibe' was defensive and hurtfully dismissive: which perhaps indicates the social origins and dynamics of our cultural superiority syndrome.

We do not stop being racist exploiters simply by calling ourselves socialists or anti-racist. If we continue to rely on the fruits of colonial expropriation and exploitation for our own lifestyle, we are failing to face up to a pretty basic contradiction in our values and situation.

A hearty laugh at ourselves now and again would return us to reality. But if we make things more unreal by sounding off about equality while accepting our own elite standard of living as 'normal', we are actively perpetuating the global lie that West is best.

Spotting specks of dust in others' eyes while overlooking the plank in one's own is a fault shared by our Rhodesian cousins. White Zimbabweans were very quick to satirize ugly, arrogant behaviour in the new black Zimbabwean bourgeoisie. African political leaders, for example, regularly keep huge crowds waiting in the sun for hours without shade, food or drink. All of these are, however, generously provided for the VIPs by the struggling people they are deigning to visit - if and when they show up, in their gleaming cavalcades.

In cases like these, settlers could see that the ones lacking dignity and grace in these encounters were the rude VIPs, not the patient, respectful poor. They would get quite indignant.

Yet they could not see the ugliness and arrogance of their own ingrained racism, a much more extreme example of systematic denial of respect. Many of these settlers seemed to be living in a state of siege behind mental barbed wire. They were nervous talking to a foreign white, whom they correctly assumed to be critical of them. Many constantly commented on the things that Africans couldn't or wouldn't do like Europeans, to justify their sense of superiority, their bitterness and separatism.

Their very eagerness to justify themselves seemed to admit a subconscious discomfort with their own cramped and rigid attitudes, as well as childlike dependence on international white opinion - a dependence which must have helped to bring the South African apartheid regime to an end.

Since the Rhodesians had already lost their war, I felt more sad for them than angered by them. Indeed, some paid unexpected tributes to the liberation of their country and its character since independence, even confessing their own previous errors. One young white farmer who gave me a lift told me he had lost a lot of good (white) friends in the war - 'But we've got a better country for it now', he said (and I found I had to choke back tears).

Others, however, cherished everything about Zimbabwe - its landscapes, climate, vegetation, animal and bird life - everything, that is, except its people.

Some of these old Rhodesians reminded me of my own Ulster Protestant roots. I recognized the same obsession with 'them' - the blacks, the Roman Catholics (never just Catholics). It is ironic: to the 'outsider's' eye, both Ulster Protestants and old Rhodesians come over as 'regressive', in relation to mainstream European culture, precisely because of the way they *voice* their conviction that their ways are more advanced than those of the community they have oppressed, and must now learn to share their country with.

The Rhodesians can see the ugliness of the new Zimbabwean ruling class' arrogance towards the rest, but are blind to the ugliness of their own attitudes towards blacks. Middle-class blacks know the weight of racist elitism, but cannot help venting their newly-acquired, imitative sense of superiority on those now 'below' them in the modern hierarchy of power.

And what of expatriate whites like myself, who can see settler and black bourgeois arrogance clearly enough, standing outside, but not so easily the arrogance and superiority syndrome of our own habitual European attitudes to other societies? Like the northern Irish Protestants and the white settlers in Southern Africa, we 'innocent' Westerners have oppressed and colonized other societies in the past, and we too must now learn to share the world with them.

As I mentioned in chapter seven, the South African left used to maintain that culture was not a factor in politics and economics. The whole concept of culture was branded a tool of apartheid, to be thrown out with racist legislation. That meant, people's inherited customs, values and beliefs, and their way of looking at the world were ruled out of court, as if the left-right political agenda did not have its own (Western) cultural roots.

The adjective coined by left-wing anti-government forces to describe the longed-for New South Africa was *'nonracial'*. Not 'nonracist' but 'nonracial'. The word 'multiracial', was apparently rejected because it smacked too much of separate assemblies.

The 'nonracial' concept seemed a stunning denial of reality, in a centuries-old melting pot which brings together Indians, Chinese, Malaysians, Africans and Europeans, and where styles of music and dress jostle and blend with one another in a riot of colours and cultures.

Yet such denial is itself part of a strong tradition. Being aware of one's regional or 'tribal' traditions and culture has long been associated in 'progressive' thinking with reactionary nationalism, even with fascism. Both the Afrikaner Nationalist government and the Zulu leadership have helped to confirm this opinion by their incitement and sponsorship of Inkatha (Zulu) violence in Natal.

The atmosphere in the New South Africa is however already so radically changed, so Africanized, that culture can no longer be denied.

Although the dangers of cultural belligerence are only too evident to Europeans, the post-revolutionary effects of denying cultural variety are also well known. Just as the South African left called all citizens to march as one people into a future of justice, equality and brotherhood over the graves of their 'outdated' beliefs and cultural differences - so the Soviet and Chinese Communist Party vanguards before them had called the peoples of Eastern Europe and most of Asia to stamp out their cultural differences in the cause of unity, solidarity and modernization. The Tibetans are still suffering for their commitment to their cultural traditions, their faith, their way of life. Many Eastern Europeans and Central Asian peoples are now reasserting their identities after decades of official denial.

The Inkatha killings of ANC supporters, which accounted for hundreds of lives, went largely unnoticed in the West. This may have been because the people being killed were not white, or because the people killing them were not white. Perhaps these events upset our simplified categories of good and evil in South Africa, suggesting that things might be more complicated and confusing there than we wanted to know about.

Whatever the reasons for it, the conspiracy of silence about Inkatha has united left, middle and right in the West. I cannot pretend to understand the internal dynamics of black South Africa, but what I learned of Zulu history and culture in Zimbabwe and Malawi helps me imagine something of what may have been going on in the townships of Durban and Pietermaritzburg.

By embarking on this description, I am breaking a strict left-wing taboo on cultural comment. The official, left-wing explanation of events in Natal is that Inkatha has always been a puppet organization, set up and paid by the apartheid regime to be a front for the security forces in their killings of the UDF and ANC members.

I do not deny the truth of this, but I believe that the cultural awareness being so manipulated and abused is important enough to merit consideration rather than silence. It should not be ignored as an unmentionable embarrassment.

The Zulus constitute the largest single cultural group in South Africa, and in Natal they are the vast majority. They have a very different past from many of the people they share the region with.

Through severe military training and discipline, this people developed a culture which contrasted with those of their neighbours, in that many of these other African cultures sought to live by consensus and to avoid conflict wherever possible. The Zulus came to rely for their livelihood on their superiority in armed conflict. They were feared raiders who were accustomed to stealing cattle, and young women, from those they conquered.

But the Zulus were also driven to extremes by European migrations and expansionism in Southern Africa. Zulu aggressiveness reached its apotheosis in Chaka. This brilliant and brutal chief led the Zulus in battle against the whites, but his paranoid feuding also caused the break-up of the Zulu people. The pressure of white settler movement and land hunger contributed to the panicky atmosphere that brought a man like Chaka to power; as, in Europe a few decades later, the pressure of unjustly extorted war reparations, and terrifying rates of inflation created the atmosphere that brought a dictator like Hitler to power.

To solve the problem of Chaka, many of the Zulus themselves resorted to the more usual African method of conflict avoidance - they moved away, and formed new groups. However, on their long trek north, out of Chaka's reach, the Zulu subgroups, among them the Ngonis of Malawi and Ndebeles of Zimbabwe, struck terror into the people they encountered, whose cattle they took, whose daughters they kidnapped, and whose neighbours they became.

Such 'tribal' or 'post-tribal' conflict is the kind of thing Europeans are used to hearing about Africa from right-wing journalists - which is precisely why 'progressive' commentators censor themselves about it. The prejudice-confirming stories *can* be countered by referring to colonial legacies and outside aggression, though there still remains, for the left, an embarrassing amount of oppression and violence.

One of the most interesting things I learned about 'Rhodesians' while I lived in Zimbabwe was that they, and the men in particular, felt a special respect for their Zulu-related Shangani and Ndebele workers. 'You know where you are with them', they would say, 'if Joseph disagrees with me, he will look me in the eye and tell me straight out what he thinks. He won't smile like these Shona people do, and say "Yes, *baas*", and then go away and do something different behind my back'.

It is easy, from a Western point of view, to see how such a direct approach would appeal to our forebears, as it does to us now. (Although I am sure Joseph didn't allow himself to disagree with the *baas* too often.) But can we appreciate the cultural parallels between ourselves and the Zulus that is highlighted by this special bond of mutual respect and recognition?

Indeed, we have much in common. Like the Zulus, we Europeans have become used to charging into other people's home areas and grabbing what we want, telling people what to do rather than sitting around for months negotiating boundaries, mutual obligations and so on. To people like us, the virtues of consensus and conflict avoidance seem time-wasting and insincere.

But from the point of view of a peaceable and conquered people, their only way of maintaining integrity in the face of coercion is by evasion and passive resistance - and so, through the period of their colonial oppression, they have become masters at these tactics.

Meanwhile, the habit of provoking and winning military conflicts has encouraged in us and in the Zulu people a sense of superiority over the more peaceable losers. Such a culture as ours or the Zulus' can easily be fired into nationalist aggression towards anyone threatening this sense of superiority, or having the cheek to tell us what to do.

The cycle of violence is self-perpetuating. *Violence, physical and psychological, brutalizes first those who inflict it*. Those who suffer the violence may also be brutalized, but they are not *necessarily* brutalized. If they have enough loving support from an unbrutalized culture, they can absorb the violence and transmute the pain into struggle, music, faith and patience.

I learned this from the palpably celebratory atmosphere in newly-independent Zimbabwe, from the tolerance and forgiveness in the air there. Once, less than five years after the end of their war of liberation, I arrived in the home of one of my students, their first white visitor, and the grandmother greeted me with the words (in chiKaranga): It is good that now we can sit like this together under one roof, and eat and talk together'.

I learned the same thing again from the gracious, gentle Malawians who have suffered, on top of their extreme material poverty, fear and indignity for over thirty years at the hands of their first national regime - a regime which perfectly internalized colonial attitudes, and imposed them on its people, for it valued white comfort and approval far above the comfort and approval of its own ordinary citizens.

I also saw, in Zimbabwe and Malawi, how Ngoni and Ndebele people, the Zulus' relatives there, had radically renounced violence as a means to achieving their ends - without however losing their cultural self-awareness, or indeed their tendency to look down on their neighbours!

The following is one of the favourite stories told by Ngonis about their relations with the Scottish missionaries to Malawi (then known to Europeans as Nyasaland). An Ngoni chief was asked to drum up some recruits for the British army in the First World War. He told the missionary issuing the request: 'You came and told us to lay down our weapons and study the Bible, and we listened to you. We are not going to take them up again to fight your wars for you!' This is a good example of Zulu directness. I cannot imagine a Shona chief saying this to anyone.

Cultural commentaries like the above find no place in 'progressive' writing or thought, nor do they find a place in nation-building propaganda. For the sake of the abstract values of humanity and Progress, the way people actually are and feel is overlooked, even denied and suppressed.

Certainly, we in the West have grounds for our distrust of nationalism and 'culture'. We are rightly terrified of fascism in our midst.

Fascism is very difficult to think or write about clearly, being both so evil and so close. If I can hazard one observation, it is that I do not believe that fascism grows out of confident cultural self-awareness: rather, it seems to grow out of the opposite - out of insecurity.

Laurens van der Post linked the rise of fascism in Germany (which he witnessed) with fascist tendencies among his own people, the Afrikaners. Van der Post, who was influenced by Jung, writes about the cultural importance of myths and the need to transform those myths at the right time.[1]

Since the Great Trek, the Afrikaners have felt themselves to be a Chosen People, like the Israelites. In the 1950s, van der Post was calling them to recognize the end of the 'Old Testament' era in their history, and to open up their inheritance to the rest of the peoples of South Africa. Otherwise, he foresaw a dreadful cultural regression ahead of the Afrikaners, like the regression the Germans had entered under Hitler.

The new South Africa points the way towards transformation of the West's cultural myth of Progress, for this country embodies in starkest terms the central paradox of Western-style Progress: that economic growth goes hand-in-hand with human degradation. The apparently conflicting ideologies of the Afrikaners, the liberal West and the new South African governments all claim to represent the forces of Progress and economic development, which will generate a better 'standard of living' for everyone. Absolute good is conceived, by all three, in economic terms.

I am arguing that on the contrary, this very process of 'economic development' has been responsible for the impoverishment and violence of South African township and 'homeland' life.

Urban poverty is dehumanizing. Your poverty has to do with your lack of power and dignity *in relation to the society you live in*. As South African economic development by its *de facto* Westernization of the country disempowered even its relatively rich township residents, as well as those left behind in the 'homelands', so Westernizing economic development in Kenya, Malawi and even Zimbabwe likewise leaves behind and disempowers ordinary people, both rural and urban, in spite of those countries' political independence. For you cannot shop in the supermarket if you have no shoes to put on.

Shoes, for that matter, are far cheaper and more plentiful in South Africa than in Malawi. Indeed, for all their political disadvantages, black South Africans have long felt far more sophisticated and confident, in terms of 'international' urban culture, than their neighbours to the north have done.

Zimbabweans, Malawians, Zambians and Batswana look south and east to their shopping and pop music metropolis, while black South Africans look down on their northern neighbours - in the same way that city people everywhere look down on country people, as backward, naive, slow and simple.

The long-standing contradiction between South Africans' political powerlessness and their economic clout and confidence vis-à-vis the rest of Africa is something the Western media has found hard to grasp. We have been used to sentimentalized images of

South Africa's oppressed masses unbalanced by matter-of-fact accounts of how South Africans actually live, and see themselves in relation to their own history and to that of their neighbours.

The contradictions of South Africa for the rest of Africa are like those of the USA for other countries: both represent the land of gold and opportunity where violence, craziness and death lurk around every corner.

A Zimbabwean friend told me with shock of his first visit to Soweto: 'We were driving home one night, and there was a body lying in the road. My friend refused to stop the car, and we just drove past. That could not happen in Zimbabwe'.

The point of what he was saying is not that the body was left lying because South Africa was at that time still a racist police state, whereas Zimbabwe was already independent. The point was that such a thing could *never* have happened in either Rhodesia or Zimbabwe, and that it probably still happens in South Africa, through pure, unpragmatic fear of crime.

Once basic social taboos are broken by an inhuman social system and once brutalization sets in, it is hard to recover the sense of shame and decency that keeps everyone respecting and observing traditional social values.

Racism has not been the only wrecker of communal life in South Africa - the blame must surely be shared by industrialization.

T hough apartheid theory claimed to be concerned with maintaining the integrity of different cultures, its real intention was to pursue an industrial economy while keeping the majority disempowered.

You cannot take away people's best farming land, force them to work for you for inadequate wages, treat them like slaves, and then tell them to 'go home and farm and preserve their culture' - for you have tried to impose your own society's values on them, by dispossessing them of their independent livelihood, and destroying the dignity of their self-reliance. You have done all you can to liquidate their culture.

Only the tiny Pan African Congress Party (PAC), which refuses to admit whites to its ranks, has raised the land question as a central issue of liberation in South Africa. By the rest of the political parties - and by middle-class radicals and reactionaries alike - the settler land grab is accepted as the necessary social basis of an industrialized economy which they regard as essential to South Africa's 'development'.

Both the Afrikaners and the liberal West seem equally embarrassed - albeit for very different reasons - by the enthusiastic and energetic Christianity of black South Africans. The Afrikaners are probably offended because it subverts their own use of the Bible to justify their thoroughly unChristian attitudes to their countrypeople; the Western left because it is an affront to their modern, materialist rejection of Christianity as the opiate of the people, and of the spiritual life as a reactionary pastime.

A few years ago, I was in a packed Edinburgh church where, as part of the Festival Fringe, a choir from Soweto was rocking the rafters with good gospel music. Although they had encouraged the audience to dance, only two of us got up. Yet the rest were enjoying the music, whooping and clapping furiously at the end of the songs.

I guess there were two inhibiting factors preventing people from letting themselves go: first, the feeling I shared, until I lived in Zimbabwe, that gyrating around to music is for Saturday night at the disco, not Sunday morning in church; then, our discomfort at being told, in sermon or in song, by no matter whom, 'This is the day of salvation'. With beautiful historical irony, such a pronouncement is nowadays as bemusing and culturally irrelevant to an average Western 'world music' audience as it must have been to an average African audience 100 years ago!

Every aspect of life in South Africa raises deep questions about the impact of European colonialism, the encounter between Westerners and the native inhabitants of other continents. As a postcard printed in Cape Town in the 1980s wisely declared, 'If you're not confused, you're misinformed'.

Except in Zimbabwe, we Westerners have never before had to parley like this with a native population, in a land we have settled and industrialized. We have not had to do it in North America or in Australia, for our pioneer cousins have simply walked into those continents and *outlived* the locals. But the Africans - unlike the native Americans and Australians - did not lie down and die of disease and despair, when they were confronted by our forefathers' irresistible fire power and fire water. Nor did they give themselves up to a living death in alcohol and violence.

Instead they have endured and learned to adapt to our ways, taking on the parts of our culture they find amusing or inspiring. They have survived on their own terms. And because they are still there, in their own country, *we have to deal with them*.

Of course this feels difficult and challenging. But surely it is a healthier and more genuine encounter than what can take place nowadays in America and Australia.

Some Westerners know how to live with confusion, but it offends our tidy minds. Our organizing intellects find it hard to include all sides of an issue, so each political interest group tends to stick to one side of the issues and ignore the others.

In relation to the South African struggle for independence, the left and many political leaders concentrated on political rights and economic justice, while the Nationalist regime and Westerners like Britain's Margaret Thatcher focused on *political order* and on *economic performance*. Each side was convinced it was more right than the other.

In the South African struggle for liberation, there was no question which side was 'more right'. Though the right were not completely wrong when they accused the liberal West of naiveté and economic irresponsibility over sanctions, and told us that they would hurt the blacks most. Economically speaking, and in the medium term, black workers certainly lost out through sanctions - as they did in disinvestment decisions like Barclays Bank's, which forced workers to exchange relatively liberal American or British bosses for hard-line local ones - or for unemployment.

It does seem to me that Western radical support for the struggle in South Africa came relatively cheap, for we had little to lose by freedom coming. The apartheid government and its ordinary and poor white supporters, on the other hand, like the ordinary and poor blacks resisting oppression, were all fighting for their lives.

This struggle for survival deserved, I think, more respectful attention, from 'enlightened' and privileged whites, perhaps even some horrified and sympathetic silence.

Too-easy solidarity can be a shortcut to complacency and hypocrisy, if we avoid looking at our own Western role in the status quo. For one person's surplus is another's survival - one's cup of coffee is another's plot of land.

Radical rhetoric - even activist activity - can assume the right to live in affluence and privilege among the dispossessed.

While we may scoff at the settlers for making excuses to justify their exploitation of Africa, and put their words in ironic quotation marks, someone else may question our version of what we are doing: whatever it looks like to us, it may look like an excuse to someone else.

Throughout this chapter I have criticized the Progress ideology which continues to grip Southern Africa as well as ourselves, and which makes discussion of land right impossible, both there and here. The vision of consumer durables for all is a necessary fiction to the affluent, for without it, how can we keep claiming more, or even the same amount of extra helpings, for ourselves? Very few of us, if we are honest, would like to see our material standard of living and our expectations axed to the level of 'ordinary' people in any global sense.

This was the fear which transfixed most white South Africans and galvanized them into brutal and psychologically desperate defence of the indefensible. The same quandary still besets ruling elites in cash-poor countries from Brazil to the Philippines. It is no joke to be threatened with ordinariness when you have grown accustomed to privilege.

In fact, living with modest means is much harder for us who have lost the subsistence skills, the support networks and the social values that still sustain the 'poor' of the earth.

To really understand Southern Africa, I believe we need to acknowledge the fear that has motivated white South Africans. For only when we admit the common ground between them and ourselves will we be ready to reassess the history that binds us all to the moving staircase of Progress.

Recognizing our own anxious faces in the grim, set expressions of the Afrikaners is a shock. But that shock may help to shake us free of our attachment to our standard of living and to the unending quest for more that are draining our lives and our culture of joy.

When this happens, we can become less introverted and more ordinary - less typically middle class and more generally human. Woody Allen-style isolation and insecurity recede as we begin to feel other peoples' joys and faith and suffering with new empathy.

We may also experience a relief and releasing of tension as we gradually realize it is not, after all, up to *us* to sort out the world - for real progress can only be brought about by the poor.

9

Coming Round

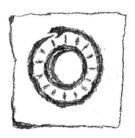

Do less, accept more - A South African sermon - What price the microchip? - Progress reassessed - Western passivity -The clock winds down - A cautionary tale - Green philosophy - Give back the land - Change is coming

SOME PEOPLE MIGHT LIKE TO FIND A PLAN in this concluding chapter, a list of things to do to help improve matters - another blueprint for Progress. We modern Westerners like tasks and solutions: it is hard for us to stop doing and be. But we have to remember that our very cleverness at doing and solving things is what has got us into the problems that face us now.

I believe that for things to change in the way they urgently need to, we Westerners need to learn to *let things be*. Letting be includes letting ourselves be, *as we are*, and getting to know ourselves better, as we are. It also implies not interfering with other people, or trying to control them, but allowing them to live their own lives.

In this book I have tried to look more deeply at how we are, as a culture, in the West, and at how we have come to be this way. A wise counsellor doesn't give answers because each of us has to find our own way through life, and this is another good reason for not offering a list of suggestions here. The miracle of change is that by learning to see and accept ourselves more and more honestly, *as we are*, we become more and more able to grow.

'Personal growth' can be seen as a very private affair - even as a way of avoiding political responsibility. But I hope I have at least begun to show how political even our most personal experiences are, and how personal politics always becomes.

I don't believe the situation is hopeless: life is full of hope. Yet I feel it is important not to tag our hope onto ways we Westerners might be able to *make things better* with our Western skills and advantages. I believe our urge to 'help' in classically Western ways is bound to end in futility, and in an increased sense of helplessness.

I am not dismissing or belittling anyone's work. Every life prolonged or enriched by Western intervention, education or medicine, is priceless. But best of all, efforts to help often lead to good relationships between Westerners and their hosts, through which we all have our horizons extended and our awareness of life deepened.

But we have to be careful not to get things out of proportion, as we so often do. We are not the world's saviours. We were never meant to be - for nobody can save anybody else. And we are not 'ahead' of other cultures - only different in our priorities. Indeed we have done a great deal of damage with our efforts for civilization and Progress, damage which continues at least partly out of our control. We cannot make up for these mistakes by more effort in the same direction. We can only try to turn around in the opposite direction, towards a more humble, renunciatory and peaceful attitude. We can let the snake take its tail in its mouth. Then, hopefully, we will no longer feel the need to plunder - or save - other peoples in order to express our cultural identity!

While I was still in Zimbabwe, an English friend in Harare told me about a funeral she had attended in a South African township. A black youth had been killed by a white policeman, for no reason. No apology had been offered by the police. The atmosphere in the crowded church was electric: she felt the congregation's grief, anger and unwavering will to resist with dignity the degrading treatment to which they were daily exposed.

Some of the preacher's words had stayed in her mind, and since she repeated them to me, they have also stayed in mine: '*Without confession there can be no repentance; without repentance there can be no forgiveness, without forgiveness there can be no salvation, and without salvation there can be no eternity*'.

We Westerners have not yet repented as a culture for our crimes towards other peoples - for we have certainly not confessed them. Rather, we have kept on pronouncing ourselves converted and saved, without ever addressing those we have harmed, or listening to what they have to say to us in reply. In Old Testament terms, we in the West need to repent and return to God for forgiveness. But we don't have a God any more - or if we do, we don't have that kind of relationship with Him/Her.

It is just possible that our lurking awareness of the awfulness of what we might have to confess to our God has contributed to our growing Western neglect and trivialization of religion.

For real regeneration to happen, the preacher prescribed five steps: confession - repentance - forgiveness - salvation - eternity. Nowadays, we Westerners shrink from strong words like salvation and eternity, and we resist the 'outdated' indignities of confession and repentance. But whether our embarrassment about traditional Christian terminology is based in agnosticism, atheism, or in a more 'progressive', politicized approach to Christianity, it seems to fit well with our culture's abdication of moral responsibility for the global system we have developed and by which we profit.

We have removed ourselves to a safe psychological, intellectual and spiritual distance, we think, from such direct challenges to our peace of mind as the preacher issued. And yet neither my friend nor I have forgotten his words.

When the South African preacher set out the five steps needed for peace and reconciliation in South Africa, he did not have to say, 'This is a political metaphor'. Nor was he simply burying subversive politics in safe religious language which the churchgoing white regime could not fault. No doubt he was also doing that, but the words he used insist on the indivisible unity of politics and spirituality. He is talking about the *condition of the human being committing or suffering oppression.*

This is what the abducted and enslaved Africans and their descendants sang about on the American and Caribbean plantations, and what the Israelites sang in Egypt - the pain of captivity which strikes spirit and flesh as one.

Our Western distaste for spiritual language and feeling was brought home to me recently at a choral concert in Edinburgh. The choir sang music from different cultures, and after a varied programme of Eastern European, African and Gaelic songs, some 'Negro spirituals' were introduced. I was amazed.

The woman making the introduction on behalf of the choir then went to some lengths to distance herself, the choir and the songs themselves from any specifically religious content. Spirituals were, she explained, vehicles for *political* messages, telling people in the fields that someone was escaping, or that a visitor would be arriving that night, or some such practical information.

But when the choir sang the so-called spirituals, the music spoke for itself, thankfully suspending silly distinctions between faith and activism.

Like the South African funeral oration, spirituals are neither political metaphors, nor religious escapism. They are direct expressions of longing, of pain, of reassurance and perseverance, and of dignity in suffering. They are reminders of the truth.

This whole book has been mainly concerned with the first two steps named by the preacher. Confession means naming and acknowledging what we have done as a culture. It means naming and acknowledging our Western violations of human rights, and also naming and acknowledging the attitudes that have incited us to these crimes, justified us in them, and in turn been confirmed and intensified by them.

With regard to slavery, for example, we need to say clearly to Africans and blacks everywhere: we did this. Our people enslaved and sought to degrade your people. We know it was wrong. We are sorry for it. Yet we are still doing it, by different means and by different names. We are responsible. It's us, it's us O Lord, standing in the need of prayer.

Until we are able to confess, without excuses or qualifications, we will not be in a position to repent, or to apologize for the damage our culture has inflicted and is still inflicting on the rest of the world.

But according to the preacher, confession opens the way to repentance. And repentance implies a change of heart, an about-turn, and new growth as a result of this change. I have tried to write about what our repentance might bring us, in the way of new relationships and perspectives on the world.

Few of us have got as far as receiving forgiveness, the third step, from those our culture has misused. But in Northern Ireland, in Israel/Palestine, in former Yugoslavia and in South Africa, people are trying to learn about forgiveness and reconciliation.

I hesitate to write anything about steps four or five. Salvation and Eternity are big words, and in a sense they speak for themselves, even if we seek to understand them psychologically or politically rather than spiritually.

By way of owning up, and also to give a concrete example of continuing slavery, let me lay before you an ethical issue that concerns the technology of book publication. With neat irony, by typing this manuscript onto disc for the publisher, I will become more directly involved than I have ever been before in one particular Western economic abuse. The microchip industry of the 1980s and 1990s is an example of an immoral economic practice about which we are not yet prepared to have scruples.

At the moment, nearly every computer and word processor we use involves the labour of young women - girls, really - in South East Asia, who are employed because of their cheapness and manual dexterity to assemble microchips by hand. They run away to the city, or are sent from their village homes to earn money, and they last, on average, two to five years in the factory.[1]

By then they have often been blinded or semi-blinded by the intricate benchwork and are fit only for the streets and bars of Bangkok, or another city. They can't go back to the village, for the road to town is a one-way street for women. Once they have left home, they are assumed to be 'fallen'.

These facts have been well-known, at least in activist circles, for fifteen years. I have told them to several friends, who have re-acted with surprise and concern - but there the response has ended. No-one has started or joined a campaign, and no-one has not bought a word processor because of what they found out, not even the radicals!

It is astonishingly difficult, in the era of information technology, to find out if there are any computers which do not involve this form of labour. But whatever I decide to do, Western society's decision is already clear: 'We can't do without microchips. They're so convenient, they're the cheapest option presently available' (thanks to the workers' poverty) - and they're the next step in our Progress.

Perhaps once we have found an even cheaper way of manufacturing microchips which is less embarrassing, we will suddenly be reading exposés in the Sunday papers about the iniquities of the old sweatshops and brothels in South East Asia - but for now, it seems, we can't afford to be that squeamish.

Slavery is still with us, and acquiescence in it is still normal in Western culture. The practice of using human beings as a means to economic ends - their lives, our ends - is intrinsic to our commercial system. The real work of antislavery reform, of inward change, is work we still have to do.

What I decide to do about word processors matters; but my decision will not exempt me from participation in the use of word processors by my society, for these will continue to affect my life wherever and however I live, short of a hermitage. If we decide not to eat meat or dairy products, and not to buy cars, this is not the end of these matters for us - we are still involved.

Taking an ethical stand on an issue does not mean we pro-nounce ourselves individually 'not guilty' or stand in judgement over others. (We can judge a practice, but not a person). Rather, our awareness *requires* us to do, or not to do, something *in order to remain true to ourselves.*

This awareness is itself a gift, not an achievement - something to be grateful for rather than proud of. Even awareness which seems to be at odds with our society has actually emerged through our experience in our society into us.

Acknowledging this, we will realize when difficult issues arise with those around us that our understanding and our actions, and theirs, are coloured by all kinds of *subconscious* needs and fears which we can only begin to unravel.

Also, because of our social inheritance and inextricable involvement in our culture, we know about the issues that trouble us because *they are inside our own minds.* We have not learned about them by study or hearsay, but from our own childhood experience, from the crucial moments of developing selfhood. We know our culture's norms from the ways we were taught, by example, to feel and think and to relate to people - and were taught *not* to feel, or to think, or relate to people.

Our personal involvement in all this gives us both the right and a duty to address our society on issues where we know that we ourselves have been hurt and damaged by its attitudes. We are not only preaching politics, but also trying to *heal ourselves* by finding other norms - other ways of feeling, thinking and relating to people.

An American Catholic counsellor (Henry Nouwen) has written a helpful book called *The Wounded Healer.* Perhaps there can be no other kind of healer.[2]

Admitting our woundedness, however, does not mean posing as the injured party, for we are perpetrators as well as victims of white cultural crime.

W hen we own up to our own role in history, this puts us and our culture in proper context and should check our strong Western impulse to speak for all humanity. We have a terrible habit of universalizing our conclusions - political, economic, philosophical or religious - to cover the whole human race, the whole earth, the cosmos even!

Yet however dominant we are, we Westerners represent just one minority culture among hundreds of others. Peoples with different histories are not like us and do not *want* to be mistaken for us. By automatically applying our norms to everyone else (thinking, as often as not, that we are doing them a favour!) we violate other peoples and their natural rights - and so further violate our own innate sense of justice.

Seen in this light, development - the continuing internationalization of our Western form of Progress, is bad news for everyone - psychologically as well as economically and environmentally. But also, seen in this light, other cultures come into their own, so that we can learn from them.

We do not have to regard them as childlike, so that their positive qualities appear to us like the lost innocence of childhood; we do not have to be embarrassed by their apparent technological simplicity or feel that their systems of knowledge and belief are primitive and cannot be of legitimate interest to us.

No culture or society is more advanced, in an absolute sense, than any other - though some may be more advanced in some aspects, others in others. And so all can, and do, enrich each other.

A friend told me the other day how, at a conference she had attended, one of her civil service colleagues patronizingly lectured a visiting Indian architect about 'developing countries like yours', speaking loudly and slowly. Finally, she turned round and, very politely, in perfect English of course, told him that India has an extremely ancient and unbroken civilization.

Europeans notice when Americans assume the superiority of *their* home culture to everyone else's. I spent two years travelling and working in the USA after I finished my studies. I was made very welcome and continually asked how I liked the States. But when I started preparing to leave, many people (though not my close friends) reacted strangely, expressing surprise and disappointment. They seemed to take my impending departure as a personal criticism, a vote of no-confidence in their beloved country. Was America not paradise? How could I think of going home again once I had tasted life there?

Such emotionally-charged encounters are usually pre-verbal. These people didn't spell out their feelings in so many words - they didn't have to. I felt awkward, ungrateful - but also exasperated. For clearly, they assumed that nothing significant or enjoyable could go on anywhere outside the USA.

I must confess that I have caught myself in a similar state of mind to those Americans, in relation to African students in Scotland who were looking forward to going home. I have found myself unreasonably hurt by their eagerness to get back to their families and real lives. What's wrong with Scotland, I hear myself asking, in my head. Yet I don't get this feeling talking to North Americans or New Zealanders who are planning to go home. Why not?

I suspect I am hurt by the Africans' impending departure because, like my own departure from the USA, it breaks the circle of illusion that 'We are it'. By all means come and join us in our Western paradise, whispers the British and North American subconscious, only don't threaten our conviction that we are the world's happiest and best by choosing to leave us.

Even though I believed, from a young age, that Africa must be a wonderful place to live, because of my parents' favourite stories about happy missionary life in West Africa (before their children were born), part of my own social programming still insists that life in the West *must* be preferable to life in Nigeria, Togo or wherever.

Given my own views, and my experiences in Zimbabwe and Malawi, I am ashamed of harbouring these Western prejudices, and relieved to notice that they seem to have eased off a bit during the last few years. But I have to accept that not everything in my mind is of my responsible adult choosing, or even a family legacy. We inherit the contents of our minds to a large extent from the *general atmosphere* in which we grow up (our culture). And unless a new awareness spreads wide enough and runs deep enough to fundamentally change the cultural atmosphere, our children will inherit the same old subliminal prejudices as we did.

I have mentioned the medieval sense of the word Progress, which predates our linear notion of what this word means - the circular route of the royal Progress around the kingdom. In our modern Western sense, Progress moves in a straight line. It means an advance from something bad, or less good, to something good, or better; an improvement, development, unfolding of potential, amelioration of ills, banishment of disease, drudgery, infant mortality, malnutrition, poverty, slavery, inconvenience, and all forms of suffering and inhumanity. The past is seen as a nightmare from which we have emerged - into present ease and the promise of future bliss.

We Westerners apply this concept of absolute improvement to the whole of our history, particularly since the Middle Ages, and particularly in its innovative aspects.

Though we may not go so far, these days, as to specifically celebrate our dominion over other peoples, we do believe that our culture has achieved some sort of absolute improvement in human life over the centuries. We have been taught, as schoolchildren, that this is what Western culture stands for - indeed, this is why we go to school, and what education is all about.

Yet we often use the word Progress with a wince and a shade of irony because many Westerners feel a little dizzy from the accelerating pace of change in our society, and hurt by many of its 'side effects'.

Moving on, then, from irony to enquiry, let us now look briefly at some specific areas where our Progress is considered most visible.

We tend to think we in the West enjoy unprecedentedly **good health**. As we look around us at the dead, dying and damaged ways of life which share the earth with us, we feel confirmed in our 'advanced' health status. Development agencies talk piously about health care - meaning 'modern medicine', or at least, clinics - as a human right. Immunization for all by the year 2000 has been a UN objective for nearly twenty years.

We Westerners *have* managed to add a few centimetres to our average height. We are statistically less likely to die of problems in childbirth, childhood diseases, domestic accidents and some adult diseases, than before and than most people in many other cultures nowadays. We can be kept alive almost indefinitely, in spite of all sorts of normally death-triggering body failures.

But do all these statistics and technical means of prolonging life add up to better health? We are also statistically likely to drive everywhere and to sit watching TV for several hours a day. We have heart attacks, road accidents, strokes, cancer, MS, ME, Alzheimer's, rising incidence of diabetes and allergies. Our immune system is becoming ever more vulnerable as we dose ourselves with antibiotics (deliberately and through the meat and eggs we eat), and face the bombardment of pollution, radioactivity, exhaust fumes, agrichemicals, additives in our water and stress.

Are we really healthier? If you watched the people walking along the roadside in Zimbabwe, you would immediately feel they looked a lot healthier than people in a Western shopping mall or a London train station. It took me quite a while to stop gawking at the general health and beauty of people's faces and bodies in Africa! Possibly my incredulity was due to Western indoctrination about African starvation and misery.

In case I should be accused of idealizing African health, I must point out that there are indeed eye ailments and insect-borne diseases in Africa that can be cured by Western-produced drugs and operations - although some immunization programmes store up as many problems as they solve. There is also dreadful and unnecessary ill-health, usually with clearly identifiable political causes like war, government priorities that benefit the few and disadvantage the majority, or a history of migrant labour set up by the mining industry or commercial farming.

As Progress both improves and undermines our Western health, so it does to Africans - only for them it brings more undermining and less improvement.

What about **energy**? We Westerners have unlimited amounts of electricity at our disposal - with unsightly pylons straddling the loveliest areas of our country, and introducing powerful electro-magnetic fields. Another invisible menace, radioactivity, pollutes the sea, the beaches and the areas around our nuclear reactors. We have scarcely any mining jobs left, in Britain at least - though that is surely a mixed curse.

The oil, like the coal, is finite. Nuclear energy creates problems we cannot solve. Yet the expectation of more and more demand for energy is used to justify more and more oil exploration and more nuclear installations.

Is this Progress?

We have freed ourselves of much physical **work**, by inventing ever more gadgets and machinery. We have aimed to do away with drudgery: yet our factory-computer-supermarket-motorway of life demands that people spend their working lives wired up to machines. We have lost the natural balance of mental and physical work, and of work and celebration. Many people's leisure activities and hobbies end up as competitive and exhausting as their working lives, for they have come to crave adrenaline. We need our daily fix of stress to make us feel alive, or so we are told.

But as more and more people experience unemployment, we are gradually learning to reassess the importance of a job for life and to use 'unemployment' more creatively. In the area of work at least, the snake of Progress is beginning to reach for its tail.

And **education**? We have access to more 'information' about the world than ever before, we think. We send our children to school for most of their childhood. Our schools, colleges and universities produce a few intellectuals, more professionals, plenty technical experts - and masses of people inured to boredom and failure.

We spread our ideas of education to every country on earth, persuading other peoples that, unless they are educated to *our* norms and standards, they are unfit to teach their own children what they need to know for adult life. By 'adult life' we mean life in the modern West.

Progress?

We know we are rich. Our supermarkets glisten with goodies, every year our cars get faster, quieter and more comfortable, our computers and sound systems cheaper, smaller and more and more 'sophisticated', our holidays more exotic. But our **wealth** is costing the earth. And our anxiety to taste everything on offer, and to maintain or improve our 'standard of living' can easily squeeze the meaning out of our lives and leave us feeling we are running desperately just to stay still.

The massive budgets of the advertising industry are spent expressly in order to perpetuate this anxiety, so that we will keep buying things to reassure ourselves we have status, we belong, we have power, *we exist*. 'I buy, therefore I am'. If we stopped buying, we would indeed soon stop existing.

Advertising does in the economic sphere what education does in the cultural one. First it steals our birthrights (self-confidence, acceptance, sexual attractiveness, conviviality) so that we will then pay money in order to feel these things, buying back our birthrights in small, expensively-packaged units. This vicious circle of motivation keeps the economy running, which is generally considered to be a good thing - though it is meaningless in itself, and destructive both of our own contentment and self-esteem and of the world we live in.

Our Western **media and communications** are often held up as an achievement. Using faxes, mobile phones, the internet, videos and satellite TV, we have more and more ways of talking to and hearing from each other. Or do we? Besides the odd thoughtful or beautifully-made TV programme, the occasional heartening phonecall or good newspaper article, we are also more and more exposed to each other's demands and deadlines, prejudices, sales pitches, intrusive and abusive images, stories and films.

We make corporations money by listening, watching, reading - just by *being* Westerners and belonging, or trying to belong, to this money-obsessed culture of ours.

These are a few of the areas in which we Westerners pride ourselves on our Progress. I would argue that they are all, at best, of very mixed value.

But real progress does happen - progress without an ironic capital letter. Where, then in our Western history, does *real progress* lie?

This morning on the radio I heard a reggae song called *Runaway Train of Freedom*. The title and two of the lines have stayed with me: *No matter how you try/You can't stop history.*[3] The song brings me back to the conversation about the elite school board that opened this book.

'Look how far we have come', my friend said. These black politicians, never mind how opportunistic and unprincipled they are, could never have been on this school board ten years ago. Progress!

What made me uneasy in that conversation was the way the grasping, elitist behaviour of the new black Zimbabwean bourgeoisie was being offered, even ironically, as proof of Progress. At least, my friend was saying, blacks were now getting the chance to do the same things that they could only watch their white oppressors doing before.

I wrote the last two paragraphs in October 1988. Now, years later, I can see that my Zimbabwean friend was saying more or less what the reggae song I heard this morning is saying - *No matter how you try/You can't stop history* - and I, with my Western mind, was resisting this soul-truth by criticizing the continuing materialism of the liberated: *'Does it surprise you that people want the same things?'* I find it both apt and moving that this singer/songwriter, Zeke Manyika, who caught my attention just at the right moment, is himself a Zimbabwean.

With the help of that song, I have made a little real progress. For I have realized something I had not seen before about my motivation in writing this book. The first step is confession, always a humbling experience. *No matter how you try/You can't stop history.*

We busy Western strivers tend to think of ourselves as *propelling* history by our efforts, forging ever onwards and upwards, into the future. Yet in truth, our strenuous efforts are more likely to be directed *against* history's own irresistible and real progress. History happens at least as much in spite of us as through us. Western-style Progress will be unmasked eventually, whatever efforts we make, or do not make.

It is not a matter of figuring out what we should do to save the world. We have *done* more than enough already: our doings are destroying the world. We need to learn to *do less*, and to *stop doing things to others*. We need to stop trying to control everything and learn to *let* progress happen, to allow the runaway train of freedom to come on down the track. It is coming anyway.

(In this context, even ethical investment can be counterproductive, if it persuades us that no damage is being done by our affluence, so we can hang onto our capital and reap the interest with a clear conscience. Of course, ethical investment is probably better than unethical or don't-care investment. But it scarcely breaks our cultural pattern of self-serving moral righteousness!)

I am not saying that we Westerners are helpless. We are not. But we do, characteristically, *feel* helpless, which is ironic, given how powerful and active our culture has been and continues to be. Partly we feel helpless because the economic forces we have set in motion are now unstoppable, we fear, and out of control. Many of us feel politically disempowered and demotivated.

But I think that most of all we feel helpless when we think about global issues or even local issues of poverty because of strong, buried feelings that are taking a great deal of mental energy to deny. This alienation from our own feelings makes our society dangerous. For often, the right hand doesn't know what its left hand is doing. Our conscious minds are 'innocent' - or genuinely ignorant - of what our own subconscious minds are driving us to do.

I believe this alienation lies, for example, at the root of our society's completely irrational willingness to spend trillions of pounds we would grudge for hospitals or welfare benefits on deadly, faulty, obsolescent nuclear weapons. Our real motivation for this suicidal and patently absurd cultural choice - a desperate sense of insecurity - is so deeply hidden in the minds of the powerful that it is out of reach of reasoned argument.

This dangerous irrationality of the powerful is also what makes a third world war so very possible. Wealthy nations have seen the folly of taking on other wealthy nations. We will not fight with Germany again, nor with Japan. But we will not hesitate to hammer poorer nations, if they threaten our wealth by withholding oil, or interest payments, or have the temerity to speak the truth to us.

Another example of alienated feeling and its grotesque results in Western culture is the violence of imagery we tolerate around us. When I returned to the UK from living in Zimbabwe, I was much more shocked than I had been before by eye-catching images of suffering - say, in Amnesty International publicity; or by the crass, degrading sexuality of advertising. I could scarcely believe the levels of misery that were considered acceptable viewing for children and adults alike in our culture - pictures of abuse, starvation, mutilation and disability. Human suffering was clearly being used to make money, whether it be attracting donations or selling products.

We must have become very desensitized to be able to look at these things with equanimity, and to let our children see them. We think we need reminding of harsh facts, for we know we have become complacent. But there is terrible irony in the fact that *because we deny* the inhumanity of our economic system, we have to rub our noses in gory stories and pictures to reawaken our deadened sensibilities.

We Westerners are not simply helpless individually or politically to change things; and we are not merely selfish, reluctant to give things up in order to share the world's resources. To some extent we are both of these, but at a deeper level, we are also paralysed by our refusal to confess and repent, turn back, change. This is what lies behind the strange contrast between the insatiable, rapacious activity of our economic culture and the awful passivity of Western people - politically, emotionally, spiritually.

The missing link between the system's cruel greed and our own acquiescence is supplied by our soothing belief in the myth of Progress, the fiction that reassures us that it's all been for the best and we are justified.

Progress ideology shields us from the truth that it has not all been for the best, and we are not justified; and so it stops us getting to the roots of our cultural problems.

And yet deep down, we Westerners *do* know our own history - we know about slavery and colonialism, and now about international debt repayments and arms sales - and at some level we feel very bad about it all.

There are three ways we can deal with this bad feeling. The first, and most usual unfortunately, is to repress and deny it. But painful, repressed feelings fester and get twisted into other, self-damaging or destructive feelings. I believe a lot of Western stress, compulsive 'busy-ness' and inability to relax come from just such denial and repression. Our buried unease has also led to crippling fear and hatred of those we have misused: in particular, white fear of black anger, which is so dominant in the USA, and which has been a huge factor in Southern Africa.

A second, more constructive response to our uncomfortable knowledge of history, is to try to make good our past mistakes by moving towards activism, or at least by giving money to alleviate some of the suffering we hear about. This is good, as far as it goes, and can help to raise consciousness - both our own and others'. The danger of activism is if it serves as a distraction from our underlying discomfort about our position in the world. Or worse, if it convinces us that we are now on the side of the angels.

The third response is to acknowledge the bad feeling and sit with it, denying nothing, and let this true feeling teach us what we should do. As we admit our feelings, they help us grow in self-knowledge and understanding, and this will help us live more authentically and effectively than trying to follow a programme. Every person will have their own road to travel, which no-one else can prescribe.

I believe that by admitting our 'dis-ease' we open ourselves to the processes of history that are bringing about real progress. What may in the end be required of us Westerners may be simply to *embrace* what is coming, not resist it. A radical change of attitude in the West, a self-humbling frame of mind, may be our only hope of avoiding a Western-initiated third world war over resources and maintaining unjust differentials.

Looking back over the eras of our history touched on in this book, it seems as if the extreme pressures and humiliations of our early European experience have accustomed Westerners to having our natural energy, our dignity and self-reliance violated by an oppressive authority (State, Church, landowner, father).

As time passed, the pressure of our blocked energy rose like water behind a dam wall, and when eventually we found ways and means to vent our pent-up energy, out it came in a rush of exploration, violent conquest, slavery, reckless profiteering and unprecedented inventiveness.

In another image, our early trials and indignities have acted like a key on an old grandfather clock, winding up our cultural springs and storing up massive reserves of energy. We have gone on to expend this energy in brilliant and disgraceful ways, with the characteristically European mixture of repressive authoritarianism and rebellious innovativeness that I have discussed.

But ever so gradually the clock has wound down, the river is broadening out to a slower stream. We have become gradually less repressed and repressive, less sure of ourselves, more tolerant. Our own authoritarianism has come to look less and less defensible to us, while at the same time, our innovativeness has slowly undermined our happiness by making our lives ever more bland and isolated and beginning to threaten our very survival. (This, ironically enough, is real progress.) By the time all our stored-up aggression has expended itself, and we are at peace again, both we Westerners and much of the earth will quite likely be exhausted.

So real progress in Western history is, I believe, a kind of 'koan' or self-contradictory truth. Real progress lies in the gradual but inexorable unmasking of the crimes which permeate our unreal, though much-vaunted Western Progress. Real progress lies in history's unravelling of the initial knots of pain, injustice and misery that bred the class-based society that sponsored our early, angry and arrogant forays into the rest of the world. Real progress lies under the runaway train of freedom.

While this real progress is happening, slowly, on the large scale, often by a process of three steps forward, two steps back, false Progress continues to confuse us.

We Westerners have become used to presenting ourselves as enlightened - much more enlightened, indeed, than we know ourselves to be. If you scratch the surface of an apparently liberated, democratic, secular Westerner, you are quite likely to find racism, sexism, religious bigotry, class prejudice and of course, the all-embracing cultural arrogance I have described as cultural superiority syndrome (CSS).

I believe that Westerners have been spiritually and emotionally deadened, or at least anaesthetized, by our denial that there has been anything fundamentally wrong with the last five centuries of Western economic growth.

We are prepared to admit that there have been terrible cruelties and injustices: child labour, slavery, opium wars, indentured labour and so on. But the very fact that we have gradually come to perceive these things as abuses, and abolished them, surely proves that we are progressing, does it not? Yes, to some extent it does. But what do these abuses tell us about the intrinsic nature of our economic growth?

Westerners have always been much too quick to sidestep this question when history challenged us, too concerned with salvaging our self-image to stop and wonder whether we should not re-evaluate our whole Progress project.

Ever since the profits of industrialization and Empire started rolling, in, we have not seriously considered changing course, or abandoning our pursuit of technology-led economic Progress. Even the terrible warnings of two world wars, the Depression and the atom bomb have not led very many people to move beyond our self-destructive society's own familiar paradigms in search of solutions.

We started out the modern era confident in our vocation and ability to perfect human life through science, technology and good organization; sometimes, shaken by the frightening 'side'-effects of Progress, we have hastily sought to reform and re-legislate our society's affairs along more 'humane' and secure lines.

Working within increasingly economic parameters, we have analysed causes for failure, incorporated criticisms, broadened definitions, and produced new packages for 'structural adjustment' or 'sustainable development' or something, to suit our political self-images as progressives or conservatives, pragmatists, socialists or free marketeers.

All along, we have been restructuring rather than repenting. We have adjusted our parameters slightly, in order to preserve our material security on the best terms we could get. We have not even considered giving up the game.

Whenever history has forced us to reclassify an economic 'necessity' as an inhuman practice and ban it, the powerful have turned, not in gratitude to the radical protesters who have been campaigning against the abuse, nor in humble apology to the oppressed whom they have decided to relieve slightly, but rather, they have turned towards one another, in pious self-righteousness: 'Haven't we done well - again!'

The powerful in our society have never dwelt on how wrong they had been before, but rather congratulated themselves on their new-found enlightenment - be it last-minute opposition to slavery, or acceptance of universal male suffrage, or of votes for women, or of letting the colonies have their independence - or, let us hope some day soon, of the need to look after the ozone layer, stop destroying tropical forests, cut down drastically on private motor transport, air transport and industrial emissions, and ban nuclear technology. This attitude of self-congratulation, we may be fairly sure, will remain characteristic of our ruling orders.

These complacent reformers have borne none of the pain and humiliation of ostracism, marginalization and imprisonment that they inflict on those who protest against abuses. Such easy, last-ditch conversions do not mean that our society itself, that is most of the people within it, have changed. What these changes do show is that real progress happens in spite of those who don't care whether it does or not, or who would really rather it didn't, if change threatens their privileges.

Our failure to confess and be humbled is our Western tragedy as well as our sin, for every evasion of responsibility and understanding diminishes our lives. To keep ourselves safe from the truth and avoid the humiliation of admitting we have done wrong, we barricade ourselves into busy, cluttered, well-organized little routines where there is no time or room for anything unforeseen to unsettle us.

We construct meaningless rituals so we can feel we are earning our way, being worthwhile, making ourselves indispensable. We cannot relax or the uncertainties come flooding in, so we must keep chasing our tails, refusing to be distracted.

If you listen to a radio report about racist attacks or violence done to women and children, or harassment of homosexuals, you are more likely to hear righteous indignation or solicitous concern than the voice of troubled acknowledgement that the attitudes which lead to these crimes are well-known to both commentators and audience *from within*, from our cultural conditioning. But they are.

All this dishonesty is the result of trying to find a shortcut from our shameful past into a blameless future - or preferably, present. But the South African sermon holds good: without repentance there can be no forgiveness. Without accepting the public humiliation of admitting how wrongly we have acted and still act, as a society - with no excuses - there can be no regeneration, and no moral beacons lit by our governments for the rest of humanity to look to. This repentance and humiliation must be felt in our hearts by each of us singly. It cannot be felt on our behalf by politicians or activists or church people, or by our children, or our parents, or our friends. We ourselves must be humbled and, in a sense, broken by the truth, so the truth can lift us up.

Jimmy Carter was thrown ignominiously out of office by a society which refused to be humbled, in favour of a business-sponsored actor turned political frontman. Carter's name still has a ring of defeat in Western ears: and his global humiliation is an example of the public suffering I refer to.

The same rejection awaited Gorbachev. This did not indicate his failure, in terms of what he tried to achieve, but rather the authenticity of his effort. For, to be ultimately honest, renunciation of power must go further than any power-retaining group will willingly accept.

In the end, only history itself - the self-liberation of the powerless, the end of the oil, climatic changes - can help things forward. We can only go on hiding from the truth for so long. If we adopt the same skin-deep, pretend-Progress approach to the ecological disasters that are well on their way towards us, our culture will simply not survive in its present form.

As long as we remain only as Green as we think we can afford to be, will we continue hurtling towards the cliff-edge. As Jesus said, 'The one who seeks to save his life will lose it'.

African children's stories contrast with the Western fairytale, in that they often end quite nastily, in order to teach their hearers the survival virtues of prudence and respect for tradition.

Once upon a time, a man was out hunting in the forest when he came upon a lioness, lying dead on the ground, with one of her cubs trying to suckle her. Feeling sorry for the helpless little creature, he took it home and reared it by hand, feeding it with milk from his cattle. His wife mocked him, saying, 'Do you think you can keep a lion like a dog? Everyone knows a lion is a wild beast which does not live with people'.

But the man ignored her words. As the young lion grew, he became attached to it, and it would follow him around like a dog. He kept it in a pen next to the cattle *kraal* (stone enclosure). His wife warned him: 'You will regret this foolishness, and we will all be ruined because of it. A lion is not a dog - don't think you can change its nature'. But the man would not listen to her.

Then one night, he was wakened by a terrible noise outside, and running to see what had happened, he found the lion had attacked and killed one of his cattle. Yet still he refused to listen to his wife and get rid of the lion.

This story continues until the family is reduced to abject poverty because of the husband's misplaced trust and stubbornness. In a European version of this story, we can easily imagine that the lion cub might have turned into a handsome prince, who would repay the man's kindness by marrying his daughter and saving them all from drudgery and want for ever more.

The feel and outcome of this African story is more or less directly opposed to the usual pattern of Western tales. In its affirmation of unromantic, feet-on-the-ground common sense and caution, this story holds out an apt warning against self-deluding optimism - the kind of happy ending fixation that keeps Westerners hooked to the comforting illusions of false Progress. Someone who grows up in a culture which tells such stories will know in their bones that there are no quick fixes or miraculous cures for life's problems, and that the long view is the only reliable judge of what is real and lasting.

The emerging Green perspective on history should reintroduce the survival virtue of prudence to our criteria for thought and action. (What I am calling 'Green', by the way, is to the Green party itself in any country what 'left' or 'socialist' is to any left-wing party, or what 'Christian' is to any real, existing church - an attitude of mind rather than a particular organization, an essence broader and deeper - and purer - than any single political manifestation of it can be.)

The only end, or goal, that Greens should recognize is the quality of life lived daily by all life on the planet, an end so all-encompassing that it has to include the means towards realizing it. Every person who comes to see things from a Green perspective should feel moved to make changes towards enacting their philosophy in their daily lives.

In Green thought and action, the end and the means should always be working towards unity: for the end is not 'the revolution'; the end is here, today, you and I and everyone else, each day. The end, in the sense of 'the goal', is now. I believe the Green approach is both more optimistic and more realistic than the 'There is No Other Way' philosophy of the machine-led culture of economic-technological determinism.

Conventional Western Progress thinking, of left and right, has assumed that *more* must be *better*. That is, however destructive and alienating our past economic growth has proved, there is nothing else for it but to try and right the wrongs by achieving *even more economic growth*. This is the lemming run - a suicidal refusal to accept the consequences of our knowledge.

By contrast, Green philosophy maintains and Greens know from experience that choosing to have *less* can *improve* our quality of life. When we consume less and thereby control less of the world's resources, life becomes more personal and less focused on possessions; we find fresh and simple food tastes better than processed and expensive food, and making our own music is more satisfying than listening to tapes. Being less plugged in to the noise and demands of the twenty-four hour sales system frees us to enjoy ourselves, each other and the world around us more, and gives us peace to *become* ourselves, on our own terms.

Green activism also needs to include an acceptance of the proper limits of activism. We are learning to *give up control* in order to *give back power* that, thanks to Progress, has been steadily concentrated in fewer and fewer hands.

To use a Zen phrase in a Green sense, activism that resists exploitation and defends autonomy is right effort; but Green political activists must guard against being sucked into the same old power games which have corrupted other movements. Their touchstone should be, 'To what extent are we living what we believe in?'

This emerging, integrating 'Green' perspective owns up to our society's historical responsibility for the economic and environ-

mental crisis the world is now in, and faces the practical consequences of acknowledging and responding to this crisis.

More humble and respectful attitudes to non-Western cultures
are already emerging among Western musicians and craftspeople,
for example. Once these attitudes spread and become established,
I believe we in the West will experience an important shift towards a more balanced and realistic appreciation of our role and
relationships in the world. Our values will have a chance to re-
root themselves in a common human ground instead of being
cramped in corsets of assumed superiority.

At the start of the twenty-first century, the West stands between two eras: immediately behind us, around us, on our TV
screens and in our minds, is the era of postwar North American
cultural and economic dominance. Behind that, and throughout
the ex-colonial world still, is the era of European colonialism.

Ahead of us is an era we are beginning to sense, where the postwar power blocks have melted away and the global balance of
power has changed. East versus West, left versus right no longer
jostle for the moral and military high ground. Stripped of ideological buffers and blinkers, rich and poor look each other increasingly directly in the eye. Will we realize, before it is finally
and irrefutably proven to us, the bankruptcy of pure economics?

Both the flavour of the past and the seeds of the future are among
us. But the new tendencies are not yet firmly established. The
shift in values is only beginning to be felt, and there will probably
be a backlash. We can expect the pro-Western superiority backlash to be at least as powerful and pervasive as the anti-feminist
one has been.

But with or without Western support, the runaway train of freedom is moving, and we will either go on paying mere lip service
to real progress, as we have done hitherto, or else learn to move
with our hearts, and get on board.

If we care how the rest of the world feels, and want to stop
acting like ridiculous, greedy bullies, we also need to try and *take*
on board what others can tell us about our past, and allow ourselves to be put in context.

Though I have explained why there is no ten-point plan in
this book, I would like to make one radical political suggestion
which some may feel is highly impractical. In my view, the most
necessary and practical step towards reinstituting a just society
where everyone has the means to dignity is to *give back the land*.

We need to recognize the human right to a place to live - not a site-and-services stand in a town planner's grid, or a council flat, but a piece of land, a *place* that means something to people and which, given proper work and care, can feed a family. We also need to ban further private accumulation of land and reverse the accumulation that has already, and literally, *taken place.*

There *are* ways of doing this. The land tax movement has a simple formula for making it expensive to own more land than you are using productively.

Such changes would put Euro-Americans and Euro-Australians, not to mention Euro-Africans, in a very awkward position vis-à-vis the indigenous populations of those continents. But no doubt land could be leased from its original 'owners', or else agreements could be reached about sharing the land more equitably among the present inhabitants.

Although this may seem far-fetched - utopian even! - I believe the land question lies at the heart of our Western cultural malaise. However rich we Westerners have become, we have remained, at heart and in fact, dispossessed and alienated. And so we will remain, I believe, until the original feudal rip-off is reversed. Certainly, land reform in the UK seems unlikely in the near future. Perhaps Southern Africa will show us the way.

It is time for Westerners to recover respect for the values of previous eras and of other cultures. We have plenty evidence in our medical and crime statistics, and in our social work records, of our urgent need for different values. Though nearly all of us survive infancy, adolescence and adulthood have become nightmares of false choices and socio-economic pressures for many Westerners, undermining their will to live. Teenage and young adult suicide is on the increase.

It gets harder and harder to become and remain ourselves in this culture, for in spite of our apparent power and freedom, we have less and less room to manoeuvre.

Those who live and work in London may make heaps of money (or they may not) but many hate the dirty, noisy, high-pressure environment. So they buy houses in relatively quiet, 'unspoiled' places up and down the country, pushing prices out of reach of local people there, who in turn are forced to go to London to look for work!

One day as I was working on this book, in Edinburgh, I watched Safeway shoppers trying to drive away from the supermarket in the next street. An enormous red truck that had just left its load there could not get round the street corner of Victorian tenements - a queue of cars waited behind while the truck driver manoeuvred, pumping exhaust into each others' radiators, getting harassed. Truck drivers, I thought, are nice people, on the whole; so are shoppers. All these nice people making life nasty for each other and themselves because they cannot see any other way; because we lack the courage to 'not-have'.

There are other ways to live! We can work part-time if we accept a drop in earnings. We can grow a bit of food at least in the summer, if we can find access to some unused land. We can think about the amount of travelling we do and whether we need a second car - or a car at all. If we are lucky enough to live in the country or in a village, we can get involved and contribute to the community's life. (We can do all this in towns and cities too.) Many people are already doing these things - living where they are, to the full.

The South African and South and Central American liberation movements have shown those who got involved with them a kind of revitalized social activism that celebrates our whole humanity - our love of music, rhythm and dance, our love of festivals, of children and family. Surely most Westerners can go along with most of this, and also acknowledge, *with the world's majority*, our basic human attachment to the land: not to the 'countryside' of the Countryside Commission, but to land that is tilled in little plots to provide us with food and work and beauty, and with the lessons of nature.

At heart, I believe we are all farmers or nomads, or a bit of both. Stuck in offices, factories, cars and aeroplanes, we wither away. The 'easy life' is actually very hard on us, both emotionally and physically, because it deprives us of things we need in order to feel happy, balanced and content.

Fifteen years ago, I heard a pavement preacher in New Orleans tell a streetful of shoppers: 'Yous all think yo' *want* is greater than yo' *need* - But I tell you - yo' *need* is greater than yo' *want*!'

We need: constant and intimate contact with many people, including large families, within a culture of respect that protects personal space and privacy; satisfying (that is, productive and creative) physical work that supports our own subsistence and humanizes our surroundings; and constant, intimate contact with the rhythms and textures of the earth.

The threatening ecological situation, and our own cluttered yet impoverished lives both cry out for radical changes that go beyond our familiar frameworks. Better management techniques will not address the issues at all.

Even if we ourselves do not feel the need to change, the big *political* questions facing the world today demand to be dealt with in non-Western terms. We must try to remember that *middle-class Westerners are a minority* - and an atypically affluent, rather out-of-touch minority at that.

Having said this, it is clear that this writing cannot - and should not - 'answer' these questions either: the answers will come from as many places as the questions do. All I have tried to do here is suggest to a Western audience reasons for reaching beyond our usual Western frames of reference, and ways of freeing ourselves, at least momentarily, from our cultural superiority syndrome, so that we can think more clearly.

Although Margaret Thatcher's new brutalism was timely, in pulling the benign mask off welfare capitalism, it is very unlikely that she will be proved right in the longer term about capitalism's capacity to sustain itself and all of us indefinitely, by the free operation of market forces.

The view of history I have been working towards in this book suggests that we in the West should not be worrying any more about how to promote development. It is more to the point to ask: 'How can we *stop* doing to others, and stop forcing others to do to themselves, what we have already done to ourselves in the name of Progress?' - that is, turning life from a cycle of seasons and mysteries, celebrations and mourning, work and rest, eating and fasting, into a linear, economic seventy-year-plan.

The point is not to grant or to deny anybody anything, but for us Westerners to take an honest look at the whole process of our development - or Progress - including the industrialization of our own society, and try to assess what it has brought us and what it has taken away.

I believe that our Western middle-class Progress thus far has involved us in *regressions* at least as significant, in terms of human culture, as the material and intellectual *advances* we have achieved; also that these human regressions are the direct result of the *inhuman* socio-economic policies which the powerful in our society have pursued up till now.

What we do about these realizations is up to us. It is enough for me if this book helps some readers to bring their political analysis and insights home to their own troubled psyches and family relationships, and some other readers to bring their personal psychological difficulties and efforts at growth home to the public, political world they have been formed by. For we and the world are at home in each other, and we cannot tackle either our own or the world's problems in isolation from the other.

Once the unity of personal and political is experienced, new respect for the neglected non-material and extra-rational factors in human happiness becomes more possible and likely.

Real change starts inside people: not 'privately' as opposed to 'publicly', but *in the consciously-experienced integrity of public and private*. This experience provides the energy for a lifetime of continued learning and practice - of more fulfilling and challenging personal relationships, of work and encouragement of others.

We should be sceptical about backpackers' guides to Nirvana that promise a cheap and exciting journey and do not refer to the political and historical dimensions of our lives. Some philosophies of personal growth go no further than condemning, or else seeking to redeem the miserable, guilt-inducing Calvinism or Catholicism many Westerners have inherited. They encourage us to be happy and serene, because the world and we are basically good.

'I'm OK, You're OK' is true on one level - the most important, and the very deepest - but on many other levels it's not. You and I were born OK - innocent - but we're not OK now: and the world is not OK, nor was it when you and I were born. That is why you and I don't feel OK now either.

We are not hypochondriacs, nor are we alone in our psychological distress and disturbance: we and our society *are* distressed and disturbed, at a deep and pervasive level, and for good reason - or rather, for reasons that are not good, but sufficient.

We all need healing, which is a big word, connected to 'whole' and 'holistic'. Healing is bound to take time, and each of us must find our own path to wholeness. I do not claim to have found my own wholeness, and I do not manage to practise even a fraction of the little I understand to be necessary to wholeness in my own life.

Without claiming to be an authority, or appearing to offer solutions where there can only be admissions, here are some suggestions for moving towards cultural healing:

Divest yourself of some privileges, and so get closer to the perspective of the majority, the outsiders - everybody except white, middle-class Westerners.

Watch, listen to and read what outsiders have to say.

Put yourself in real-life situations where *you* are the outsider, the learner, the receiver - even the exploited: relinquish control over other people.

Giving up control in real social and work situations leads to a completely fresh perspective on life, a perspective more open and less alienated, more joyful and more painful than the old one. Breaking the circle hurts, but it is a 'good hurt'.

Perhaps, as the Myth of the Fall suggests, our loss of joy is a condition of our humanity from which we can never completely recover.

But remember the South African preacher's words, which, though negatively phrased, hold out more hope than Genesis: 'Without confession there can be no repentance; without repentance, there can be no forgiveness; without forgiveness there can be no salvation, and without salvation there can be no eternity'.

This means that *with* confession, there *can* be repentance; with repentance, there can be forgiveness; with forgiveness there can be salvation, and with salvation there can be eternity.

I believe we *can* make true progress, step by step, back to the deepest level where we are all OK: but we need to make a journey to get there, a journey full of faith and humility.

Reading List

Chapter One
1. All Biblical references are from the *New English Bible*. *New English Bible* © Oxford University Press and Cambridge Press 1961, 1970.
2. Alice Miller, *For Your Own Good* (Virago Press, London, 1987)

Chapter Two
1. Lucy Goodison, *Moving Heaven and Earth* (Allen & Unwin, London, 1990)
2. For a contrast, read *Montaillou: the World Famous Portrait of Life in a Medieval Village*, written by Emmanuel le Roy la Durie, (Penguin, 1980); also recommended is *Civilisation and Capitalism* by Fernand Braudel (trans. S Reynolds), (Fontana, London, 1985)
3. Edwin Muir, *An Autobiography* (Hogarth Press, London, 1954)

Chapter Three
1. Jean Liedloff, *The Continuum Concept* (Penguin, London, 1989)
2. Maria Mies, *Patriarchy and Accumulation on a World Scale* (Zed Books, 1986)

Chapter Five
1. See Raymond Williams, *Culture and Society* (Chatto & Windus, London, 1963)
2. Samuel Butler, *Erewhon or: Over The Range* (Richards, London, 1901)
3. *The Revolt Against Change*, by Trevor Blackwell and Jeremy Seabrook (Vintage, London, 1993) offers an incisive study of this switching of terms, together with an excellent critique of 'economic development' North and South, and its social costs.
4. Toni Morrison, *Beloved (Chatto & Windus, 1987)*.
   Also recommended is: Zora Neal Hurston's *I Love Myself When I Am Laughing* (Feminist Press, New York, 1979) and *Their Eyes Were Watching God* (Virago Press, London, 1986); the autobiographical *Equiano's Travels*, written by Olaudah Equiano (ed. Paul Edwards) (Heinemann International, 1967); and the work of James Baldwin, Alice Walker and Maya Angelou.

Chapter 6
1. See John Pilger's *Distant Voices* (Vintage, London, 1992) and his issue of *New Internationalist* on Cambodia, May 1996

Chapter 7
1. See *Under The Eagle,* by Jenny Pearce (Latin American Bureau, 1982)
2. James Baldwin, *Notes Of A Native Son* (Corgi, London, 1965)

Chapter 8
1. See *The Dark Eye In Africa*, written by Laurens van der Post (Hogarth Press, London, 1955)

Chapter 9
1. *New Internationalist*, no 263. January 1995. *(Unmasked; The East Asian Economic Mistake)*
2. Henry Nouwen, *The Wounded Healer* (Double Day Publisher, New York, 1972)
3. Zeke Manyika, *Runaway Train of Freedom*, EMI

The Iona Community

The Iona Community is an ecumenical Christian community, founded in 1938 by the late Lord MacLeod of Fuinary (the Rev. George MacLeod DD) and committed to seeking new ways of living the Gospel in today's world. Gathered around the rebuilding of the ancient monastic buildings of Iona Abbey, but with its original inspiration in the poorest areas of Glasgow during the Depression, the Community has sought ever since the 'rebuilding of the common life', bringing together work and worship, prayer and politics, the sacred and the secular in ways that reflect its strongly incarnational theology.

The Community today is a movement of some 200 Members, over 1,400 Associate Members and about 1,600 Friends. The Members - women and men from many backgrounds and denominations, most in Britain, but some overseas - are committed to a rule of daily prayer and Bible reading, sharing and accounting for their use of time and money, regular meeting and action for justice and peace.

The Iona Community maintains three centres on Iona and Mull: Iona Abbey and the MacLeod Centre on Iona, and Camas Adventure Camp on the Ross of Mull. Its base is in Community House, Glasgow, where it also supports work with young people, the Wild Goose Resource and Worship Groups, a bimonthly magazine (*Coracle*) and a publishing house (Wild Goose Publications).

For further information on the Iona Community please contact:

The Iona Community,
Pearce Institute,
840 Govan Road, Glasgow G51 3UU

T. 0141 445 4561; F. 0141 445 4295.

Other Titles available from WGP

SONGBOOKS with full music (titles marked * have companion cassettes)
THE COURAGE TO SAY NO; 23 SONGS FOR EASTER & LENT*John
 Bell and Graham Maule
GOD NEVER SLEEPS – PACK OF 12 OCTAVOS* John Bell
COME ALL YOU PEOPLE, Shorter Songs for Worship* John Bell
PSALMS OF PATIENCE, PROTEST AND PRAISE* John Bell
HEAVEN SHALL NOT WAIT (Wild Goose Songs Vol.1)* J Bell & Graham
Maule
ENEMY OF APATHY (Wild Goose Songs Vol.2) J Bell & Graham Maule
LOVE FROM BELOW (Wild Goose Songs Vol.3)* John Bell & G Maule
INNKEEPERS & LIGHT SLEEPERS* (for Christmas) John Bell
MANY & GREAT (Songs of the World Church Vol.1)* John Bell (ed./arr.)
SENT BY THE LORD (Songs of the World Church Vol.2)* John Bell (ed./arr.)
FREEDOM IS COMING* Anders Nyberg (ed.)
PRAISING A MYSTERY, Brian Wren
BRING MANY NAMES, Brian Wren

CASSETTES & CDs (titles marked † have companion songbooks)
Tape, THE COURAGE TO SAY NO † Wild Goose Worship Group
Tape, GOD NEVER SLEEPS † John Bell (guest conductor)
Tape, COME ALL YOU PEOPLE † Wild Goose Worship Group
CD, PSALMS OF PATIENCE, PROTEST AND PRAISE † Wild Goose
 Worship Group
Tape, PSALMS OF PATIENCE, PROTEST AND PRAISE † WGWG
Tape, HEAVEN SHALL NOT WAIT † Wild Goose Worship Group
Tape, LOVE FROM BELOW † Wild Goose Worship Group
Tape, INNKEEPERS & LIGHT SLEEPERS † (for Christmas) WGWG
Tape, MANY & GREAT † Wild Goose Worship Group
Tape, SENT BY THE LORD † Wild Goose Worship Group
Tape, FREEDOM IS COMING † Fjedur
Tape, TOUCHING PLACE, A, Wild Goose Worship Group
Tape, CLOTH FOR THE CRADLE, Wild Goose Worship Group

DRAMA BOOKS
EH JESUS...YES PETER No. 1, John Bell and Graham Maule
EH JESUS...YES PETER No. 2, John Bell and Graham Maule
EH JESUS...YES PETER No. 3, John Bell and Graham Maule

PRAYER/WORSHIP BOOKS
PRAYERS AND IDEAS FOR HEALING SERVICES, Ian Cowie
HE WAS IN THE WORLD, Meditations for Public Worship, John Bell
EACH DAY AND EACH NIGHT, Prayers from Iona in the Celtic Tradition,
Philip Newell
IONA COMMUNITY WORSHIP BOOK,
WEE WORSHIP BOOK, A, Wild Goose Worship Group

WHOLE EARTH SHALL CRY GLORY, THE, George MacLeod
PATTERN OF OUR DAYS, THE, Kathy Galloway (ed.)

OTHER BOOKS
EXILE IN ISRAEL: A Personal Journey with the Palestinians, Runa Mackay
FALLEN TO MEDIOCRITY: CALLED TO EXCELLENCE, Erik Cramb
REINVENTING THEOLOGY AS THE PEOPLE'S WORK, Ian Fraser
PUSHING THE BOAT OUT, New Poetry, Kathy Galloway (ed.)
WHAT IS THE IONA COMMUNITY?
COLUMBA, Pilgrim and Penitent, Ian Bradley
EARTH UNDER THREAT, THE: A Christian Perspective, Ghillean Prance

WILD GOOSE ISSUES/REFLECTIONS
WOMEN TOGETHER, Ena Wyatt & Rowsan Malik
THE APOSTLES' CREED: A Month of Meditations, David Levison
SURPLUS BAGGAGE: The Apostles' Creed, Ralph Smith